W9-BYW-439

Hampshire County Public Library
153 W. ___ Street
Romney, WV 26757

3/2014

To Have and to Hold

To Have and to Hold

Motherhood, Marriage, and the
Modern Dilemma

Molly Millwood, PhD

HARPER WAVE

An Imprint of HarperCollinsPublishers

HarperCollins books may be purchased for educational, business, or sales promotional use. For information, please email the Special Markets Department at SPsales@harpercollins.com.

FIRST EDITION

Photograph on page iii by itlada/Shutterstock, Inc.

Library of Congress Cataloging-in-Publication Data has been applied for.

ISBN 978-0-06-283865-0

19 20 21 22 23   LSC   10 9 8 7 6 5 4 3 2 1

For Ari, Noah, and Quinn
my teachers, my inspirations, and my reasons for pursuing an ever-greater understanding of what it means to love and be loved

Contents

Introduction

When my first son was born, I lamented the scarcity of books about what motherhood is really like. Why, I wondered, were there so many books dedicated to pregnancy, childbirth, and caring for a baby, and so few books that explored how a woman's internal experience changes so radically when she becomes a mother? Eventually I discovered that several such books do exist, and in the last few years, there has been a flurry of honest writings (largely in blog or other online forms) about the actual—not romanticized—experience of becoming a mother. Why are these kinds of accounts—full of the promise of restoring sanity to new mothers everywhere—so heavily outnumbered by the "how-to" books about parenting? Why are they not standard baby shower gifts, and why are their titles not nearly as familiar to all pregnant women as, say, *What to Expect When You're Expecting*?

I believe it has something to do with the fact that our culture values a mother's skill at parenting over her well-being as an individual. Nobody recommended these other books to me as I approached motherhood. I had to dig deep to find them.

The taboo against exposing the complexity of motherhood has a long history in our society. I am not forging any new territory by acknowledging that such a taboo exists or by offering candid accounts of maternal suffering in these pages. I am simply adding my voice to a chorus that's too small, a chorus we must strain our ears to hear amid the much louder sounds of how lucky we are to have a new baby and how we should go about taking care of that baby.

As a psychologist, I find the secrecy and shame surrounding the struggles faced by new mothers both crippling and dangerous. As the mother of two young children, I wanted to write the book I longed to read when motherhood was brand-new to me: a narrative that explores the emotionally and psychologically complex terrain of new motherhood. In that terrain, we encounter not only a woman's internal experience of herself, her child, and her radically changing identity, but also her experience of her marriage or intimate partnership.

Too much of the existing literature on motherhood, both scholarly and popular, diminishes or completely overlooks the relational context in which motherhood occurs. Certainly, mother*ing* is recognized as relational in nature; mothering is about interacting with our children. What gets less attention is that mother*hood*, as an experience and identity, usually unfolds within the context of an intimate adult relationship. Experiences of loss, separation, power, control, autonomy, dependency, and conflict within a woman's romantic partnership are, at various times, either background or foreground in the experience of motherhood. These issues simply cannot be disentangled from the supposedly "individual" ones that characterize new motherhood, like mental and physical exhaustion and loss of personal freedom.

So this book is not about women's individual happiness within motherhood, or about marital happiness after the transition to parenthood. It is about both.

Too often, personal contentment and relationship harmony are pitted against each other, as if we must sacrifice one, at least to some degree, in order to achieve the other. Likewise, a woman's desire to mother and her desire to do other things are also pitted against each other. These are false dichotomies.[1] What if we could instead occupy a mental space in which there is room for all our loving, nurturing feelings toward our children and our partners *and* room for all our other, less socially acceptable feelings, too? We get tired of nurturing. We long for freedom and breathing room. We savor opportunities to become immersed in other kinds of tasks and experiences that are meaningful to us, yet we often feel guilt or shame for prioritizing our own needs and desires.

What if we could be free of confusion about these seemingly incompatible sets of feelings? What if we could be free of the self-disdain that says, "If I were a good mother, I would want to stay home full-time with my baby" or "I shouldn't meet my friend for dinner when I barely have time to cook or have dinner with my husband"? What if we could trust that as long as we are intentional in our choices and clear about our needs, whatever it is we are doing to take care of ourselves also makes us better mothers, and that whatever time we take away from our partners to do something meaningful actually breathes new life into our relationships?

So many of the women who come to me for therapy are tormented by their own ambivalence. They want more time with the baby, but also more time alone. Their children bring them indescribable joy, but also make them crazy. They are grateful for their husbands' calm and stability while simultaneously resenting them for being less affected by the transition to parenthood. They are crying in hopeless frustration one moment and feeling surges of love and affection deeper than they've ever known in the next. "I'm losing my mind," these women say. "No, you're not," I respond. "You've lost many things now that you're a mother, but your mind is not one of them." In actuality, these women have *found* their minds; they have found crevices and corners they didn't know existed and hadn't planned to visit. The same is true of their hearts.

I'm guessing you picked up this book because, like the women I've just described, you're wondering what's become of your life and your marriage since you've become a mother. You think maybe you're losing your mind, too. In this book, we will take a look at what you *have* lost: a great deal of your personal freedom, any sem-blance of order and simplicity in your life, your idealized pre-baby notions of what kind of mother you would be, your pre-baby fantasies about the ways parenthood would enhance your marriage, and many other things you held dear. Those losses need to be recognized and grieved, but even more important than this is the need to make sense of what new things you've *found*. We will shine a light on the thoughts, feelings, and parts of self you have discovered since be-coming a mother, and look upon them with curiosity and acceptance rather than shame. We will look bravely at the emotional chaos of motherhood and tame it with meaning. Reading this book won't make the chaos go away—much as I wish it would—but my hope is that it will become much more bearable. All of what's painful, messy, and confusing in life becomes easier to bear when we stop trying to make it go away, when we learn that others have found themselves in the same tangle, and when we find words to bring us reasons and meaning.

Everything in this book is written from my vantage point as a clinical psychologist who has spent many an hour in dialogue with new mothers and couples muddling their way through the haze and emotional turmoil of early parenthood. I write also from my vantage point as a psychology professor and scholar with special-ties in intimate relationships and the transition to parenthood. But perhaps most important, I write as a mother and a wife.[2] I would be doing my readers a great injustice if I pretended that my psy-chologist status somehow rendered me immune to all the struggles described in the pages that follow. After all, greater transparency about the many ways in which motherhood rattles us is the very thing I wish for. What plagues so many new mothers, what adds a layer of unnecessary suffering to the inevitable pain, is the shame in which they are enshrouded because they think they are the only ones having such a hard time. If I maintained a fully professional voice throughout this book, describing my observations from a detached, clinical, or academic perspective and never speaking of my personal experiences, I would be reinforcing the misconception that most women are sailing smoothly through the seas of new motherhood and only a few unlucky ones are floundering. So, although this book incorporates research findings, the narratives of my clients, and the themes that arise with such regularity in my clinical practice, my own stories will reveal that I relate to those themes on a deeply personal level.

In the beginning stages of writing this book, as I spoke compassionate words to clients in my therapy office about the weight of sleep deprivation, I was functioning on more cups of coffee than hours of sleep because at home, I was mothering a baby for whom no "sleep training" strategy ever worked. Far from being removed from my clients' experiences, a veteran mom who survived the battles and emerged no worse for wear, I have been right in the trenches with them. The moments in which I was not enjoying motherhood are depicted throughout the pages of this book, right alongside similar moments experienced by the women who come to me for therapy. This book is about giving those moments a voice, the collective voice of so many new mothers who falter and ache through the transition to motherhood but can say so only in the safest and most private contexts, if at all.

Much of the time, these women who came to me for therapy probably held the illusion that I had no mothering challenges of my own.* If they are reading this book, perhaps my self-disclosures will catch them by great surprise. I hope the surprise is a welcome

---

* A very interesting and reliable phenomenon in psychotherapy is the tendency of clients to idealize their therapists. There are many reasons for this phenomenon, including the need to believe that the professional is relatively free of her own personal problems and so is better equipped to offer help. But the reason closest to the heart of

one. Author and poet Adrienne Rich said it best forty years ago: "I believe increasingly that only the willingness to share private and sometimes painful experience can enable women to create a collective description of the world which will be truly ours."[3]

Some Caveats

For a majority of women, the experience of becoming a mother is embedded in a heterosexual relationship; the two are inextricably linked and both deserve our simultaneous attention. Since this is not a book about *only* motherhood (in which case, its contents would apply to all women, straight or gay) and since it is not a book about *only* couplehood (in which case, it would be crucial to tailor the material to same-sex as well as straight couples), it contains a bias I could not avoid without defeating the purpose of the book. The bias is this: *In this book, heterosexuality and a committed relationship status of "married" or "partnered" are assumed.*

While I hope this book will have value for women in same-sex relationships, women whose male partners are the primary caretakers of their child(ren), as well as single or separated or divorced women, I acknowledge from the outset my bias in writing most of the time about *motherhood as it unfolds within the framework of a married or committed heterosexual relationship.* When I use the words "husband," "wife," and "spouse," I do this for simplicity and ease of communication, not because I am excluding the huge numbers

---

this book is *how readily we make assumptions, in the absence of any obvious data to the contrary, that other people are doing better than we are.* The psychotherapy relationship is set up in such a way that the therapist, disclosing so little about herself, is a bit mysterious to the client. Faced with that mystery, most clients conjure up fantasies of the therapist's life in which she is infinitely competent, even-keeled, and free of turmoil.

of couples who are raising a child or children together but are not married. Please consider these words to be interchangeable with "boyfriend/girlfriend/partner," and please consider the word "marriage" to be interchangeable with "long-term committed relationship."

Another strategy I have applied in the interest of clarity is to devote several chapters in a row to the "we" aspect of *motherhood in the context of couplehood* after focusing primarily on the "me" aspect of motherhood. Since the very premise of the book is that the two are inextricably linked, separating out marriage/couples issues into their own chapters was a difficult organizational decision to make. I hope I have done so while managing to preserve one of the fundamental messages of the book, which is that *women's individual well-being and the well-being of their marriages are not at all separate matters*. In turn, I hope devoting multiple chapters to a deep exploration of new parents' marital struggles sends its own message. If marital strain is not just part and parcel of a mother's difficult adjustment but often a central reason for it, understanding that strain is important in its own right.

To protect confidentiality, I have changed names and other potentially identifying details within the case vignettes. Though not fictitious, occasionally the vignettes are composites of several different women's experiences woven together into a single tale. The decision to create composites is rooted partly in the interest of protecting my clients' privacy, but it serves another purpose as well. Composites capture and emphasize the universality of women's struggles. With no intended disrespect to the uniqueness of each human life, as a psychologist and therapist I am most interested in our shared humanity. I am interested in just how deep our shared experience runs, and especially in the struggles we have in common. When we bring those struggles into the light, their weight is lessened. Their hold upon us is loosened. We see something of ourselves in someone else, and instantly we find some relief, even in the absence of an obvious solution to the struggle.

Finally, I am passionate about the influence of science and scholarship on the well-being of couples, families, women, men, and children. Research findings are arguably the closest thing to "truth" we have about, at least in a general sense, how large numbers of people out there in the world are functioning, and truth is power. However, many authors struggle to convey scholarly work and research findings in a way that's accessible to everyone. They fear either "dumbing down" the science in a way that is insulting and unfulfilling to their readers or writing a tome of incomprehensible, unrelatable scientific findings that nobody outside their field will ever read. In this book I have tried to use science and theory mainly in a supporting role, to underscore and bring meaning to the stories being told about real women and real couples. Readers who want to know what voice that science would have if it were in the starring role should look to the endnotes. In those notes, findings and theoretical constructs are further elaborated upon, and references are provided so that readers can dig deeper if they choose.

To Have and to Hold

I

Women Transformed

Having a baby is a psychological revolution that changes our relation to almost everything and everyone.
—ESTHER PEREL[1]

Women in contemporary Western society are not permitted to grieve or mourn when they become mothers as they might with other life changes. If they do, they are seen as "ill" or "unnatural" in some fundamental way. So strong is the taboo against appearing unhappy after having a baby that women themselves frequently fail to admit their sense of loss to themselves, at least in a conscious way.
—PAULA NICOLSON[2]

I am a fundamentally happy person. I come from a family prone to depression and other mental health issues, and I weathered some very difficult storms as an adolescent when long-brewing problems in my family erupted and ultimately rendered my parents' marriage unsalvageable. But I have always been, at my core, a content and glass-half-full person with a mostly unwavering sense of gratitude for what is good in life. Far from bubbly and effusive, I haven't been one to shout from the rooftops how joyful I am or to go out of my way to cheer others with jokes and uplifting sentiment. But it seems

I have always exuded a kind of quiet, peaceful contentment that others readily detect, enough so that as a teenager my demeanor earned me the nickname "Molly Feel Good."

In early adulthood, there were many instances in which I wandered far outside my comfort zone. For graduate school, I moved to a state in which I knew not a single soul. While others might have approached such a move with a sense of liberation and enthusiasm, my introversion and my enmeshment with my family meant that I had to work exceptionally hard to combat fear, anxiety, and loneliness beneath the big sky of Montana as a first-year graduate student. Yet that is exactly what I did. I did not sink into sadness and I did not lose my footing. Certainly, I was anxious at times, especially as I faced the very significant challenge of teaching a class of sixty-some undergraduates when, as an undergraduate myself just a couple of years before, I had barely spoken a word in class unless forced to by a professor. My shyness meant teaching did not come the least bit naturally to me. So on top of the stress of a demanding graduate school workload, the daunting responsibilities of being a psychotherapist in training, and the adjustment to an entirely new social circle and community, several days a week I had to ignore the anxious rumblings in my stomach and the loud voice in my head saying, *Don't go into that lecture hall and teach that class!*

Through this chapter of my life and the ones that followed, transitions and challenges abounded. Most of these were fortunate challenges. Getting married; moving away from the Montana I had come to cherish and saying good-bye to the graduate school friends I held so dear in order to pursue an internship in San Francisco; moving again, this time cross-country, to settle into the unknown of a new life in Vermont as a professor while starting a private psychotherapy practice. All that time, my core contentment prevailed. My positive outlook remained. If silly nicknames were part of the vernacular of thirtysomethings, I probably still would have been called Molly Feel Good.

I paint this picture not to say, "Look at how marvelous I am to have navigated all these challenges so gracefully!" I was far from graceful during many of those tough times, and my husband will attest that transitions are very hard on me. But if there were lapses in my usual emotional stability, my clarity and comfort with who I was and where I was going, they were just that: lapses.

And then I had a baby.

The moment I gave birth to my first son, I fell in love with him. I don't think the visceral memory of those first moments will ever fade. Slimy and wrinkled and smooshed and purple, he was the most beautiful thing I had ever seen, smelled, or touched. My bond with him was intense, and instant. The depth of joy and gratification I felt as I rocked him and nursed him, as we held each other's gaze, as I bathed and dressed him, was unlike anything I had experienced before. It was reminiscent of the way I fell in love with my husband, except it was so unguarded. So limitless, and so much more powerful than any inclinations I might have to be careful about loving some-one else so much. This element of unabashed, uninhibited delighting was new, and it was palpable to others. I remember a close friend commenting, "You look like you are genuinely relishing the daily stuff of motherhood." And I was.

Except when I wasn't.

The dark and vexing moments of mothering existed side by side with the moments of joy and fulfillment, but because they were not sanctioned and because they were invisible to others—except my husband, to whom my suffering was perhaps more obvious than it was to me—they took a slow and silent toll. A year into mother-hood, I could no longer construe my negative moods as lapses; they had become the norm, and for the first time in my life, I had lost my footing. Though I wasn't exactly *sad*, I was grouchy much of the time. I was withdrawn, socially and emotionally. I was chronically fatigued, even though I was sleeping much better than when our son was first born. I was irritable, doubtful, and skeptical, and I just wanted to be left alone.

Like many of the women I see in therapy, I had none of the risk factors for postpartum depression (PPD) and none of its classic symptoms. I had not been depressed prior to pregnancy, I had a lot of social support, I was not having trouble bonding with my son, I was not unable to find pleasure in life's daily activities, I was not lethargic or unable to concentrate or fearful or anxious. Even as I recall the extent to which I was unhappy, I am aware that I was still quite capable of joy. I do not look at photographs of myself during my son's first year and see a face of despair, and that's not because I was wearing a mask of cheeriness the way many depressed people do. I see a young mother who was genuinely taking pleasure in her new role, sometimes even glowing with the joy of it. The change was in the balance, in the frequency with which I felt listless, angry, and numb compared to the frequency with which I felt energized, peaceful, and content. For me, the scales had always been tipped in favor of contentment, and this was no longer true. It was a painful realization. I came to it slowly, and only with much prompting by my husband, whose view was less clouded. He told me I was negative, hostile, and cold, and that he barely recognized me anymore. I hated him for holding up a mirror to me that way, the way our spouses so often do. But for the good of all three of us, somebody needed to acknowledge this new state of affairs. And it wasn't going to be me.

It's not that I had done a 180-degree turn from happy and kind to unhappy and mean. But I had come to inhabit a far more complex emotional world, and I moved among different mood states in a rapid, often unpredictable fashion. *I see this now as really rather normal.* I see that a transformation of enormous proportions was under way.

It was not that the dark moods and the agitation defined me, but they existed alongside my more customary neutral and happy states. The problem was that they were so foreign to both my husband and me that we felt threatened by them. They were not consistent with earlier incarnations of me, and they were certainly not consistent with the picture we both had of how our lives, as parents, would be enriched. I coped mainly by ignoring and denying. And as is so often the case with whatever we try to ignore or deny, the darkness managed to grow ever more pronounced. I now find myself wondering, *What if my darker moments hadn't been so threatening?* What if I had found a way, earlier on, to make sense of them? What if I had been able to recognize them as well within the range of normal for a woman adapting to motherhood, rather than as indications that I was somehow flawed? The dark moments felt like uninvited and unwelcome visitors, but *what if I had known they were coming?*

I didn't know, because nobody talks about it.

I didn't know, because I had navigated so many other major transitions without much internal upheaval; why should the transition to motherhood be any different?

I didn't know, because I had navigated the early postpartum period—the first few months when moms are expected or "allowed" to have a little case of the blues—without a hint of the darkness that was to come later on. My colicky baby cried incessantly and I was physically taxed by him more than I ever could have imagined, but by all accounts I was coping well with having a difficult infant.

Not Postpartum Depression, but Postpartum *Transformation*

In one of the most important, honest books about childbirth and motherhood available to us, *Misconceptions*, author Naomi Wolf uses the term "postpartum grief." She uses it almost in passing, but when I first read it, it stopped me in my tracks for all its accuracy and significance. Though Wolf uses the term to describe what *depressed* new mothers feel, I propose that we embrace it as an accurate label for the *perfectly normal* emotional state in which a new mother frequently finds herself, much like we view grief as the perfectly normal state that follows the death of a loved one. The term captures a core aspect of the transition to motherhood, but it is one that nobody likes to talk about. It captures the *fundamental sense of loss* associated with becoming a mother.

When my first child, Noah, was about six weeks old, I wrote the following in my journal:

Moments ago, I was sitting on the back stoop, drinking a beer and listening to the crickets. It's an unusually hot late-summer evening. I'm sticky from the heat, exhausted from caring for my very fussy son all day, and the tension in my back muscles is fierce. As I sat staring at the moon during the first peaceful moment I've had all day, I found myself missing Life Before Noah. And then came the wave of guilt for feeling such a thing. Certainly, I am a guilt-prone person anyway, so the feeling is quite familiar. This, though, was different. More intense than any wave of guilt that's ever washed over me before. What kind of person, what kind of mother, would long for the life she had before her child was born?

After sitting with this feeling of guilt for a minute, feeling disgusted with myself, it occurred to me that maybe it's okay for me to feel this way. Why shouldn't I miss all the things about my life that I cherished before Noah came along? I had a pretty wonderful thing going, and for the moment, much of that wonderful stuff has vanished. I trust that a lot of it will return, but honestly, it's nowhere around right now and I miss it. The beer I was drinking tasted mighty fine, and I sure would've liked to have more than one. I can't do that without tarnishing the breast milk that nourishes my baby. The quiet of the evening felt so cleansing, and I sure would've liked to spend the whole night out there enjoying it, instead of wearily grabbing just five minutes of it when the long battle to get Noah to sleep was over. Everything I hadn't been able to get done all day was waiting for me inside, and I had to tackle it now that the baby was sleeping.

With the creation of a brand-new human being, there is so much emphasis on what is gained. New mothers bring home their little "bundles of joy" and all the gear that goes with them. A couple grows into a family. Diapers, toys, clothes, strollers, baby carriers, and high chairs fill the house. Visitors bearing casseroles and baby gifts appear at the door. The phone rings with inquiries and well wishes, and Facebook pages spill over with congratulatory posts. Feedings, diaper changes, cuddles, and naps fill the hours. All these additions to a woman's life can obscure what is lost and what feels damaged, altered, broken, disrupted. Autonomy and personal freedom. Restful sleep. The familiar and predictable routine of life without a newborn. Confidence in one's appearance, comfort in one's own skin, a sense of oneself as feminine and sexual. A sense of connection to, and participation in, the outside world. Occupational identity. The time, and maybe even the interest, to be close to our mates.

Pregnant women are not sufficiently warned, if they are warned at all, about how a person so tiny can play havoc so enormous on the lifestyle they once knew. We speak in vague language like, "Oh, your life is about to change!" Everyone knows to expect a big change. Hardly anybody knows that that change can feel a lot like grief.

Every new mother mourns the loss of her personal freedom, more or less consciously and to varying degrees. Some women are acutely aware of their feelings and their longings and feel entitled to them; these are the luckiest among us, able to experience the joys *and* the pains of motherhood without self-scorn or denial. Others are aware but shame themselves for feeling what they feel, believing they are supposed to love every minute of motherhood or that they are selfish if they want just to be left alone for a while or that they should never have had children if they'd rather return to work than stay home with them. Some may view the feelings as perfectly reasonable for *other* mothers to have, but they stir up harsh self-criticism about perceived weakness or failure when the feelings belong to them. Still others are vaguely depressed or anxious without much insight into why. All are experiencing a profound kind of loss that, as a culture, we have conspired to keep secret. Motherhood, so they say, is supposed to be about the *addition* of a bundle of joy, not the *subtraction* of anything important or significant.

It has been pointed out that one of the reasons so little has been written about what it is like to mother a new baby is that the time to reflect on this experience, let alone put those reflections into words, is an unavailable luxury when one shares a home with a newborn. Author Louise Erdrich writes that she responds to the needs of her new baby without even translating the baby's cries into words; she "bypass[es] straight to action."[3] As she does so, she occupies some sort of Neverland: "My brain is a white blur. I lose track of what I've been doing, where I've been, who I am."

I have a similar memory from my earliest days of motherhood. I was sitting on the couch in our living room, nursing my son and looking out the window, when I saw some people walk by. I had a sudden realization that the same old world was continuing to go on out there and *I was no longer a part of it*. That moment captures how drastic the change from non-mother to mother really can be.

For me, this observation was not attached to any kind of emotion other than surprise. I was not (yet) sad or lonely or angry about existing in a separate dimension with my new baby. I did, however, lack the awareness that this pronounced sense of separation from the rest of the world was only temporary. I had the impression that this was the new, permanent state of affairs, much like I later had the impression—when my baby established himself as a truly terrible sleeper—that I would never again sleep.

And so the facets of loss in a new mother's life are many. This is not to say that the average new mother is in an acute state of mourning, let alone in a state of full-fledged depression. Like I was, most new mothers are vacillating, constantly, between states of joy and other emotions so varied and complicated that, for now, we'll just call them "non-joy." The trouble begins when we judge the non-joy states. We see them as bad, wrong, and shameful. We view them as indicative of our competence at mothering or our suitability for the job ("I feel so overwhelmed. I'm just not cut out for this."). We see them as unwelcome intruders on what is supposed to be the pleasurable, fulfilling stuff of motherhood.

The good news is that as a society, we are no longer silent on the topic of postpartum depression. Even in the decade or so since the words by Paula Nicolson quoted at the start of this chapter were published, the taboo against unhappiness in a new mother has begun to loosen its grip. Books like Brooke Shields's *Down Came the Rain*, essays and candid disclosures in popular magazines by Chrissy Teigen and Adele, and other celebrity accounts of PPD have done much to normalize the experience of mood problems during and after pregnancy. New research identifying just how commonplace emotional problems are in new parents, and how many different forms they can take, is getting some much-needed publicity, and public health campaigns reflect our growing commitment to addressing women's well-being in early motherhood. In many states,

laws require pediatric and obstetric health care providers to screen
for PPD at standard checkups, such as the baby's one-week visit and
the mother's six-week checkup with her OB-GYN. It is no longer
quite as shameful for a new mother to suffer debilitating depressive
symptoms in the wake of giving birth. After all, she is undergoing
tremendous hormonal changes as well as lifestyle changes, and
either of these could leave even the most psychologically healthy
woman susceptible to the "common cold" of mental illness, as depression is sometimes known.

However, overly simplistic explanations for PPD are part of a set
of myths that continue to distort our view of what changes within
a woman when she becomes a mother and what constitutes a "normal" transition into motherhood. Our improved awareness and
acceptance of PPD has brought with it an unfortunate consequence:
another false dichotomy that distorts our conceptualizations of
motherhood, this one distinguishing between the small minority
of women who suffer from PPD and the large majority of those
who do not. If you are lucky enough to fall into the latter category,
the assumption is that your newfound motherhood is generally not
marked by darkness, agitation, loss, helplessness, or despair. It is
assumed that your transition is a joyful one, maybe with some exhaustion on the side. This misconception of the difference between
those struck with PPD and those who are not masks the complexity
of the *typical* transition into motherhood, a transition that has the
potential to rattle and rearrange a woman more than anything else
she has faced before or will ever face again.

Where does this leave the large majority of new mothers, spared
from clinically detectable or diagnosable postpartum depression but
nonetheless suffering in various ways, often on an unpredictable
timeline? The mothers who are fumbling, doubting, and hurting
even as they smile, laugh, and genuinely treasure their new babies?
The mothers who are wondering, sometimes with profound angst,

who this person is in the mirror looking back at them even as they rejoice in their new role as nurturer? The ones who, grateful though they may be for their coparent, are distressed about varying degrees of anger or disinterest toward their partners and worried about what will become of their marriages? Their stories are the norm rather than the exception.

Yet *these* stories are so rarely told.

Anna came to me for therapy when her baby girl was five months old. I will never forget the look in her eyes as I greeted her in my waiting room that first day. A beautiful woman in her early thirties, with long brown wavy hair and a gorgeous curly-headed baby to match, she spoke to me before even opening her mouth. Her eyes said, *"I've been putting on a brave face and I can't do it anymore. Can I tell the truth to you?"* Anna's truth was that she felt utterly overwhelmed by daily life with her daughter, Gracie. She loved caring for her, and there was no shortage of joy in interacting with her— Anna wanted to be sure I understood that. But lurking beneath her pleasure in mothering was a pervasive sense of discontent. Each new day meant another opportunity to get "caught up on life," as she put it; she wanted to get the bills paid, return her grandmother's phone calls, clean the house, schedule that overdue lunch date with her coworkers who hadn't seen her since the baby was born. But each evening brought the same familiar disappointment. All her hours were filled with the endless stuff of parenting an infant, and when the baby slept, Anna collapsed in exhaustion and stared out the window, thinking about all the things she should be doing. "I used to be so energetic," she told me. "It makes me feel crazy to fall behind—to owe people emails, to see dirty dishes piled in the sink, to get phone calls about overdue bills. I keep waiting for things to get easier, but they don't. I want my old life back."

As soon as those words came out of her mouth—the wish for her pre-motherhood life—Anna began to cry. The emotion resided there, in the place where she couldn't bear her own words because of what she feared they meant. "How can I even say that? I love my daughter. I would do anything for her. I can't stand the thought of losing her. But sometimes when I look at her, all I can think about is who I used to be. I didn't know what I was giving up to become her mother. I didn't know how lost I would feel."

It wasn't long before the conversation turned to her marriage. Anna's husband, Pete, had been the one to call me about the possibility of seeing his wife for therapy. "I think she's either depressed or having anxiety attacks, or both," he had said to me over the phone. "She told me she was open to seeing somebody, but that calling to set up the appointment was just one more task that would go undone. So I offered to make the call for her." When I talked to Anna on the phone after that—to ensure that she did, indeed, want to set up an initial appointment with me and to transfer the control and responsibility to her—she told me she had agreed to let her husband make the call in hopes that maybe this would set the stage for him to be involved in therapy. "He thinks I have a problem, and I guess that's true. But something's not right with our marriage, and I wanted him to want to come with me."

In that first session, Anna told me all about what "wasn't right." Anna and Pete argued far more than they used to. They often went their separate ways in the evenings after the baby was in bed; Anna would immediately go to bed herself, and Pete would stay up until midnight playing guitar or watching movies. They hadn't had sex since their daughter was born. Pete had tried, many times, but Anna couldn't muster enough interest or comfort in her own body to be sexual with him. Pete felt rejected and angry. Anna felt guilty for hurting him by rejecting his advances, but also angry and resentful about his interest in sex. "I have nothing to give him. I can't even find the time or energy to take care of myself. When he inches closer to me in bed and tries to kiss me, it feels like just one more demand placed on me."

Though it took a little longer to find a way to talk about it, eventually Anna also told me about a nagging, and sometimes seething, anger toward Pete for the way he seemed to be carrying on with life as usual since Gracie was born. "He comes home from work and immediately asks what he can do to help. He usually takes Gracie off my hands and plays with her while I make dinner, and it's nice to have that time to myself in the kitchen. I know I should feel grateful. He's a good dad. But his life is pretty much the same as it was before she was born. He goes to work, he goes to the gym on his lunch hour, he sleeps all night long while I'm up breastfeeding. He doesn't even hear her cries, or if he does, he just moves her over to me and then rolls over and falls back asleep. Sometimes I lie there awake, nursing, thinking about what an asshole he is for being asleep. What is wrong with me?!"

Much like Anna saw each new day as an opportunity to finally "get on top of things," she also felt each new day would be the day she initiated a conversation with Pete about all the unsettling feelings that had been haunting her since their baby was born. She wanted desperately to give her feelings a voice, and Pete had always been the one to whom she turned when she needed to talk. But something was different now. He felt so far away, and she felt so confused and ashamed by her misgivings about motherhood that it just didn't feel safe to talk to him. Sometimes she tried to hint at her underlying feelings. "Do you ever miss life before Gracie?" she asked him one day. "I can't even remember what it was like before her," Pete had replied. "I can't imagine life without her." This was a sweet response in some ways; here is a dad who has welcomed his new daughter into his life so fully that it's as if she had always been there. But for Anna, it also fell flat; there was no sign in Pete's response that he shared any of her ambivalence. She felt more alone than ever.

Anna was tormented by her own mixed feelings. She felt guilty for feeling anything other than happiness about parenting. She felt a deep sense of loss about all that had changed for her since her daughter was born, right alongside a genuine sense of joy and gratitude for the addition of her daughter to her life. She resented her husband for seeming immune to the ambivalence that pervaded her experience of parenthood; he seemed so infuriatingly *not rattled* by their daughter's birth. And until our therapy conversation started, Anna didn't dare mention any of this to anyone else. Everyone else saw a beautiful new mother caring for a beautiful baby girl, with her stable, caring, involved husband in a supporting role. And as Anna looked around at other new mothers, she saw the same illusion: women everywhere with smiles on their faces, delighting in their babies, apparently free of the inner turmoil and marital problems that plagued Anna.

The assumption that motherhood is unfolding relatively seamlessly inside the walls of homes besides our own is a damaging misconception held by too many of us. There is so much anguish associated with this assumption, and such deep shame. If I had to identify the single most common cognitive distortion or false belief held by the new mothers who come to me for help, it is that other mothers seem to be having an easier time, and that consequently there is something wrong with them. What are the roots of this belief? Why do women assume their maternal struggles are singular or abnormal and that, therefore, they should keep them under wraps?* The women in my therapy practice who hold this belief are

---

* It is worth stating the obvious here, which is that a classic catch-22 explains the existence of this erroneous assumption. When women suffer during the transition to motherhood, they generally keep it to themselves because it does not seem that others are similarly suffering. Why not? Because other women are keeping their suffering to themselves, too.

not necessarily prone to other sorts of cognitive distortions. These are not "faulty thinkers" or "depressive" women who see everything through a negative lens. Rather, these women are victims of a fallacy that permeates our society at every level. As Naomi Wolf puts it in *Misconceptions*, "It is not the depressed new mother that is aberrant; it is her situation that is the aberration." There is nothing easy or normal about caring for a helpless, demanding infant, especially in the compromised physical and emotional state that results from the act of childbirth, and *especially all alone*, as is the typical scenario in American culture.

To witness my clients abandon this crippling assumption is to witness a remarkable transformation. Much of my work as a therapist is related to chipping away at this misconception that their daily foibles with their young children are unique to them, or at least worse and more numbered for them compared to others. I have this fantasy that all mothers—new and more established— could see into one another's lives, to achieve a sense of really knowing about this shared, universal fumbling through the territory of motherhood, especially in those early weeks (and months, and years). Imagine the rejoicing! Imagine the reassurance, the affirmation, the empowerment.

Sadly, this is not a reality. We don't often get a clear, unobstructed look into the real lives of other women besides—if we are lucky—a few close friends. Most of the time, we're limited to little glimpses and hints—glimmers of possibility that others are struggling the same way we are—that are usually dismissed in favor of the default assumption that motherhood is easier for other people than it is for us. I hope the stories I share in this book will provide a window into the truth of things, which is that the struggle is alive and well *in just about every other mother out there.*

2

_____

Out of the Shame Hole

Nothing is so painful as the pain that cannot be acknowledged, the pain of which we are (for whatever reasons) ashamed or that we construe as weakness or aberration.

—SUSAN MAUSHART, *THE MASK OF MOTHERHOOD*[1]

Rachael first came to me for therapy when her daughter was seven months old. She was haunted by images of harm coming to her baby, and much of the time, in those images, she was the one doing the harming. She pictured putting her baby in the dryer and turning it on. She pictured dropping her on the floor. She pictured driving off a bridge with her baby in the back seat. Sometimes she thought she might throw her baby against the wall. I can't imagine that any of us, parents or not, wouldn't cringe at these images. It's terribly unnerving to think of precious, innocent babies being harmed or killed. So imagine what it was like for Rachael when the images were about her own treasured baby girl. She loved her daughter deeply, and nurtured and protected her daily. Rachael's problem wasn't that she wanted to bring actual harm to her daughter (though sometimes, in severe cases of postpartum depression or psychosis, a mother actually does want to harm or kill her child). It was that she had no intention of hurting her daughter yet was terrified she might. That somehow she would "snap" and lose control and do the unspeakable.

As a therapist, I was immediately aware of what Rachael *wasn't* saying. I wondered about the pieces missing from Rachael's story of what the transition to parenthood had been like for her. It was clear to me that she was working hard to maintain the shiny veneer of a new mother thrilled to be staying home with her baby. Each time a darker aspect of Rachael's subjective experience rose to the surface in our conversations, it was quickly tamped back down: "Sometimes I feel like my husband isn't doing enough to help, but objectively I know he is. He's awesome. I shouldn't complain." Rachael was adept at denying her struggles both to herself and to others. So those struggles found the only outlet they could in her conscious awareness: the intrusive images.

As Rachael learned to give voice to the aspects of her experience that were taboo, the images began to fade away. Though intrusive images are what brought her into therapy, the real work we faced together was finding ways to help her access and express the complete truth of her experience as a mother. The images had completely disappeared within the first six months of therapy, but our work together has continued for another six years. These many years of therapy work could be characterized as a long, slow climb out of the "shame hole."*

One of my favorite lines in a book about mothering comes from Shirley Jackson's *Life Among the Savages*. She describes so well the cluttered, maddening, messy, joyful mayhem of her life as a mother of young children in rural Vermont in the 1950s. With the irreverence that characterizes her entire memoir, she states,

---

* I borrow this term from Brené Brown, author of *Daring Greatly* and other excellent books.

"I cannot think of a preferable way of life, except one without children."

What I love about this line is how efficiently it captures the ambivalence of mothering. Jackson was a renegade, giving voice to her mixed feelings at a time when women were not supposed to long for anything other than a life as a housewife and mother. Furthermore, she voices her ambivalence without equivocation; she says it like it is. Writing like Jackson's is so refreshing and, sadly, so rare. At least to her readers, she appeared to ride the waves of motherhood, marriage, and domesticity with a sense of humor and an openness to whatever feelings washed over her, without guilt. Her life of chaos was at once sublime and insufferable; there was no competition between the two states. Unlike Rachael, it seems she was nowhere near the shame hole. How can we help more women claim, as matter-of-factly as Jackson does, their mixed emotions about motherhood?

When I was training to become a psychotherapist, one specific area of study that interested me greatly was group therapy. The principles by which group therapy works are significantly different from the principles of individual therapy. In *The Theory and Practice of Group Psychotherapy*, author Irvin Yalom, one of my therapist-scholar heroes, describes what group therapy uniquely offers. Chief among these unique offerings is a ladder out of the shame hole.

Imagine that you are staying home with your new baby and struggling in silence with feelings of boredom and isolation. In your new role as a mother and in your intense adoration for your child, you have many beautiful moments, of course. You savor those moments and cling to them like buoys in the dark sea of stress, tension, exhaustion, and uncertainty you entered when your baby was born. But those moments seem few and far between, peppering what you would otherwise describe as an expanse of boredom.

Boredom is, in itself, unpleasant enough. But because you feel caught off guard by your boredom, and because you have an immediate judgment about it—*I should not be bored. I have this beautiful new baby, and I have the good fortune of being home with her. I must be a terrible person, or at least a terrible mother*—now you are not just bored. You're also ashamed. And because you're ashamed, the last thing you feel like doing is putting words to this experience. You probably won't tell your husband, and you definitely won't tell your mother (who has mentioned how lucky you are to get to stay home with your baby because she didn't have that luxury when she was a new mom), or the two mom acquaintances you met in childbirth class (who always look like they are having the time of their lives with their babies). No, you'll keep this secret to yourself. Your shame secret.

Now imagine that you are sitting with a group of other new mothers in a therapist's office, all gathered around for a first session to begin to process, and support one another through, the stresses of early parenthood. (We won't bother ourselves with how much trouble it took you to get there, how you thought you shouldn't need to do such a thing, how if you were a natural at mothering like everyone else seems to be, the flyer in your baby's pediatrician's office advertising this group would not have grabbed your attention, and how you felt so uneasy pulling into the parking lot at the therapist's office that you almost turned around to go home.) Imagine that, somewhere near the end of the hour, one woman says, "I never realized how long the days at home with my baby would feel." You experience a flash of recognition. You think, *I wonder if she feels bored, too. Nah. That's not what she said. She simply said the days feel long. She's probably just exhausted.* But in response, another woman says, "Me neither! I catch myself looking at the clock and can't wait until he falls asleep because I am just so tired of holding him." *Hmm*, you think. *That sounds a little like boredom to me. But no, maybe she just feels pulled in too many directions.*

She wants her baby to sleep so she can get the laundry folded or take a shower. Still, you drive home from that first group session wondering about the possibility that these other moms are bored sometimes, too. You have no solid evidence yet, but a seed has been planted.

If you go back to the group, you'll hear more of the same, and eventually you'll realize you are most certainly not alone. Your experience of boredom will be reduced to just that—boredom, not boredom coupled with shame. But if you don't go back to the group and instead keep your boredom to yourself, you'll retreat further into your shame cave.

Rachael had found her way into that cave very soon after giving birth, when she encountered a whole host of feelings she wasn't expecting. They were the same kinds of feelings Anna had experienced, the same kinds I had experienced, the same kinds *most, if not all*, new mothers experience at some point. Feeling exhausted and overwhelmed, sometimes resenting her baby, often resenting her husband, sometimes fantasizing about running away, hating the enormous discrepancy between the mother she envisioned herself being and the mother she actually was—these are all feelings shared by many new mothers.

Unfortunately, Rachael did not have the benefit of a peer group as transparent as the one in that hypothetical group therapy scenario. She perceived every other mother she encountered as competent, happy, and "on top of things," which only worsened her shame. Unable to face these feelings herself, let alone express them to her husband or anyone else in her life, Rachael kept them hidden from view. And until she began to tell her shame secret in therapy, it poisoned her. It undermined her confidence in herself as a mother, and it planted horrifying pictures in her head of harming her daughter.

Another client who suffered from a similar sense of shame and guilt about her perceived inadequacies as a mother was forty-year-old Jasmine. When I first met with her, she burst into tears as she told me that parenting seemed to come more easily to her husband than it did to her. She saw him as being "a natural"—a doting father who was able to remain calm and patient even when their babies presented the greatest challenges—and wondered if she was simply not cut from a mothering cloth. She couldn't understand how someone who had worked for years as a pediatric nurse as she had, genuinely enjoying the company of babies and kids, could find the idea of staying home with her own two small children so unpleasant.

Jasmine's husband had a well-paying job, and they lived comfortably—there was no economic imperative for her to go back to work. In fact, doing so might even mean they would lose money due to steep childcare costs. Jasmine admitted to me that she worried what other people would think if they knew she would rather go to her mediocre job every day than stay home with her kids. She wondered if maybe she had just waited "too long" to have children and having many decades of comfy child-free life under her belt impeded her maternal instincts from kicking in more strongly. She feared she would never be the kind of mother her children needed her to be.

In fact, Jasmine was a wonderful mother who was extremely self-critical and held herself to exacting standards. For far too many women, feelings of shame and inadequacy shape the words they use to describe their experience of themselves as mothers. With each internal telling and retelling of the shame story, the fundamental sense of being "bad" at mothering—or, at best, the sense of isolation in *struggling* with mothering—grows stronger. And like every other mother plugged into social media, Jasmine found that she didn't even need to leave her living room to see an image of a woman who appeared to be more competent at mothering, and a lot more blissful about it and gorgeous while doing it, than her.

Shame and Social Media

I n the current digital age, we cannot have a discussion about the sources of women's shame, anxiety, and self-criticism without addressing, at least briefly, the role of social media. What are most breastfeeding mothers doing while immobilized on the couch with a nursing infant? Chances are, they're not spending the whole time staring at their baby's face, or reading an absorbing novel that allows them some escape from the relentless inner dialogue about how well they're performing as mothers. More likely, they're scrolling through their Facebook or Instagram feed. And I hear regularly from my clients about how this habit makes them feel: lousy.

No matter how informed we are about the hazards of social media, no matter how strong our intellectual understanding that it is a performance-driven medium in which people airbrush their lives with the images and filters they choose, most of us are still likely to fall into the comparison trap. An isolated new mother is likely to contrast other people's idyllic posts with her own messy, confusing, overwhelming life. In a perverse irony, the sense of isolation she is attempting to counter by turning to social media only deepens her feelings of otherness and separation. Confined to the house with a napping baby, or too constrained by the dual demands of work and motherhood to fit in face-to-face time with friends, she enters a digital world that promises connection and sharing. More often than not, she emerges feeling lonely, anxious, and unsure of herself.

With the staggering popularity of social networking sites and our increasing reliance on them as a means of social support, there is reason to be curious about how our online behavior affects our emotional well-being. Research on the psychology of social media is still in its infancy, and so far it is inconsistent and contentious. One large-scale study demonstrated that the more time a person spent on social media and the greater the number of social media memberships he or she had, the higher that person's stress level and the lower his or her quality of life.[2] Some scholars have used the term "internet paradox" to refer to the set of findings that reveal an inverse relationship between online networking and offline social connection and psychological well-being.[3,4] Others have found that some forms of social media can improve the mental health of people with certain conditions that make face-to-face interactions difficult.[5] Still others have shown that although social media involvement increases one's sense of *online* social support, this has no direct bearing on one's overall well-being.[6,7] While the jury may still be out with respect to any definitive causal relationships between social media use and psychological health, at a minimum the correlational findings indicate that we are not likely to find the antidote to what ails us by logging onto Facebook. A fair assessment of the current state of affairs in research might be put this way: Face-to-face social interactions and perceived social support have long been established as crucial to psychological well-being, and scientific investigations have yet to generate any compelling evidence that cyber interactions yield the same benefits. Further research will help to parse the lack of benefits from possible detriments.

From my vantage point as a therapist, I worry most about social media's capacity to fan the flames of shame. The social media habit provides an abundant supply of "evidence" that others are doing better, and it moves us further away from honest dialogue about the underlying issues that are aching to be acknowledged. Even when people post photos that expose the chaos of their home life, with self-deprecating and funny captions like "#parentingfails" or "#Calgon-takemeaway," there is a playful tone that belies the more unsettling feelings that lurk beneath. It feels to me like the din of daily superficial posts is drowning out the sound of hearts quietly breaking. Painful truths get buried beneath the censored, enhanced, or patently false fronts we project. Among the painful truths are these:

"I am not the kind of mother I thought I would be."

"Having a baby has not brought me and my partner closer. Actually, I feel further away from him [or her] than ever before."

"I don't feel like myself anymore."

"Sometimes I wish I could go back to life before children."

"I'm not sure I'm cut out to be a mom."

I'm pretty sure we won't see any of those statements as status updates or hashtags. From behind the safety screen of social media, we either put our shiny happy faces forward, or we vent about the superficial messes and stresses of parenthood. Both practices cloud our view of our *deeper* shared experiences as mothers. Our trouble with emotional vulnerability and authenticity has been around a long time, and it won't vanish anytime soon. Social media has intensified it, creating a whole new invitation to wear our masks and indulge our perpetual temptation to deny or distort the feelings that unsettle us the most. We now spend increasing proportions of our lives in this strange new online world, where it's so easy to trivialize or exaggerate and so hard to be real.

I like to imagine what could happen if just a fraction of social media posts were replaced, or at least supplemented, with time spent writing a few pages in a journal. Or with intimate, unhurried, brave conversations with friends and partners. In those mediums, we are far more likely to remove our masks and begin to connect to the current of our deeper emotions.

In my fantasy alternate universe in which all women are transparent about exactly how hard mothering is and every mother feels full permission to have and to voice any emotion, Jasmine's story would sound very different from the shame-saturated one I de-scribed earlier. She might say, upon arrival to therapy, "I need a little support as I attempt to adjust to my life as a mother. It's a much bigger transformation than I imagined it would be. I've got a lot of mixed emotions, and I'm exhausted." In those words, there is an absence of judgment, self-criticism, and shame. The words depict in a matter-of-fact way how hard it is to do the work of mothering and to regain equilibrium within such a radically changed identity and lifestyle. In an ideal world, women would have access to this kind of language to describe their experience of motherhood.

As both Rachael and Jasmine hinted early on in our conversations, the experience of motherhood wasn't the only shameful part of their lives; their private concerns about their marriages also fueled their shame. Like Rachael and Jasmine, many women feel shame and guilt for resenting a "good" husband. Rachael recognized the many helpful contributions Scott made to their daughter's daily care, which made her feel worse about being unable to let go of her ir-ritation over all the ways he *wasn't* helping. It was up to Rachael to figure out alternate arrangements when the nanny was sick. Rachael was the one who heard their daughter crying in the night. Rachael spent weekends catching up on laundry, cleaning, bills, and every other thing that slipped through the cracks all week, while Scott spent weekends catching up on sleep.

As long as we are keeping our problems to ourselves, we stand no chance of learning that these kinds of issues are common and that there are good reasons for them. If, instead, we share our stories with other women, we are almost sure to discover that their strug-gles are remarkably similar to our own. Sometimes our husbands are even the ones to help us out of the shame hole. When Rachael found the courage to tell Scott about the horrible intrusive images she'd been having, he looked her in the eye with loving compassion—not fear or disgust—and suggested, gently, that she seek help. He told her she was a wonderful mother, and he sat beside her on my couch during that first therapy hour, helping pave the way for the long journey that has brought her out of shameful darkness and into the light of ordinary, universal struggles.

Silence—our own and others'—keeps us stuck in shame. False, distorted, and censored accounts of motherhood—our own and others'—keep us stuck in shame. Only when silence is broken and secrets are revealed can we begin to revise the shame story. Thus, this seems like as good a time and place as any to let some big cats out of the bag:

1. Sometimes we resent our babies.
2. Babies do not equal happiness.
3. Babies do not bring couples closer together.

Sometimes We Resent Our Babies

> I didn't know she had colic; I just thought she was an asshole.
> —*The Longest Shortest Time*, episode #10

I recently listened to a podcast about a mother whose newborn baby started crying one day and didn't stop for six or eight weeks. During that time, the mother very persistently had the thought that she should probably give the baby to her sister. She was at her wit's end, utterly exhausted by her attempts to soothe a baby who could not be soothed. Her thought that she should give the baby to her sister originated in part from a sense of incompetence; surely her sister (older than her, and an established mother) could do a better job of caring for this fussy infant. What interested me more, though, was that this new mother did not even *like* her baby. She did not feel connected to the baby and did not have fond feelings for her.

Her courage in revealing this to a potentially enormous audience of strangers was refreshing. I think that perhaps one reason she had the ability to do so was because more than a year had passed since those difficult days. In that time, she had bonded with her baby and gained hard-won perspective. She could look back and laugh a little about how terrible the experience was.

A good friend of mine told me about the night she angrily dropped her two-month-old baby onto a mattress while declaring, "I hate him." Like the woman from the podcast, my friend was drained of her usual mental and emotional resources by a baby who would not stop crying. When she told me about this—without a trace of shame, because she is a rare and wonderful bird—I remember filing it away in my brain as evidence of how much better off we are when we can voice our emotional truth, *however taboo it may be*. She did hate her baby in that moment. She is also a loving mother. Those two things do not cancel each other out, and she knew that; otherwise, she would never have told me the story. She had climbed out of the shame hole a long time ago, if she had ever fallen in it. Because of her uncommon and unapologetic candor, I picture her standing at the edge, aboveground, shouting down to the mothers trapped within, "Come on up! I hate my baby sometimes, too!"

Another friend tells me that she locked herself in the bathroom for longer than she cared to admit, with her preschooler and toddler knocking on the door, because she could not stand another minute of their demands. On a different occasion, after a particularly stressful early morning, she went to the garden with a beer at nine a.m. She relayed this to me with a little bit of a nervous laugh, wondering if I thought she was crazy or horrible, and said, "I have *never* done something like that before. I have never even *considered* a drink in the morning, but it was like I needed medicine. I needed something to calm my body." Again, our children have the ability to rattle us like nobody and nothing else can. This friend is an extraordinarily responsible person, lovely in all ways, playful and fun and creative and nurturing. And sometimes, when her husband is not around to share the parenting burdens, she locks herself in the bathroom and cries, or downs an early-morning adult beverage.

Of course, for nearly all women, loving feelings prevail in the unfolding emotional drama of motherhood. We are devoted to our children, we gladly make sacrifices for them, we protect them fiercely, and we delight in them like we delight in nobody else. But it is the coexistence of the loving and the less-loving feelings that is so difficult to tolerate. It's as if we expect the resentment will run amok and destroy the love if we acknowledge it. Maternal ambivalence remains a highly uncomfortable concept despite its having been explored by many writers before me. From this intolerance for ambivalence is born the pursuit of perfection, and a great deal of suffering. We shame each other and ourselves for harboring negative feelings about our babies and our roles as mothers, even though maternal ambivalence, at its core, is nothing more than a conflict between our needs and the needs of our babies. Both sets of needs are legitimate, and both warrant fulfillment. It is quite inevitable, then, for this ambivalence to arise. It is an inherent condition of motherhood, reflecting the simple fact that our needs do not cease to exist when we become responsible for a needy infant.

Babies Do Not Equal Happiness

Popular culture tells us that having children is one of the key ingredients (along with a satisfying career and a solid marriage) of a happy, fulfilling life. Adults past child-rearing age who never had children are often regarded with suspicion or pity; we wonder if these poor childless souls experienced infertility, or what less-than-optimal personality traits they possess (selfishness, immaturity, curmudgeonliness) if they voluntarily opted out of the child-rearing enterprise. But according to Harvard researcher and bestselling author Daniel Gilbert, those non-parents have an edge over the rest of us when it comes to happiness. Using a research tool called experience sampling, in which people's moment-to-moment happiness levels are assessed as they go about their daily lives, Gilbert and his colleagues have established that adults without children are happier than parents. Least happy of all are parents of young children, and among women, spending time with a child generates about the same degree of joy as vacuuming.

In Gilbert's keynote address at the American Psychological Association's annual convention a few years ago, he likened parenting to a no-hitter baseball game. The moments of excitement and pleasure are dwarfed by the moments of boredom. We may be reluctant to embrace this metaphor, but it rings true, and his research certainly backs it up. Is there any truth, then, to the folk "wisdom" that children bring their parents happiness? Research tells us that in old age, looking back retrospectively upon parenting is, indeed, a central source of happiness. Gilbert proposes that in order to cope with the extreme hardships of parenting, we need to *believe* our kids bring us happiness. He states, "We don't value our children in spite of how difficult they are, we value our children *because* of how difficult they are."[8] It's as if we are playing a little Jedi mind trick on ourselves, saying, "If children cost me so much, they must be worth it. They must be an amazing source of happiness." Coupled with our collective silence about how hard it is to raise children, this mind trick keeps us sane but perpetuates the myth that parenting is bliss.

None of this is to say that children are *not* a source of joy. There's another, critical component of Gilbert's analogy of the no-hitter baseball game: *In the bottom of the ninth, with two outs, somebody hits a home run. Maybe even a grand slam.* That one hit makes the whole game worthwhile. Now we don't resent being there for those nine monotonous innings. Our children seem to deliver these "home runs"—a perfectly timed kiss or cuddle, a shining accomplishment, the most hilarious question, a stunning observation—when we least expect them, and perhaps just when we most need them.

In her bestselling book *The Happiness Project*, author Gretchen Rubin coins the term "fog happiness." She writes, "Fog is elusive. Fog surrounds you and transforms the atmosphere, but when you try to examine it, it vanishes. Fog happiness is the kind of happiness you get from activities that, closely examined, don't really seem to bring much happiness at all—yet somehow they do."[9] Rubin suggests that parenting small children falls into the category of fog happiness. If we train our close analytical eye on any given ordinary interaction with our children during any ordinary day and examine our emotions, "happy" is not very likely to be in the mix. It's even less likely to be the prevailing emotion, the one by which we imagine we will remember that moment if we had a snapshot of it to return to years later. Wrestling our toddlers into their car seats? We feel irritated, frustrated, impatient. Reminding our fourth graders that their homework isn't going to do itself? We feel annoyed and resent the sound of our own nagging voices. Holding back a child's hair while she crouches over the toilet vomiting at three a.m.? We feel exhausted, maybe a little grossed out, and worried about canceling all the work meetings we have scheduled for the next day. As Rubin states, zoom in on any one of these moments, and there is nothing happy about it. But zoom out and ponder the big picture of parenthood, and almost invariably we construe it as a source of tremendous happiness. We ascribe meaning to the small moments that may not be a party while they're occurring, and it is within that meaning-making that the happiness arises.

Often, parents whose children are grown seem to recall even the most challenging aspects of early parenthood—sleepless nights with infants, endless diaper changes, caring for sick children—through a rosy lens: "Oh, how I miss those nights of rocking my baby to sleep over and over again, holding her close." They miss these experiences because of the meanings they ascribed to them, meanings centered around nurturance, intimacy, and pride. Those meanings are, almost always, more accessible after the moments have passed. The cliché "You don't know what you've got until it's gone" is perhaps nowhere more apt than in the realm of parenting small children. Parents with grown children always seem to be cautioning in-the-trenches parents about how fast the time flies, how important it is to slow down and savor the experience.

In her memoir of motherhood, *Operating Instructions*, Anne Lamott writes, "It's so easy and natural to race around too much, letting days pass in a whirl of being busy and mildly irritated, getting fixed on solutions to things that turn out to be just farts in the windstorm." It's true. Even a relatively small passage of time is often enough to alter, dramatically, the way we think and feel about a parenting experience. Just yesterday, my mother, who has a strange but endearing practice of archiving and frequently resurrecting past emails, stumbled upon an email I had written to her a couple of years ago:

Quinn was behaving very badly on Saturday in numerous ways when we were out and about, but let me tell you about the straw that broke the camel's back and sent his beloved fire engine to the basement (which he had been warned would happen). In Barnes and Noble, I was keeping a tight grip on him because he has such the tendency to run off. He kept complaining about that and saying "LET ME GO!" and I was saying "I CAN'T LET YOU GO BECAUSE YOU WON'T STAY CLOSE AND YOU NEED TO STAY CLOSE." Eventually this exchange was happening while we were standing in line to pay, and he convinced me to let go and promised me he would not run away. The instant I let go, he bolted like a bat out of hell, ran directly behind the cash registers, then all the way across the store to the farthest away corner, laughing and squealing with devilish delight all the while, knocking a couple of books over in the process and almost knocking some people over, too. Meanwhile Noah was standing alone in the line while I was chasing Quinn; we had been in this long line for a while and I didn't want to lose our spot so I told Noah "STAY THERE" and when I returned with Quinn, poor Noah was standing at the front of the line, with our items to purchase in hand, meaning it was our turn, and he was looking all worried. Jesus.

I remember that as I wrote that email to my mom a day or two after the incident had occurred, I could already see the humor in it. I couldn't *feel* the humor, though. The stress of the situation was what figured most prominently in the way I was carrying it with me mentally. I was aware not only of the feelings I had (anger, exasperation, embarrassment) while at the store chasing my three-year-old, but also the swirl of negativity that surrounded the incident immediately afterward and beyond. My bad mood in the car on the drive home and the bad taste in my mouth from the harsh talking-to that I gave Quinn. My follow-through, once we got home, of taking away (temporarily, of course) his treasured ride-on fire engine. My ruminating about why it has to be so difficult to have a nice outing to the bookstore with my children on a cold winter day. My ridiculous, neurotic internal questioning of *what is the matter with my child that he cannot obey a simple command when I am very serious about its importance, and worse, why does he not have the* instinct *to stick close to his mother while out in a crowd?*

I know that as I wrote the email to my mom, I thought, *One day I'll think this is funny.* And as predicted, when the email appeared in my in-box yesterday and I opened it, I experienced only positive emotions. *Quinn is such a rascal,* I thought with a smile. What felt stressful and very much un-fun in the moment is now a memory that captures Quinn's great sense of freedom and adventure—something I have come to celebrate—and the "full catastrophe" of parenthood. It *is* a funny story. I don't love the way I reacted at the time—particularly all the needless contemplating of Quinn's possible defects—but there is no temptation to revisit the negative feelings from that day. There is only a sense of looking back on a classic tale of the perils of navigating a big store with an active, curious toddler, and a realization of how much he has already changed and grown and how much I have come to value his defining features rather than worry about or resent them for the parenting hardships they generate.

Rubin's conceptualization of fog happiness helps resolve what appear to be contradictory research findings about the happiness of parents. Ask a young mother to pause from playing with her fifteen-month-old at eleven a.m. and indicate her current happiness level, and her answer will be about the same as when she's vacuuming at four p.m. Ask that same woman when she's eighty-five years old what her top three sources of happiness were, and "being a mother" or "caring for my children" will surely make the list. Vacuuming, not so much. *Immediate* joy and fun in parenting are scattered stars in the great black sky of strain, boredom, and unrelenting responsibility in parenting. But when the joy comes, it comes insisting. And when we take the long view and ascribe meaning to our life's activities, little else competes for first place with raising our very own human beings.

For many of us, this juxtaposition of dull or difficult moments against fundamental joy and fulfillment is visible every single night in the sleeping faces of our children. So many nights, exhausted or just impatient, I have been eager for my children's bedtime. One son's chatter barely registers in my ear because it's the same chatter

I've been hearing all day. The other son's chain of requests—for a sip of water, to be tucked in (again), for another sip of water, to turn the hall light on—feels like fingernails on a chalkboard. Minutes later, as I peek into their rooms and see that they have each fallen into slumber, I see all sweetness and splendor in their faces. I want to lie down next to them and hold them close. I wonder what that last bit of chatter was that I tuned out, whether it was something important about my boy's world that I missed. A tiny voice saying, *"Can I please have another sip of water?"* echoes in my head, and I hear it more clearly now as, "It makes me feel secure and cared for when you get me a drink of water." Their well-being matters more to me than anything, and I feel at a cellular level the honor and joy of being their mom . . . now that they're asleep.

Babies Do Not Bring Couples Closer Together

Often, newly-in-love people describe their certainty that they have found "the one" with some statement along the lines of "I want to have his baby" or "I just know she's going to be the mother of my children." This kind of sentiment conveys how much emphasis we place on child-rearing as the ultimate achievement of a romantic union. For 90 percent of adults, when we find ourselves deeply in love and maybe even convinced that we've met our soul mate, we set our sights on making and raising a baby with that person. It *is* a beautiful fact of nature that children are living, breathing products of a union between two people. I am not here to undermine the beauty—one might even say the miracle—of human life arising out of love. But I do want to counter a very pervasive myth, and I want to articulate one of life's greatest ironies. The myth, which somehow persists even though the strains of parenthood are well known, is that having a baby cements a couple's bond. The irony is that children quite often threaten the very connection from which they came. The intimate, sexual, emotional tie between their parents that led them to make a baby in the first place begins to unravel when the baby materializes. This is usually true for even the happiest and sturdiest of couples, so imagine the rude awakening in store for those unstable couples who, searching for remedies for their ailing relationships, say to themselves, *Maybe a baby will bring us closer together.*

Study upon study shows that marital happiness takes a significant hit when spouses evolve from partners into coparents. Their sense of intimate connection, emotional and sexual, drops precipitously. Their level of conflict rises sharply; new parents argue nine times as often as they did before they had a baby.[10] Problematic communication patterns—like one partner pursuing contact while the other withdraws—happen far more than before the baby was born. Self-reported marital satisfaction levels are significantly lower than those of childless couples, especially among women, and especially in that first year after the baby's birth.[11]

Even when we broaden the scope beyond just the initial transition-to-parenthood years when couples are destabilized the most, we see that the strain of parenthood shapes marriages in a lasting way. Just like research demonstrates that personal (individual) happiness is higher for non-parents than parents, we also have an abundance of studies showing that *marital* happiness is higher for non-parents than parents. And while a lot of couples recover at least partially from the disruption of their marriage brought on by the birth of their first child, many do not. The divorce rate among couples with children is highest in the early parenting years, and the parents of young children are overall more likely to divorce than their childless counterparts.[12]

Interestingly, the decline in marital satisfaction for new parents is sharper now than it once was. Compared to the new parents of the 1960s and '70s, today's new parents take twice as steep a nosedive in their marital adjustment. As we will see later, because our ideals about marriage have shifted, the losses ushered in by parenthood hurt more than they did in previous generations. More than ever, marriage is expected to bring emotional support (not just, or even necessarily, financial support) and intimate companionship. Add a baby to the equation, and the support and intimacy for which we strive in our marriages become much harder to generate.

In my experience, women tend to be more vocal about this particular "secret" of new motherhood. It is relatively easier to air gripes about one's partner or husband and to confess to feeling disinterested in him than it is to reveal feeling disinterested in, and destabilized by, motherhood itself. It is less shameful to hit a rough patch in one's relationship than it is to question one's competence as a mother, or to wonder whether one is "mother material" when motherhood is exalted as the ultimate source of meaning and identity for women. What so few people seem to realize, however, is exactly how much these marital changes affect, and are affected by, their own well-being as women and mothers.

For decades, marital therapy has been an accepted form of treatment for women's depression. Studies show it to be as effective as other forms of therapy in alleviating symptoms of depression in women.[13] This isn't rocket science. If strengthening a marriage alleviates depression in a wife, then depression has at least some of its roots in an ailing relationship. And there's a great deal of research to support that idea.[14] Furthermore, the links between *postpartum* depression, in particular, and marital health are many and undeniable. Women who experience PPD report lower marital satisfaction, compared to mothers who do not meet the criteria for depression, as many as five years after the initial episode of

PPD.[15] Among the strongest statistical predictors of PPD are marital distress and poor social support, particularly lack of paternal involvement in the care of the baby.[16, 17]

Evidence for the role of relationship distress in mothers' depression pours in from all different angles. For instance, women who feel less secure in their relationships are more likely to suffer PPD, and when women diagnosed with PPD are offered a short-term course of therapy designed to help them cope with caring for an infant, their depressive symptoms improve more when their partners attend therapy with them than when they attend alone.[18] Everything about this makes sense, and yet a woman's depression is still primarily regarded as a "woman's problem," something originating within her rather than within the space between her and her mate or in the impossible standards to which she is held. When husbands do not see their role in their wives' suffering—both in contributing to it and in having the capacity to help her out of it—women are at even greater risk of falling into the shame hole. Sometimes it might even seem that our husbands are kicking the ladder out from under us as we try to climb out, because they tell us our feelings are unfounded, ridiculous, or wrong. Responses like those, while perhaps offered in the hope of alleviating some of our pain, only reinforce our sense that something is wrong with us. And they most certainly don't generate feelings of closeness in the relationship. As we will continue to see in subsequent chapters, *the extent to which our partners stay close* as we navigate the uncertain territory of new parenthood makes all the difference, not only in our sense of well-being as women but also in terms of our marital health and happiness.

3

The Full Catastrophe

To opt for kids is to opt for chaos, complexity, turbulence, and truth.

—Harriet Lerner

There is a wonderful collection of essays called *Finding Your Inner Mama* that I wish all new moms knew about and had the time to read. In one piece, "A Crash Course in Vulnerability and Other Lessons," renowned psychologist Harriet Lerner says this:

When things go by the book, which statistically speaking they are likely to do, pregnancy is still a lesson in surrender and vulnerability. Your body is inhabited; you live with the realization that childbirth is a wild card; and you know at some level that your life will soon be altered in ways you cannot even begin to imagine. No matter how well you prepare yourself, you are not going to be able to run the show. You're in the thick of a full catastrophe, and change is the only thing you can count on for sure.[1]

As Lerner implies, the metamorphosis that motherhood brings begins not when the baby is born but during pregnancy. My client Julia came to me when she was about three months pregnant with her first child. A little depression-prone all her adult life, she now found that she was anxious, too. Many women become pre-occupied with their developing baby's health and worried about the act of childbirth, and this was true for Julia. But her anxiety also ran deeper. She had recurring dreams about her baby being a girl, and she said to me, "I realize I want so badly for this baby to be a boy. Because I think sons look more to their fathers and daughters look more to their mothers as they are forming their identities. I'm terri-fied that if we have a girl, I'll ruin her."

Julia's fear made me very sad. In so few words, she told me a great deal about how she felt about herself. I assumed that as we talked further, I'd hear more and more about her negative self-image and all the ways this had hindered her long before getting pregnant. I was wrong. As I got to know Julia, I found that she was a self-possessed, energetic, gregarious, determined woman who—though often contending with low-grade sadness and irritability—was genuinely proud of her accomplishments and felt well liked by her peers and her family. It was only during pregnancy, as she started to imagine herself as a mother more vividly and to contemplate the influence she would soon have on a brand-new human being, that she began to encounter some very dark facets of her self-image. These facets weren't accessible to her before. She'd never had a rea-son to doubt herself as seriously as she now did.

Fast-forward about a year, and Julia is sitting on my couch breast-feeding her five-month-old son, crying as she tells me about her latest argument with her husband and how close she is to "losing it" because her house, her marriage, and her life are in such disarray. The concerns that brought her into therapy now seem almost existential; they have become peripheral in our work, pushed aside by the more pressing mat-ter of her overwhelming daily life. She is too busy trying to keep from drowning to worry about what kind of person her son will grow up to be under her care. Besides, she got her wish: he is a boy, and rational or not, her fears of damaging her child are less pronounced because of that.

Julia spends her days proficiently taking care of her baby. He is healthy and content and adorably chubby, and Julia exudes confidence in the visible realm of parenting. She feeds him, changes him, and rubs eczema cream on his winter-worn cheeks during our sessions while also keeping her train of thought squarely on its tracks and expressing herself eloquently. I am struck by her grace and efficiency. But this appearance that Julia projects, this air of being "on top of things," is quite the opposite of her internal experience. Julia does not recognize her own life anymore. She uses that phrase over and over again to capture just how much has changed. Normally extremely responsible and conscientious, Julia has lately forgotten to show up for doctor appointments, gotten her car towed for parking in a no-parking zone, and neglected to return important phone calls. Once a social butterfly, now she would rather stay home than meet with friends. When she does get together with others, she replays their conversations afterward in her head with self-loathing about her "verbal diarrhea." A self-described neat freak, she looks at the messes in every room of her house and feels simultaneously suffocated by them and unmotivated to clean them up. Time is too precious; when the baby is napping, she needs to take the world's fastest shower or answer her husband's text about what to pick up at the grocery store on the way home. And besides, any tidying progress she makes will just rapidly come undone by her own frenzied manner of going about the day or her slob of a husband. Before their son was born, she considered herself quite happily married, but now she looks at her husband and feels either aggravation or indifference. She's not sure which is worse. And as if all this doesn't feel bad enough as she's living it, the interpretive frame she puts around it makes her feel even worse: "I've become a different person, and I hate who I am now." There are plenty of other ways she could frame her current struggles (for instance, "Sleep deprivation has really started to take a toll"), but the interpretation she has chosen is one in which her very personhood has been altered, and not for the better. It's a frame that adds a layer of unfortunate, unnecessary suffering to the inevitable pain of her daily life.

If these words, "pain" and "suffering," seem strange, let me explain the context in which I'm using them. A certain kind of distinction between pain and suffering has proved quite helpful in the mental health field.[2] Pain is inevitable. It is part of the human condition. We will undoubtedly injure ourselves, and be injured by others, and so we feel pain; this is true both physically and emotionally. Suffering, on the other hand, comes when we do what human beings seem uniquely inclined to do, and that is to relate to the pain cognitively and emotionally. We analyze it, judge it, scorn it, resist it, try to control it, deny it, distort it, hate it, blame someone for it, scoff at it, wallow in it, scrutinize it. The realm of pain is primitive and primary; our bones ache from the piercing cold, our muscles are sore from carrying a hefty baby all day, our bodies are heavy and our heads throb from another night of insufficient sleep. The realm of suffering is auxiliary and secondary; we react to our experience of cold, aching bones with perhaps a scornful thought directed at the self ("I'm so stupid for forgetting my coat"); as we massage our tense shoulders, we drive ourselves crazy wondering why our baby needs to be held constantly; and as we face another sleep-deprived day, we dissolve into tears of frustration and anger about why the stupid no-cry sleep method doesn't work on our baby.

As Julia spoke, I heard the places in her story that gave rise to the suffering. And Julia's story very much resonated with me. While buried beneath the weight of new motherhood, I, too, experienced a profound identity shift and often felt like a stranger to myself. When Noah was seven months old, I wrote in my journal:

Motherhood has apparently transformed me from an extremely mellow, even-keeled person to a tense and high-strung person with mood fluctuations so pronounced that my husband has asked me, on more than one occasion, what I've done with his wife and when she's coming back. During my pregnancy, my blood pressure was 112/60 at every single prenatal doctor visit I had. The nurses commented each time on how amazingly consistent I was. It seems silly, but I took pride in this, feeling it was a clear physical indication of the ever-so-stable and calm person that I am. At my six-week postpartum visit, my blood pressure was so much higher that the nurse asked me if I was nervous. "Nervous?" I asked. "No, just exhausted and on edge from having a baby who never stops crying." Six months later, my baby boy is as happy as a clam, but I'm not. I'm guessing my blood pressure hasn't returned to that low number that reflected my internal calm and stability. I'm not the same, and I wonder if I ever will be. Seven and a half months into motherhood, I sometimes don't recognize myself. If a client were describing to me this same set of concerns, I would be inclined to reassure her that the fundamental person she is remains unchanged, and that this is merely an adjustment period. I know better than to assume we are that fragile, and I have a lot of faith in the resilience of human beings. Living inside my own skin, though, I'm filled with a fear that something about me—something that previously defined who I am and served me quite well—is irrevocably different now that I'm a mom.

Like Julia, I had a tremendous amount of judgment about the strange new person I had become. I did not like her. I liked my old self much better. Julia liked her old self much better. What neither of us knew, at the time, was that the very qualities we felt we had lost and were grieving were the qualities that set us up to be so discombobulated by motherhood. One of the first things to disappear when we cross the threshold into parenthood is any semblance of order that our lives may once have had. No new mother is unfazed by the changes a baby brings, but people who thrive on having a sense of control and agency, who put a high premium on productivity, and who feel calm only when "on top of things" are likely to experience significant challenges when a baby enters the picture.

Lerner cautions women, "Don't have [children] if your life's purpose is to dwell in complete stillness, serenity, and simplicity; or if you have a great dread of being interrupted; or if you are on a particular life path that demands your full attention and devotion." Of course, her advice is tongue-in-cheek. Ninety percent of adult human beings do have children, and very few people think carefully about whether they are exactly the right kind of person to be a mother or father. Nobody with a strong urge to create their own human being is going to heed Lerner's advice and say, "Oh, okay, never mind. I'd rather have a serene and uninterrupted life." We just carry on with our plans to have a baby, more or less aware that it might be a little hard on us. Indeed, whenever dissonance is caused by two competing ideas, such as "I have baby fever" and "Raising a baby is really, really hard and I'm told it will turn my world upside down," we are pretty good at negating one of those ideas in order to eliminate the dissonance. Most people resolved to have a baby (or two or three) find ways to dismiss the evidence for how exceptionally difficult it will be. We are equipped with all kinds of tricks and tools for this, because our species depends on it. If everybody got cold feet about this procreation business, well . . . we would cease to be. So we say to ourselves, *It can't be* that *bad. Everybody else is doing it.* Or *They had a tough time of it when their baby was born, but that's because their marriage was falling apart, too.* Or *They had a tough time of it, but that's because they had no family around to help. At least my in-laws live across town.* Or simply, *It'll be hard, but we'll get through it*. Vague reassurances, rationalizations, pep talks, arrogant notions that we will handle it better than others do . . . these are all effective strategies to muster the courage to plan a pregnancy, or to cope with an unplanned one.

I used these strategies myself. When I was pregnant with my first child, an acquaintance who was, at the time, an exhausted new mother told me she didn't even have time to brush her teeth anymore. I recall thinking, *Oh, c'mon now. It takes two minutes to brush your teeth*. Well, let's just say karma did its thing. While life with a newborn does allow for a "free" two minutes here or there throughout the day, usually there are far more pressing things than teeth-brushing that we choose to do with those two-minute stretches. Like peeing. And eating.

There is no question, then, that most expectant parents do not appreciate the level of chaos they are inviting into their lives. It's just one of those things that is impossible to anticipate or understand until it is being lived. But what I also know, and what Lerner's words illuminate, is that coping with this chaos is an individual endeavor that varies widely. There are some mothers for whom the chaos is barely noticeable, and others for whom it is a crippling problem. The majority of us, like me and like Julia, are somewhere in between, perhaps vacillating between tolerating the chaos just fine and feeling for a moment that we might rather be dead than continue to live amid such mayhem.

One of my oldest, dearest friends happens to be the most disorganized, fly-by-the-seat-of-her-pants person I know. She has a demanding career, a husband with a demanding career, three small children, and a tiny two-bedroom Manhattan apartment. When she came with her family to visit us for an autumn weekend in Vermont, she pulled from the trunk of their car one of those giant, cobalt blue, faux suede Amazon.com gift bags into which she had hurriedly shoved a few articles of clothing, along with a few toothbrushes, for everyone in her family. She did this after spending the morning working from home to meet a tight deadline, with all three of her children in the apartment, while her husband was at work.

If I were headed out of town for the weekend, I would have the suitcases out the night before, carefully choosing outfits for my children and myself and probably checking things off a packing list. I would find it enormously stressful to have to spend the morning at my computer, frantically completing a work project, while my children made various demands and messes, knowing I then had to pack for a trip and load up the car and drive for six hours. I would arrive at my destination exhausted and in need of a cocktail. For my wondrous friend, this was just another ordinary day. She was truly unfazed and arrived at our house late that night in her usual good spirits, three beautiful sleeping children in tow.

She and I have long teased each other about our very different ways. She aspires to have more of my planning and organizational skills, and I have always admired her relaxed, laid-back approach to each day and the attendant freedom from all the anticipating, planning, and worrying that sometimes bogs me down. In a sense, my friend dwelled in the chaos long before she became a mother, so when her first child arrived, she was better prepared to handle the ensuing disorder. She embraces the full catastrophe of motherhood in the same way that she embraces the full catastrophe of life.

The term "full catastrophe" as I am using it here, and as Harriet Lerner used it in the earlier quote, is borrowed from author and mindfulness expert Jon Kabat-Zinn. As he wrote in his classic book *Full Catastrophe Living*, the catastrophe describes the full experience of life: the good and the bad, the ugly and the beautiful, the messy and the neat. Like other Buddhist thinkers, Kabat-Zinn suggests that peace can be found in embracing things as they are, rather than preoccupying ourselves with how things ought to be, or might someday be, or should have been, or could have been. Mindfulness, as a practice of noticing and (here's the hard part) *accepting without judgment* all of what the present moment brings, was first integrated into mainstream medicine for its stress-reduction potential. What I find so valuable about it for psychological health is what happens when we apply it to emotion. A widely held misconception is that mental health means fewer negative emotions. If that's our goal, we aren't likely to embrace each of our emotions equally as they come up, especially not the ones that don't fit with our preferred notions of ourselves as mothers, like "cool, calm, and collected" or "in control" or "patient and forgiving." But inherent in the human condition is a wide and inevitable *array* of emotion; we cannot avoid pain, sadness, loss, grief, boredom, sorrow, loneliness, uncertainty, regret, and fear and experience only joy, excitement, connection, wonder, awe, and love. We encounter all these as we walk through this world. That is the full catastrophe, and nowhere, I would argue, is the catastrophe fuller than in parenthood.

In the essay collection *Finding Your Inner Mama*, writer Andrea Buchanan describes her experience of the unexpected feelings that arise within this emotional chaos:[3] "I knew to expect sleepless nights; I knew to expect crying; I knew to expect exhaustion; I even knew to expect joy. I did not know to expect ambivalence. I did not know to expect doubt."

In the early days of motherhood, we exist within a spectrum of emotional states—some spoken, some unspoken. We speak of the joys, and we mean it; the pleasures of parenting are real and deep. We speak of the practical challenges: poor sleep, sore nipples, dirty diapers, and inconsolable crying. We ask for advice about those practical challenges (Cry it out or soothe to sleep? Pacifier or no pacifier? Cloth or disposable?), and most of us hungrily gobble up any strategies or tricks offered to us that might make the logistical stuff of parenting just a little bit easier. But we rarely speak of the thickly layered and varied ways in which we feel, sometimes quite intensely, unpleasant and uncomfortable emotions in the presence of and in relation to our new babies. That is, we do not speak of the full catastrophe. Instead, we place interpretative frames around our unwanted emotions; they mean we aren't good mothers, or our marriages are failing, or we don't love our babies enough. So we pick and choose from among our feelings, hoping some will cease to be if we just push them over to the margins. The problem is that this comes at a tremendous cost.

The Freedom to Feel

The thing is, we cannot selectively mute some feelings and leave others to frolic about freely within us. We may think we're able to press the mute button on the feelings that trouble us—through denial, compartmentalization, or other attempts to ignore them— but in the process, we also block out everything else. The sounds of sorrow *and* the sounds of joy disappear. We cannot invite happiness, passion, and contentment into our lives as welcome companions but order sadness, fear, and boredom to take a hike. I'm not suggesting it wouldn't be really lovely if we could; who among us wouldn't like to avoid the feelings that are no fun and bask only in the good stuff? Too often we believe this is possible, that we can outwit or avoid our emotions, as if emotional states are a choice. Never mind the troubling consequences of this misperception (e.g., the shaming belief that a depressed person just needs to choose happiness instead), but also, psychologically and physiologically, *our minds simply don't work that way.*

In a prominent place in my therapy office, I've posted this quote: "The true opposite of depression is neither gaiety nor the absence of pain, but vitality—the freedom to experience spontaneous feelings." [4]

Many people in this world say many wise things, and it would be easy to plaster the walls of my therapy office with quotes that might enliven, inspire, encourage, or comfort my clients. But these words, from author Alice Miller, are the only ones I have displayed. In a sense, they say everything that really matters to me in my work as a therapist, and everything I hope for the people who walk through my door. I hope for lives of freedom. I hope for the heart of emotion to beat steadily inside every human being. I hope for lives lived in full color, lives unmuted, *lives vitalized*. And it is only with the willingness to feel *all* our feelings that we become truly alive and truly free.

Access to the entire landscape of emotion requires the skills of recognizing, validating, and regulating all of what we feel, and this comes much more easily to some of us than to others. The seeds for these skills are sown in childhood, when we depend on our caregivers to help us make sense of our internal worlds. Starting with our earliest experiences as babies, those who care for us play a critical role in whether we can identify and tolerate our own emotions. The popular Pixar film *Inside Out* brought this truth to light in a powerful and accessible way.

In the film, ten-year-old Riley is uprooted from her beloved Minnesota life when her father takes a job in San Francisco. Attempting to adjust to her new surroundings, Riley encounters a whole host of painful emotions, from social anxiety and awkwardness among her new peer group to grief and sadness about the life she left behind. None of this is the problem. The problem is that her parents, with all good intentions, cannot see or tolerate their daughter's distress. They want her to cheer up and embrace all her new life in San Francisco has to offer. In one pivotal scene, Riley's mother makes it known that Riley's good cheer is an important contribution to the family's tough adjustment process. From that point forward, because Riley does not feel entitled to her sadness and discomfort, her *entire emotional life malfunctions*. It is only when she can cry for what she has lost, in the comforting arms of her mom and dad, that she recovers her capacity for joy. The clear implication is that if only her parents had helped her to identify the painful feelings in the first place, and given her space and permission to feel them, she would not have fallen into such a dark place where joy was out of reach.

In the film's closing scene, when Riley's concerned, loving parents envelop her and stay close as she cries and shares the whole truth of her emotional experience, I was a puddle of tears—and I'm not sure there was a dry eye in the theater. Riley was lucky her parents were there for her, if a little late in arriving. Many of us grow up without a steady witness for our emotions, or any witness at all. Attuned parents see the fear in our eyes and say, compassionately, "Oh, is that loud sound scaring you, sweetheart?" They wipe away our tears and say, "I know you're sad. Grandma and Grandpa are so special to you, and it's hard to say good-bye." They give us names, and reasons, for powerful feelings that might otherwise be overwhelming. But no parent succeeds at this key task at all times. And many parents—whether because they're caught up in their own stressors, or they're uncomfortable with their children's negative emotions, or they never had the benefit of this kind of emotional attunement as children themselves—cannot do it consistently or skillfully. Maybe sadness is mirrored back empathically but fear is ignored or even ridiculed. A child's anger may not be tolerated so she learns early on to swallow it.

In the best-case scenario, children are encouraged to feel, fully, any and all emotions (while, of course, being guided toward a solid understanding of what's appropriate and what's inappropriate to do with those emotions). Those children are likely to grow into adults who, equipped with the capacity to recognize and regulate their negative emotions, are not tempted to hit the mute button when those emotions arise. They grow into adults whose rivers of emotions flow freely—no logjams or frozen-solid parts. They grow up to be adults who lean into the full catastrophe—neither denying their own impatience, anger, fear, or sadness nor judging it or interpreting it as evidence of some fundamental change or flaw in their character. But since that scenario is as rare as it is ideal, for the rest of us, there are many obstacles to overcome before the river can flow freely.

The Perils of Expectations

When my older son was seven years old, an acquaintance whose first baby was due in a month posted on Facebook that she was going to bed at seven p.m. and looked forward to getting her energy back after her pregnancy was over. I commented, perhaps overzealous to give this young woman a reality check, and maybe with just the merest hint of bitterness, "You may never get your energy back. I've been tired for seven years!" While I was exaggerating, of course, my attempt at truth and transparency was quickly countered by someone else's more typical, encouraging words: "Just wait until your baby is two months old. He'll be sleeping through the night by then and you'll feel like your old self again."

What? There is a guarantee that a two-month-old infant will sleep through the night? And there is a guarantee that two months after becoming a mother, this woman will "feel like her old self again"? Apparently, social media—aka the world of illusory perfect and happy lives—is not the place for a reality check. Though silent on her Facebook page after that, with a heavy heart I pictured this new mother three months later, rocking her crying son into the early morning hours, feeling exhausted and discouraged, wondering how things had gone so wrong.

For a lot of years, I've been thinking about the effects of expectations on the experience of motherhood, marriage, and life more generally. Expectations can be helpful if they are realistic—they allow us to prepare in both psychological and practical ways for what is to come, and to avoid the emotional discomfort of being caught unaware. But when they are not realistic or, worse, are simply false, they set us up for disappointment, frustration, and anger. They restrict the quality and flow of our internal experiences, because if any of those experiences was unexpected, we may view it as bad or wrong or unfair or shameful, and when we attach those labels to what we feel, we are almost definitely going to cut off or distort those feelings in some way. In short, the human tendency to expect generates a whole host of distorted perceptions and self-critical judgments, and acts as a roadblock to full-catastrophe living.

Part of the problem with expectations is that there is a whole host of things we *ought* to expect that we do not, because hardly anybody speaks of them. Remember Jasmine, who wasn't expecting to dislike being a stay-at-home mother when her previous career had involved being in the constant company of children? She was steeped in shame when she found that being with her own children around the clock was not nearly as fulfilling. I was similarly caught off guard when my once sunny outlook darkened into agitation and irritability a year into motherhood. There are vast plains in the terrain of motherhood that we simply did not know we would travel. And we trudge across these plains, wearily, uncertainly, perhaps numbly, perhaps with self-righteous indignation, thinking, *What the hell is this? Why didn't anybody tell me about this part of the journey?*

The other part of the problem is that the expectations we do hold quite often do not come to fruition. In fact, I'd argue that more often than not, whatever is "supposed" to happen in the world of parenthood doesn't happen. Our babies do not sleep through the night by three months. Our vaginas do not feel like having a penis inside them at six weeks. We do not naturally, automatically know what to do to soothe our babies' cries. Our voices are not as calm in responding to our toddler's hundredth demand for a snack as we once assumed they would be. It isn't any easier dropping off our ten-month-olds at day care than it was dropping them off at four months old. The initial breastfeeding challenges aren't any less challenging with Baby #2 than they were with Baby #1. Our progressive, well-intentioned husbands are not sharing baby care duties with us fifty-fifty.

Few new mothers are unaware of, or unintimidated by, the vast amount of parenting opinions and advice pouring from books, blogs, and magazines. There are books about how to conceive a child, how to navigate pregnancy in a healthy and happy manner, how to breast-feed, how to care for an infant, how to get your baby to sleep through the night, how to create a "superbaby,"[5] how to manage toddler tantrums, how to increase your baby's IQ, how to eliminate behavior problems through dietary changes, and on and on and on. In the classic feminist manifesto *The Second Sex*, Simone de Beauvoir describes an infant as "an existence as mysterious as that of an animal, as turbulent and disorderly as natural forces, and yet human." Though this may be construed by some as a particularly dramatic and dark depiction of human infants, I suspect de Beauvoir's words resonate with a great many mothers and fathers. Within these words we can see why there is such a market for how-to books about parenting. Who wouldn't want some explicit guidance about how to tame the turbulence and disorder, offered up by an "expert" who claims to have unlocked the mysteries of these strange little beasts who baffle us so?

Though I am the owner of a sizable stack of books about pregnancy (because it is a fascinating topic to me even when I am not pregnant) and sleep problems (because neither of my children had much use for sleep during their first years of life), over time I have become increasingly clear in my conviction that moms should not immerse themselves too deeply in how-to guides. These books carry some problematic, even dangerous, messages. Many of them convey the notion that there is a "one size fits all" solution for problems arising in infancy, or at least a "type" or "category" into which every baby fits. This implies that if you can just identify what kind of baby you have, you will figure out the solution.

Equally problematic is the pervasive message in these books that there is a solution at all. Many "problems" for which these books provide solutions are not problems at all if we do not view them as such. Is it a problem to have an infant who still does not sleep through the night by the time she is six months old? It's rough, certainly, but is it a problem to be solved, or is it just the current reality, one that will, sooner or later, morph into a different reality? Is it a problem to have an older baby who prefers to fall asleep while cradled in his mother's arms, as opposed to alone in his crib, or a toddler who clings to his father's legs at day care drop-off? Last time I checked, most of us prefer a set of loving arms around us when we're tired, upset, or scared, whether we're three months old or three years old or forty-three years old.

I think we make a costly mistake when we turn repeatedly to books that classify our babies and children and offer recipes or color-by-number-style solutions to their "problems." I dream of a world in which people's approach to parenting is as unencumbered by expectations as possible, and parenting books are counter to that cause. The great majority of them generate a host of expectations. When expectations are not met (as invariably happens), the search for the right solution begins; in turn, this search adds an unnecessary layer of suffering to what would otherwise be just the pain of motherhood. First we find that motherhood is far more difficult than we thought it would be, then we observe (incorrectly) that every other mother seems to be sailing along just fine, and finally we conclude (at great cost to our self-esteem) that we are doing something wrong. The sense that what we're doing isn't the right thing to do, or that what we're feeling isn't the right way to feel, leaves us feeling inadequate, or worse. Meanwhile, we're expending precious energy attempting to pinpoint what it is we should be doing differently to make our babies fit the mold and adhere to expectations of development or internal visions of how things *should* be.

Without the extra layers of suffering caused by unmet expectations, our misguided attempts to deny or suppress our feelings, and our self-critical interpretative frames, we would simply *feel the pain*. Of sleep deprivation. Of missing our old lives. Of not having enough time for ourselves. These things are all painful, but pain is far more tolerable than suffering.

I'm not arguing that the most emotionally sophisticated among us feel only pain and bypass suffering all the time. But we would all do well to ask ourselves, periodically, *Are there layers of pain and suffering that could be peeled apart? Might I be able to find some relief if I remove the judgment from what I'm feeling, and just notice the feeling itself?* To return to the concept of full-catastrophe living, the suffering comes when we resist, fear, or deny that the full catastrophe exists—when we favor the good and the beautiful over the bad and the ugly, as if we might somehow, if we just try hard enough, be able to experience the former without the latter.

And so we see the damaging effects of unmet expectations manifest in mothers racking their brains to figure out what they are doing wrong, what they have done to deserve this, and how they could possibly have found themselves in this situation that is so far off the mark from what they expected. When things do not go as planned, we experience not only the pure pain of the situation—a hard time breastfeeding, a colicky baby, marital tensions—but also the suffering arising from unfulfilled expectations. We attach judgment to our babies, ourselves, our husbands. "I have a difficult baby and so-and-so has an easy baby." "I don't have the patience for this. Maybe I'm just not cut out for motherhood." "If my husband weren't so self-absorbed, motherhood wouldn't be so hard on me." I once had a conversation with a colleague whose son was about a year and a half old at the time and was sleeping poorly. She was at her wit's end about his sleep problems (and her own, by proxy). She noted that, ironically, in the very early weeks and months, her son was sleeping far more poorly, but she and her husband were coping better. Now that he was over a year old and showing some less-than-stellar sleep habits, they found themselves far more distressed. Why? Because they *expected* him to be sleepless when he was brand-new. Now they expected him to sleep more, so when he didn't, they wondered and they worried and they blamed and they suffered.

What if our expectations could be more realistic, or at least less rooted in value judgments of "good" and "bad," "right" and "wrong"? Or, better yet (but perhaps next to impossible), what if we could enter motherhood unattached to expectations? What if we could completely embrace any scenario that comes to pass?

We can work on the realistic expectations part by cultivating a more honest, open dialogue in our communities about the emotional hardships of motherhood. Here we are making a bit of progress. The resisting of expectations altogether is a more individual endeavor, an internal one that requires considerable psychological effort. For most of us, this won't come easily or naturally. But when it happens, it is a beautiful thing. I have witnessed again and again that when struggling new mothers let go of the expectation that they should be enjoying their new babies constantly/better able to console their fussy babies/more grateful for being able to stay home with their babies/missing their babies more than they actually do when they go back to work, they also let go of a great deal of suffering. Sometimes this is only a momentary letting go, and sometimes it is a pivotal moment of insight that forever lessens the emotional burden they carry. Always, it comes in part from realizing that among other mothers, *things are not what they seem*. Other mothers do not succeed 100 percent of the time at soothing their fussy babies. Other mothers, despite the smiles on their faces, are not free of the occasional thought that a life without children sounds much more appealing. Other mothers, despite how serene they appear in the grocery store when their toddlers are having a tantrum, scream at their children and pour themselves a glass of wine when it's only three p.m.

I remember that during my older son's toddler years, the foulest moods I had *ever* experienced in my entire life came when he refused to take a nap. I would try for hours to shepherd him toward sleep with books, singing, back scratching, butt patting, head rubbing, rocking, and drives in the car, and I would emerge defeated, as angry as I can ever recall feeling, because he was still awake. I remember the day I recognized how toxic this scenario was and vowed I would never again have an emotional investment in whether he napped or not. I was liberated that day.

What was the problem before that? What had taken me so long to realize that this daily struggle was a choice I was making, and that I had other options? I *expected* him to sleep.* Toddlers take naps—

---

* With my second terrible sleeper, Quinn, I found that his unpredictable, ever-changing night-waking habits caused me far less anguish. I was tired, but I was not angry, confused, or searching the far recesses of my mind or the internet to figure out what may have caused him to start waking at one a.m. when he had previously been sleeping until four a.m. I was only tired. Pain, not suffering. I accepted that his changing sleep patterns seemed to have no rhyme or reason, and that just as nothing in particular seemed to have caused him to start waking three or four times a night, he would return to sleeping more solidly without any intervention on my part. I observed his awakenings, his restless sleep, his need for more nighttime nursings, with a curious nonjudgment most of the time—a skill I lacked when I was new to the trenches of parenting. "Most" really is the key word in the previous sentence. I was not immune to occasional moments of despair, anger, and righteous self-pity so pronounced that I didn't know why nobody had yet volunteered to take care of my baby while I checked into a hotel to sleep for a week.

everybody knows that! And, of course, I had my own "selfish" reasons for wanting him to take a nap; his naps meant precious freedom for me, and they meant a smoother afternoon and evening because he was less likely to be cranky. The words in my head were, *Why the f*&# won't this child sleep?* and they played over and over in the sea of anger and self-pity that was my inner experience. My expectations, my convictions about what a toddler was *supposed* to do (take a nap, even if it required a little coaxing), created a context in which I was blind to the many other options available to me. For example, I could've stopped trying to get him to take a nap at all. I could've set a timer for thirty minutes and promised myself I'd only try for that long. I could've instituted a daily "quiet time" ritual instead, with Noah in his room but not asleep, during which time I could've plopped down on the couch with a cup of tea and picked up Jon Kabat-Zinn's *Full Catastrophe Living* and said to myself, "Yep, here I am, right smack in the middle of the full catastrophe."

4

Mom, Interrupted

We are all struggling, with more or less grace, to hold on to the
tiger tail of children's, husband's, parents', and siblings' lives while
at the same time saving a little core of self in our own, just enough
to live by.

—LOUISE ERDRICH, *WRITINGS FROM A BIRTH YEAR*

When I was pregnant with my first child, I took a road trip to
Montreal with a group of close friends. The scenario was
such a positive one. I was on vacation, in great company, I had a
baby in my belly, and we were headed off on a fun weekend excursion to a city I love. And so it caught me by surprise when I had *zero*
patience for the traffic jam we encountered on the way. With good
humor but also genuinely riled by the impasse, I began pounding
the steering wheel, shouting, "COME ON, PEOPLE! We've got
places to go!!"

My friends giggled about my restless energy and agitation,
something they'd never seen in me before. At the time, I was inclined to attribute it to pregnancy hormones. Looking back, I see
this as the beginning of a whole new way of relating to time. I have
been in a hurry ever since I became a mother.

On a recent visit, my client Julia talked about her struggle with
time. "I'm constantly playing catch-up, never able to savor the

moment," she said. She imagined that if she could just get enough of a break from holding and feeding her baby, she could finally cross off some of the items on her lengthy to-do list—a constant preoccupation—and enjoy the delights of parenting. Julia told me that when she'd complained to an older friend about this issue, her friend had responded, "Enjoy this time. He won't always want you to cuddle him constantly." Of course, this friend is right: there will come a day when Julia's baby isn't a baby and will not wish to be held or cuddled by her. But this friend's well-intentioned advice also failed to acknowledge Julia's reality: the hard work of caring for her son was so draining and monotonous that she found herself unable to enjoy the sweet moments as much as she would have liked. Instead, she often found herself fast-forwarding to the next hour, the next day, the next month, when she might have that break she needed.

Julia wanted more than anything to be able to savor her abundant physical contact with her son. Like so many other new mothers I've seen in therapy, she described what felt to her like a constant struggle to maintain focus on the present moment, to see and fully experience the beauty and wonder of her children. But she was also worn from the struggle, and feeling defeated by the stubborn urge to be somewhere else, do something else, feel something else besides what she currently felt. Even as she hurried through her days, she berated herself for letting moments with her infant pass by unsavored.

For many—perhaps even all—new mothers, there is a desire to be more present with our children, coupled with what feels like a total inability to fully embrace the moment. The work of caring for a child is so all-consuming that we often struggle to stay present. That's true even when we are having a good time with our children, let alone the times when they are cranky, whiny, oppositional, or boring. Which can be often.

Wherever You Go, There You Aren't

The inability to focus on the present isn't limited to new moms. Most people are so busy anticipating what will come next, whether it is the next millisecond or the next day or the next year, that they fail to notice what is right in front of them. In his bestselling book *Stumbling on Happiness*, psychologist Daniel Gilbert described this phenomenon as "nexting." Gilbert proposes that this is a uniquely human propensity, and that while in the past it served us very well in terms of survival (we needed to anticipate whether a bear was about to charge us if we stood a shot at getting out of its way), today it may serve as an impediment to authentic, sustained happiness. Why? Because anticipating the future obscures our experience of the present moment. Although some happiness comes from envisioning good things in the future (many people say that planning and anticipating a vacation is as fun as the vacation itself), technically happiness can be actively experienced only *right now*—not tomorrow, or when our daily chores are done, or when our children are just a little older and more independent, or when we get that new job or new house, or when we retire.

According to Gilbert's research, people spend nearly half (47 percent) of their waking hours thinking about something other than what they are currently doing or what is happening around them at the time.[1] "A human mind is a wandering mind," write Gilbert and his Harvard research partner Matthew Killingsworth, "and a wandering mind is an unhappy mind. The ability to think about what is not happening is a cognitive achievement that comes at an emotional cost."

In their study, Gilbert and Killingsworth used the research methodology I mentioned in chapter 2, known as "experience sampling," to measure participants' attentiveness and its correlation to their happiness. More than two thousand participants were prompted with an iPhone app at random intervals to record what they were doing, what they were thinking about, and how they were feeling.[2] The results show that when the mind is focused on what has already happened, what will happen in the future, or what may never happen at all, happiness is lower. While it may be tempting to conclude that being discontent sends the mind wandering, thanks to time-lag statistical analyses, the researchers could pinpoint mind-wandering as the *cause*, rather than a consequence, of unhappiness. "This study shows that our mental lives are pervaded, to a remarkable degree, by the non-present," the researchers state, and in turn, "mind-wandering is an excellent predictor of [un]happiness."

Interestingly, the activity during which the mind wanders the least is sex. Killingsworth and Gilbert found that people are the happiest while exercising, engaging in conversation, and making love. These activities seem to harness the most focused attention and, in turn, generate the greatest sense of well-being. The implications of these findings for couples are quite compelling. Both common sense and research tell us that talking and being sexually intimate are important ways to nurture our relationships; couples with higher frequency of sex, better emotional communication, and better communication in general are more satisfied. What Killingsworth and Gilbert's findings suggest is that the same activities that fuel our relationship satisfaction also involve the greatest focus on the present moment, which, in turn, fuels our happiness as individuals.

The trouble is that when we are parenting babies and small children, we are not only less likely to make time for exercise, sex, and conversation, but also may be more caught up than ever in "nexting." As the minutes and hours tick by, we wonder when we will be able to put the baby down and get that report filed for work, when the next chance will arrive to tackle the pile of overdue bills, or when our partners are going to get home from work to lighten our load just a little. And as we drift away from what's happening in front of us, or drift off to sleep at night, we're often contemplating big questions about the future. We wonder when our baby will finally learn to sleep through the night, when or whether we should get pregnant again, and when we will be able to take our eyes off our danger-seeking toddler for more than two seconds at a time.

The cruel irony is that this difficulty staying present occurs right when we would benefit most from the stress-reducing effects of mindfulness. The challenges and uncertainties of early parenthood, by their very nature, position us to do a whole lot of nexting. But nexting is the opposite of mindfulness—the ability to notice and accept, without judgment, all of what the current moment involves. And the practice of mindfulness has been shown by an abundance of research studies to ameliorate stress and the symptoms of anxiety and depression,[3] all of which are increased in the transition to parenthood.

For a long time, I was too ashamed to tell anyone how much I imagined fast-forwarding time when I was home with my new baby. I often counted the hours until his next nap, or until I could put him to bed and draw myself a bath and call a friend. If there were pediatrician appointments or errands to run, I was glad, because it meant there were things to anticipate, outings for which I needed to prepare us both, drives in the car that would help the hours go by a little faster. Even though I loved my baby boy and truly delighted in him, I also found some days home alone with him interminable. Taking care of him often meant that I was exhausted, bored, or both. Similarly, with my second child, who was an extremely active toddler, the thought of the vast expanse of a day at home with him was not usually a pleasant one. I left the house more than I actually needed to, making extra trips to the grocery store because I couldn't stand one more minute of trailing behind him and monitoring his every move while he explored the sloping, rocky terrain of our yard. *I'd like to let him explore out here to his heart's delight, but I'm too bored*, I'd think.

Hanging out constantly with babies and small children is pure pleasure for only the rarest of us. Sometimes we are sad and lonely, because we long for more adult contact or the easier life we once had. Sometimes we are angry, because our children do not listen to us, and sometimes we are bored. What we don't always realize when we're in the midst of these states is that none of them will last. We assume we are in some kind of permanent new reality. Following a toddler around the yard, it can feel as if this is what life has become. Feeling lonely for adult company while playing with a baby, we might think, *My social life is over.*

Earlier, I mentioned the concept of impermanence. This fundamental truth, that *nothing lasts,* is so uncomfortable that we tend to look away from it, preferring instead to believe that we can count on things to stay the same. To some degree this denial is adaptive, for we might otherwise live in a state of relentless fretting about when we will lose each of the people and things that are so important to us. But we are so adept at denying the fact of impermanence that we also fail to reap its benefits. I remember, during the early months of my first son's life when the fog of sleep deprivation was so dense, believing with real conviction that I would never get sufficient rest again. Somehow I could not grasp that the state in which I was functioning was an impermanent one, and that at some point, this little person would learn to sleep all night long.

Indeed, the misconception of permanence lies at the heart of much of our suffering when we are new to parenthood. Great relief comes with trusting that what characterizes our daily experience now— whether it is a fatigue so heavy it threatens our sanity, a baby's cry so unrelenting it physically hurts, or a loss of personal freedom so great we are lucky if we can take a shower on any given day—will inevitably change. A toddler's refusal to move from beneath our feet as we wash the dishes becomes less an annoyance and more a sweet display of dependency when we realize we will one day be so much less needed. My younger son's favorite thing to say lately is, "Mommy, I never want to be more than one hundred feet away from you." Seasoned mother that I now am, I know for sure he will change his mind about that. And so I open my ears just a little more to the sound of tenderness in his words, even if I am trying to say good-bye so he can go to school or I can go to work.

Many of the working mothers* I have encountered, especially those who have just returned to work after having a baby, describe a frustrating inability to devote their full focus to their work. They might feel guilty or sad about being away from their children for so many long hours, anxious about having to rush through their workday to get home for bedtime, or distracted by having to sequester themselves away every few hours to pump breast milk. At the same time, many of the stay-at-home mothers with whom I have worked in my practice describe difficulty focusing on their babies because there is so much to do around the house, or they describe secretly wishing they had a job or hadn't put their careers on hold because staying home with a toddler isn't quite as fulfilling as they'd imagined it would be. In both scenarios, there is a pull toward elsewhere. And our happiness suffers as a result.

Luckily, our ability to accept impermanence does seem to improve with time and experience. Audrey, a woman I see in therapy who is followed fairly constantly by a shadow of discontent, struggled mightily after the birth of her first child. In those early weeks, her world was turned so upside down that she began to see me for therapy. She had not expected the demands of caring for her newborn to outweigh the delights, but that is exactly what happened. As much as she loved her baby girl, true joy in caring for her was

---

* I use this term because it is less cumbersome than "mothers who work outside the home," and with no implication *whatsoever* that stay-at-home mothers are not working. We are all working really hard, at home and at work.

elusive. She was anxious, distracted, and overwhelmed, and those feelings dwarfed any fleeting moments of contentment from the experience of nurturing her newborn daughter.

And yet she was at her best after the birth of her second baby. Audrey's love for him was intoxicating; his beauty and vulnerability and sweetness, and his frequent need for her milk, elicited in her a kind of mindful attentiveness, a state of being grounded, that was normally extremely difficult for her to attain. Her internal experience, typically so characterized by dark thoughts, was transformed into one of relative serenity. Caring for this newborn was the closest thing to bliss she had ever experienced. I remember watching her nurse him on the couch in my office. She gestured to him, making a circling motion to outline the invisible bubble in which they were enveloped, and said, "I am loving this." Audrey's ability to inhabit the present moment was almost palpable in the room. She glowed with the contentment that, as Gilbert and Killingsworth's research showed, is born of mindful attention to *right now*.

I experienced a similar shift in mentality with my second child. During the early weeks and months with Quinn, I was immersed in a state of loving him, coming to know every contour of his body, every nuance of the sounds he made. Many new mothers, and fathers, too, speak to this early falling-in-love period during which they could stare at their newborns indefinitely. But our departures from that mindful state are frequent, and I think much more so when we are reeling from the drastic transformation of our lives that a first baby brings. My experience of Quinn early on was one of profound and consistent delighting in him, with very little intrusion of thoughts like "I need to do this or that" or "Why isn't he sleeping through the night yet?" It was wonderful, but also bittersweet in that it brought to my attention how much less present I had been with my older son, Noah, when he was an infant. It's not that Noah needed or deserved more from me than what he got; he was very well cared for, and I soaked up his deliciousness thoroughly and often. But *I* deserved to focus more mindfully on him than I did. I wish I could go back in time and remove the discombobulation that sometimes dulled my senses or pulled me away from the present moment. Of course, there is simply no way around all the uncertainty that a first baby brings; it cannot be undone or erased, just like everything else that is momentous and unique about a first child. Perhaps the ability to savor more, and worry less, is a gift that can only come with a second (or third, or fourth) child.

Our ability to savor the present experience when we are new to motherhood is hampered not just by how difficult and disorienting the experience is, but also by cultural mores that devalue the act of nurturing. In their book *Everyday Blessings: The Inner Work of Mindful Parenting*, Jon Kabat-Zinn writes with his wife, Myla, that we enter into the monumental task of parenting "without preparation or training, with little or no guidance or support, and in a world that values producing far more than nurturing, doing far more than being." It can be exceedingly difficult to sit and *be*, whether we are attempting to meditate on a cushion or soothe a crying baby. We feel a pull toward doing something "useful" or having something to show for our day. Though the pull may be stronger for some than for others, the productivity refrain in our culture is heard by all. And it is directly at odds with our happiness. That may seem a bold statement to make; after all, we do find great fulfillment in our accomplishments, and for career-oriented people especially, our productivity at work may be a key source of self-worth. However, given what research has illuminated for us about the connection between mindfulness and happiness,* there is nothing outrageous

---

* There is also quite a lot we know from research about the connection between children's well-being and their parents' capacity to attune to them emotionally. I'll say more about this in later chapters.

about the claim that as a culture, we would benefit from being more mindful of the present moment.

Indeed, there is nothing outrageous about the claim that as a culture, we would benefit from valuing the caretaking and nurturing that sustain the human species as much as we value the workplace-work that generates income. And despite how far we have come in viewing the latter as something both women and men can do, the former remains squarely in the category of "women's work." As political scientist and public commentator Anne-Marie Slaughter points out in the TED Talk associated with her viral piece in *The Atlantic*, "Why Women Still Can't Have It All," when men choose caretaking as their primary role, they put their manhood on the line. That's because as a society, we decided a long time ago that work associated with a salary is the most important kind of work. Until we dismantle the notion that nurturing is just the runner-up, rather than the *equally necessary and equally valuable* other pillar on which societies rest, equal opportunity within each realm will remain elusive. And those of us who engage in the work of nurturing will remain vulnerable to the nagging feeling that we are somehow worth less, that the way we spend our time isn't good enough.

———

Psychologist and author Daphne de Marneffe writes in her book *Maternal Desire* that "when the activities of mothering are interpreted as self-limiting, they tend to be treated dismissively."[4] De Marneffe is referring to the broader, collective social judgment in which mothering plays second fiddle to earning an income, but of course, this attitude also trickles down to the level of the individual and impacts us in the trenches. Internally, as we go about our days with small children, we often dismiss the value of our efforts. What does it matter if we change one more diaper, go to one more doctor's appointment, fix one more lunch? We go through the motions, rarely pausing to reflect on the value and impact of each task or encounter.

If we do not attach much meaning to the seemingly mundane, then it is just what it seems: mundane. And when we're bored or frustrated with what seems like a day of accomplishing nothing, it's easy to let our minds wander into the future and perhaps even to fantasize about that future being far preferable to the present. But if, on the balance, we are able to shift our perspective and construe the stuff of mothering as not mundane at all but instead profound and meaningful work, we might well find more value in the everyday moments. And the more value a moment holds, the greater our capacity to stay present to it.

Of course, none of this is easy. As I write this, the younger of my two children is what most would label a "difficult" toddler. Quinn does not sleep. He does not eat. He does not sit still. He tests limits like it is his job (which, I suppose, it is). His frustration tolerance is astonishingly low. He is loud and volatile and reckless with his body. It is a rare day when he does not have a new injury. I have wondered, lately, what number I would reach if I counted how many times in a day I say the word "no." Each time I do so, I feel a pang of heartache, a sense of sadness about having this kind of experience over and over and over again. I did not envision myself in such opposition to my child so much of the time, and I am fearful of what stage this sets. I try to choose my "no" moments carefully, reserving them only for the times he is truly in danger. Sometimes I lapse into a kind of mindless autopilot in which I no longer even hear myself saying "no." Sometimes I harbor resentment toward him for the many ways that he makes my daily life challenging. But sometimes, instead, I try to root myself in the moment and remind myself that this work of motherhood is important, and it is deeply meaningful to both of us.

Stripped of this deeper meaning, these encounters leave me feeling angry, depleted, and at my wit's end as I mentally search for a "solution" to my son's limit-testing behavior. But when I cast a net of curiosity and sift through what's inside, I find tremendous meaning. I consider the possibility that there is no solution at all because there is no problem; there is only my inquisitive, fervent child who is just beginning to understand this world. He bumps up against the edges of it again and again to learn its shape, because what else is there for him to do? And what else is there for me to do but notice it, notice him, and breathe my next breath?

His and Her Versions of Time

My client Emily burst into tears on the couch one day when I offered a comment I didn't realize would resonate so deeply with her. I said something like, "In those rare stretches of alone time once we become mothers, the stakes feel so much higher." She had been describing a recent afternoon during which she found herself "vegetating" while her husband and their baby boy were gone from the house. Removing her head from her hands and wiping her eyes, she said, "I put so much pressure on myself to use that time 'wisely.' And I beat myself up when I didn't." Because of how I responded, Emily understood that she was not alone in this experience, and that her "vegetative" state resulted not from some shameful character flaw but more likely from the very human tendency to flounder or freeze when the pressure is too high. As we talked, Emily continued to cry softly, realizing how quick she had been to judge herself harshly, and mourning the loss of the more resolved, inspired approach she once took to her solitude.

My work with Emily has only recently begun, and she hasn't yet mentioned anything in the way of feelings toward her husband about the way *he* relates to time. But if they are like so many other heterosexual couples, it's likely that tension is brewing about this issue. If I had to guess, I'd say I'll be hearing soon that she feels some blend of dismay and resentment when she weighs her struggles with time against her husband's. Women's worlds, internal and external, are changed so drastically by motherhood, right down to the way we relate to time. Men's worlds, by comparison, are not. It's not a competition, except that it is. We cannot help but compare and contrast with our partners in procreation, and when the contrasts loom large, how can we *not* have some feelings about that?

My husband would not say his relationship with time has changed since we had kids. Sure, he is baffled and bothered by its rapid passing, just like every other adult human on the planet, but he has not been engaged in a losing battle to tame the beast of time like I have. When I am in "doing" mode, my head spinning with tasks to complete and my body flitting around the house cleaning up other people's messes, I often assess what kind of mode he is in. If he is in "being" mode, relaxing with an afternoon pint of stout and playing cards with the kids while the stew he whipped up earlier is simmering on the stove, I feel more than a little resentful. I wonder how this happened, how and why he has such steady access to slowed-down moments like this when my only access to them is near bedtime, when I've collapsed in a heap of exhaustion.

A similar resentment simmers in my client Rachael, who bristles in response to her husband Scott's seemingly supportive question, "What can I do to help?" Why, she wonders, is he not *inherently* aware like she is of the ten thousand things that need to be done? How is it that he defaults to the couch throughout the evening to relax and play with their daughter—until she gives him a task—when the couch is quite literally the last place she lands at the end of the day when she can do no more? Scott is not a couch potato, and Rachael is not a neurotic martyr. Yet this picture, in which he is relatively at ease and she is overwhelmed, depicts their life since having children. It is a common scenario that we will discuss in more detail in later chapters. My intention here is to emphasize the fundamental difference in how Rachael and Scott relate to time. For Scott, there is more of it. There is time to relax, time to play, time to work, and—if only Rachael were more receptive—time to be intimate with his wife. For Rachael, time has been a scarce commodity since their daughter was born. Though the hours passed slowly in those first weeks and months with the baby, they were hours during which she felt trapped by her baby's needs, unable to get anything else done. All those daytime hours of watching the clock tick while she nursed were juxtaposed against evening hours with a frenetic pace. Once her husband came home to hold and entertain the baby, that was her chance to do anything else, *everything* else she had not been able to do all day long. On weekends, she felt pulled in a hundred different directions. She wanted time alone, but she also wanted the sweet family outings she envisioned having when she pictured, during pregnancy, what their lives would look like when they became parents. She wanted to exercise, but she also wanted to catch up on sleep. She wanted to do some cooking since they'd been living on frozen pizza and take-out since the baby was born, but she also wanted to get out of the house and away from anything domestic. She wanted to see her friends, but she felt guilty spending time with them when Scott was hinting at how much he missed her and wanted to connect with her without the baby around.

These competing desires sometimes left Rachael paralyzed, unable to follow through with anything because she couldn't decide what she needed most. Just like Emily, she was at a loss when she finally got the time to herself she so regularly yearned for. Both women emerge from their rare alone time feeling unfulfilled, kicking themselves for not using the time well enough.

I wish we could construe this situation as a temporary loss of equilibrium, but I'm just not so sure. On one hand, some quantity of personal freedom *is* restored as our children grow older. There is no doubt that the baby and toddler years are the worst in terms of the sheer number of minutes and hours swallowed up by our children's needs for attention and supervision. As they become more independent, we recover some of our ability to choose how we spend our time. I remember well when my husband and I were able to resume our Saturday morning tradition of drinking coffee and reading magazines in bed, and how amazing it felt the first time I could say the words, "Go outside and play!" to my children. On the other hand, I think as mothers we are forever changed by the experience of being tethered to a small human who absorbs massive amounts of our time and energy. We may never relate to time in the same way again, and we certainly never return to our previous priorities around who, and what, gets our attention. Those priorities shift differently for women and men. Time is a scarcer commodity for mothers than for fathers early on, but even when or if this discrepancy becomes less pronounced later, it leaves a mark.

A couple I currently see in therapy, whose children are now teenagers, describe their central problem as difficulty connecting. He says it feels like they are just roommates; she doesn't seem to want to spend time with him without the kids around, and she's not interested in sex. She says he doesn't understand her emotional world. While she appreciates how much more involved he is now on the domestic front compared to when the kids were little, what she wants more than anything is to feel seen and *emotionally* nurtured by him. He doesn't know how he's supposed to nurture her—besides putting dinner on the table—when she sends out signals to him that seem to say, "Stay away from me." She doesn't know how she can be more receptive to him when she's so wounded by all the years of feeling alone and unsupported.

Their story is sad, and sadly common. It's not surprising at all that when I asked them to trace these dynamics back to their roots, we arrived at the birth of their older child sixteen years ago. He says, "When he was a baby, she never wanted to get a babysitter. I wanted

us to spend time without him, and she didn't want to leave him."
She says, "I was always so exhausted after we had the baby. I just
wanted to catch up on sleep, and I wanted somebody to take care of
me. I didn't want to get dressed up and go out and pretend to have a
good time when I was running on empty." Sixteen years later, very
little has changed. Their kids require far less of their direct time and
attention, but the divergent paths of need they began to follow when
their first son was born are now well worn. This couple reminds us
why we cannot make the claim—much as it would be reassuring—
that children *temporarily* disrupt lives and marriages.

A while back, some acquaintances of ours were approaching their
son's third birthday, and at a party I overheard the mother telling
our mutual friend that their son sleeps on top of her every night. Not
just *with* her in the family bed, but *on top of her*. My friend asked a
reasonable question about this woman's physical comfort: "Can you
even breathe with him on top of you?!" In my mind, I was asking a
very different kind of question: *How long are you willing to be immobilized by your child's needs?** Earlier in the evening, my friend and I
had been laughing at ourselves about all the crazy things we've done
in the name of keeping a sleeping baby asleep: "I've been known to
slither out of the room like a snake. I'm not talking about crawling
on all fours, but a full-on slither as low to the floor as possible."
Some of us who shall go unnamed have wound up *in the crib*, for
God's sake, perhaps to offer our breast or provide just the right gentle
strokes on our baby's forehead, and have then performed amazing
acts of silent acrobatics to climb out unnoticed. These are crazy
moments, for sure. But at least the ultimate goal was to get the hell
out of there, to leave our sleeping baby behind so we could do something, anything, for ourselves. Eat our dinner that's been sitting on

---

* I also couldn't help but think, *What a creative form of birth control!*

the table, cold and untouched, since the baby's witching-hour meltdown began. Take a bath. Watch a movie. Have sex. So from my point of view, the crazy behavior is understandable and justifiable, and laughing about it after the fact makes sense and feels good. But I wasn't laughing about this woman spending every night for the past three years with the weight of her child literally upon her. She was now so accustomed to sacrificing her basic needs that she could not even see the outrageousness of the situation. When she went to get a massage, which was a way for her to care for herself and get some long-overdue alone time, her son was so unhappy being away from her that she ended up FaceTiming with him through the little round cutout in the headrest of the massage table.

Research has demonstrated that mothers actually have a higher likelihood of depressive symptoms four years after the birth of a child than they do in the first year after birth.[5] Given how much publicity postpartum depression gets, most people are surprised to learn this. In my mind, it makes very good sense. Life is "supposed" to be easier four years after becoming a mother than it was at first, and remember: expectations and shoulds and supposed-tos lead to suffering. Babies are hard, toddlers are notoriously difficult (the "terrible twos"), but people talk less about what we might call the "fucking fours." Perhaps women are more depressed several years out because the marriage has not yet recovered from the blow it suffered when the baby first arrived. Maybe there is a second baby now. The cumulative exhaustion has likely taken a heavy toll. Perhaps a mother's sense of herself as still so very off-kilter, years later, is harder to bear. My friend's friend with the three-year-old sleeping on top of her and hijacking her spa day is a prime candidate for this kind of maternal depression. It's not about the hormones or the upheaval of brand-new motherhood. It's about the long, hard assault on a woman's autonomy and vibrancy.

The Longest Shortest Time

As mothers, we sometimes want to freeze time; we are aware that our children grow so fast, and even without our elders reminding us, we want so much to savor the precious moments of caring for little ones before they're no longer little. On the other hand, as mothers, we sometimes want to fast-forward into a future we envision as more comfortable and more productive. We long for escape from the truly grueling work of caring for infants and toddlers. We count the hours or even minutes until we get some relief—until our spouse comes home, until bedtime, until we go to work—only to miss our babies immediately upon parting ways and to feel guilty for letting our minds wander so much when we were with them. We cannot wait to press play on the parts of our lives we've had to pause: creativity, sexuality, careers, travel, adventure. Like with our mixed emotions, we wonder, *Which is it? Do I want time to slow down or speed up?* And like with our mixed emotions, *relief comes when we embrace the paradox*. It's both.

What if we could both *try harder* to remain in the present moment when we are mothering, and *accept that we will fail at this task* some, or even most, of the time? Better yet, what if we did not use the word "fail" at all, but rather we simply noted that sometimes we are mindful and sometimes our minds are elsewhere, and carry on with our efforts to tip the balance in favor of trying to be more present with our children?

Time elapses, and we are not always as awake to the current moment as we would like to be, because we are only managing to keep our heads above water. Time elapses, and we are not always able to participate in other realms of life and attend to vital dimensions of ourselves and our relationships.

Parts of our lives are on hold, and also, life is moving so fast we can barely hold on.

5

It Takes a Village to Raise a Mother

We need to ask the question: What do mothers deserve if they are to mother well? We need to answer: Everything. Everything that is due them.

—NAOMI WOLF, *MISCONCEPTIONS*

During my first pregnancy, I had the most extraordinary dream life. I have vivid dreams in general, and though they are sometimes a nonsensical mishmash of superficial material, often I find great meaning in them. What was so different about my dreams when I was pregnant was that just about every person I've ever known appeared in them. Each night, against the dark backdrop of my closed eyelids, I would watch scenes play out with hordes of characters from every phase of my life. I noticed that certain characters made repeat appearances—usually people with whom I'd fallen out of touch but who remained quite important to me. I would wake up with strange pregnancy cravings not for pickles and ice cream but for phone conversations and email exchanges. It seemed to me that my unconscious mind was rounding up my village, saying, "Don't forget about all the people you have in your life. You'll soon be needing them."

Given that it was cranking out these dreams night after night, my unconscious mind evidently also knew I'd need some serious persuading. An introvert by nature, I have always preferred depth over breadth in my social relationships. And I really hate talking on the phone. And I'm exceptionally reluctant to ask for favors. And at the time, we hadn't been living in Vermont long enough for me to feel all that well connected, and our families were on the West Coast, and all our good friends from graduate school had scattered to different pockets of the country to establish their careers just like we had. It was going to take some real work for me to find the village that would help me raise my child.

When I first began to conceptualize the contents of this chapter, I envisioned focusing on one phenomenon. I thought I would write about how young couples are raising their children in increasingly insular environments—geographically separated from their families of origin and their best friends from childhood and their college or graduate school mates—and the detrimental role this plays in our adjustment to parenthood. I soon realized that the situation is even bleaker than that. The "village" is lacking in so many ways, from the failure to support women well enough during and immediately after giving birth, to the laughable policies surrounding maternity and paternity leave, to the general decline in meaningful face-to-face social connection and the increasing reliance on one and only one person—our spouse or partner—to support us through hard times. It's not enough to say that the culture of postpartum care and support in the United States is subpar. It's more accurate to say that new mothers are thrown to the wolves.

Aloneness, Loss, and Shame in Childbirth

Sometimes when I am struggling to catch my breath while hiking or bicycling up a big hill, cursing my choice to take that particular route and thinking maybe I'll just turn around and head back,

I remind myself that I birthed two babies. And I think, *If I can do that, I can do anything.*

I had the good fortune of being able to give birth naturally, with no medications or medical interventions, twice. I say that I am fortunate because I recognize the likelihood that something will go awry during labor is largely a matter of luck and random chance, but I also give myself some credit. I'm proud of my natural childbirths. I was determined to give birth the way women have given birth for thousands of years, until really quite recently, when childbirth became medicalized in the Western world. When it came time for me to think about how I wanted to give birth to my sons, I did an enormous amount of reading and research. Having as natural a birth as possible was important to me, and I wanted to trust my body to do what it is designed to do. Luckily, I had two mostly uncomplicated labors and deliveries, and I know that I will always look back on the births of my children as the most amazing, meaningful experiences of my life. I drew on internal resources I did not know I had, and now, many years later, I tap into those resources in times of challenge, knowing they exist.

It often feels risky to tell this story of fulfillment and good luck in giving birth, because I know this is a sore subject for so many. My hesitation seems to be a form of survivor guilt, similar to what people feel when they emerge alive from an accident or battle zone that killed others. Many women intend to give birth without medical interventions—and they deserve that experience every bit as much as I deserved it—but for various reasons, they end up with epidurals, Pitocin, episiotomies, and/or caesareans. Often, the hope for a specific scenario of childbirth is a mighty one, cultivated over the nine months of pregnancy and held very dear. When that hope is dashed, the sadness and anger women feel can run very deep. Those feelings are obviously valid, but because they stand in such contrast to how women are "supposed" to feel when they have a healthy, brand-new baby, they very often become a source of confusion and shame.

When Natalie began therapy with me after a very difficult birth, we spent most of our first several sessions processing her feelings about her unplanned, unwanted C-section. She needed to tell me her birth story many times, often putting its details under a microscope, identifying all the places where a different decision might have meant a vaginal birth. She cried as she told and retold the story. Natalie was actively mourning the birth experience she had imagined and did not get. This made sense to me, and I was glad that coming to therapy to talk about it was helpful for her. Natalie's caesarean was six months prior to her first therapy session, but for her, it still felt fresh. It was an open wound, despite the time—and all the practical challenges of her baby's first six months of life—that had elapsed. I came to understand that Natalie had kept the wound under wraps, hidden from view, until she came to see me. It was as if, once inside my office, she unraveled the bandages and said, "See, here it is, and it has not healed at all since I wrapped it up."

Everyone heals on a different timetable, of course, but I believe one reason Natalie's pain was still so raw was because *she had never been able to express it fully*. Natalie's mother, mother-in-law, sister, and friends—all with good intentions, I'm certain—hushed her anytime she tried to talk about her horrible experience of childbirth. They all directed her attention to the thriving baby in her arms and told her to focus on that instead. But Natalie had a whole host of very strong, understandably negative feelings about how that thriving baby made his entrance into the world. She was angry at the medical professionals involved in her birth, and she was angry at her husband for not having been a better advocate for the birth they'd both envisioned. She was disappointed in herself for not having more resolve and not asserting her wishes more adamantly when the medical team began to suggest a C-section. She felt bitterly envious of a close friend whose birth experience a few months later was so much smoother. She continued to relive the intense fear she had felt when it seemed the baby was in danger, and she worried that she'd never be able to forget the scary scenes that played in her mind again and again. She hated that her memory of giving birth was so contaminated with fear. And she was also just plain sad about the childbirth experience she did not get to have.

None of those feelings had found a voice, or perhaps more accurately, the voice couldn't find a compassionate listener other than her husband. And Natalie sensed that even he was growing weary of the topic. He, too, sometimes implied that she should just be happy about having a healthy baby. She'd been very busy in the last six months trying to do just that, like everyone was telling her to do.

Studies show that when babies are born vaginally and without medical intervention, they get the healthiest possible start. Their little bodies, squeezed by contractions, are bathed in oxytocin as they travel through the birth canal, facilitating their ability to bond with those who care for them. When babies are born vaginally and without medical intervention, their mothers also get the healthiest possible start at mothering, and at physically recovering. There are no surgical wounds, no medications to clear from the bloodstream, and an abundance of oxytocin and natural endorphins to shrink the uterus, help with pain tolerance, and promote a sense of emotional well-being and connection to the new baby.[1]

These are all very good reasons for a great many women to set their sights on a birth experience with as few interventions as possible. Of course, an unmedicated birth is not for everyone, and women can and should be able to choose epidurals or C-sections or other medical procedures to increase comfort and decrease risk. But it is the concept of *choice* that matters so much, and it is there that things often go awry. After hearing from so many clients and friends about upsetting and traumatic birth experiences, I watched the documentary *The Business of Being Born*. For those who have not seen this film, it reveals how the practice of defensive medicine negatively impacts the childbirth experience for millions of women in the US. Because I was one of the lucky ones in terms of my own experiences giving birth, my intensely angry response to this film caught me by surprise. I think it came at least in part from knowing, firsthand, how birth *could* be, how the process can go when there is trust in it for all parties involved (especially the mother) and an absence of bad luck. I know I am not alone in being quite troubled about the culture that has taken shape around childbirth, undermining that crucial sense of trust in the process for so many women.

Despite recent home-birthing and birthing-center trends, the great majority of American children are born in hospitals. Among the many consequences of this is that from a liability standpoint, practitioners who deliver babies practice from a "risk management" position. Childbirth is seen solely as a medical issue during which many things could go wrong, rather than an organic, miraculous act of one human being emerging from another. Within this medical climate, not only are various preventive measures taken that end up directly affecting the course of the birth (for example, the standard practice of continuous fetal monitoring can lead to false indications that the fetus is in distress, which can then lead to an unnecessary decision to perform a caesarean), but also the air of defensive medicine is breathed by the laboring woman. She senses the concern that something may go, or has already gone, wrong. She doubts her body's capacity to deliver a baby safely into the world. She leaves the hospital feeling robbed of the birth scenario she wanted for herself and for her baby, and if that were not a difficult enough feeling to endure, she may well be blaming herself for it. The sense of perceived failure and inadequacy is very strong for many women whose births do not go as planned, and it can permeate their experience of the early weeks and months of motherhood. Preoccupied by a birth story so counter to what they had hoped and imagined, struggling to accept it and somehow integrate it into their larger life story, they often feel very alone.

Well-intentioned others, like Natalie's loved ones, tend to say things on the order of, "You have a healthy baby, and that's all that matters." Embedded in those words—"that's all that matters"—is the notion that neither the mother nor her feelings matter. Though no loving spouse or family member would actually make that claim, they often don't realize what their words imply, and it is within that implication that the pain arises. Caught in a bind between what they actually feel (a complicated mix of happiness about having a healthy baby and unhappiness about how that baby entered the world) and what they believe they *should* feel (just the happiness part), these women often get derailed in their attempts to validate their own experience. What they need is permission to feel the full range of their emotions. What they get is an implicit message that the value of their emotional and physical well-being pales in comparison to the value of a healthy baby.

A particular kind of damage can be done when one's partner is the person sending that implicit message. Natalie's husband had his own traumatic experience in the birthing room as a witness, and so she was fortunate that he could join her at least sometimes in her distress about the memory of their baby's birth. His empathy for what she had gone through and their shared sense of being shaken by what happened that day in the hospital created a safe haven in which Natalie felt mostly free to speak to her feelings with him, even if elsewhere she did not feel that freedom. Sadly, this was not the case for my client Daniela. Her husband couldn't understand why Daniela was still upset, two months later, about having a C-section. From his standpoint, the doctor's declaration that a caesarean was necessary ushered in relief—relief from watching his wife labor for a solid day with little progress, and relief from his worry about their baby's well-being. Over and over, as he listened to Daniela's frustration and disappointment about how the birth had gone, he responded with the same refrain. With tenderness in his voice, he said, "Honey, I wish you could let this go. So many people have C-sections. It's not a big deal." For Daniela, it absolutely *was* a big deal, and her husband's response—though not at all unkind, and spoken with earnest hope that it would help her feel better—left her feeling unsupported.

In a study I conducted, levels of marital distress among new moms were found to be higher in women who had undergone a caesarean than in women who had given birth vaginally.[2] This was one of those accidental research findings; I hadn't been looking for any such connection, but there it was. The study was correlational, which means that we can only speculate about whether a causal relationship exists, and if so, in which direction. Did the C-section birth contribute to marital problems? Are women with less-fulfilling marriages somehow more likely to end up having a caesarean? Or is there some separate third factor that accounts for the link? We need more research in order to know the answer, but the anecdotal evidence seems to favor the idea that C-section is cause and marital distress is effect. This is not to say that marital distress after birth is caused primarily by a less-than-optimal birth, nor is it true that C-section births automatically and always create tension in a marriage. Rather, my sense is that unplanned and unwanted caesarean births plant seeds of marital tension in a ground already fertile for this kind of tension (and we will look at that fertile ground quite closely in the next couple of chapters). Unexpected birth experiences leave an emotional mark on women, and create an opportunity for (usually) well-meaning husbands to invalidate their wives.

Women like Daniela go home from the hospital with a baby, a surgical wound, and the memory of a birth experience that did not go as planned. At best, the unexpected C-section is a disappointment and a significant physical setback for a new mother. She may feel upset that she could not give birth vaginally like she imagined, and she now has to recover from major surgery while also taking care of her new baby, but she feels blameless and trusts that the right decision was made by her doctor or midwife. At worst, and all too often, the C-section is linked in a woman's mind with the terrain of self-worth and agency. She may feel her body failed her, or that she let herself and others down, or that her wishes were not respected. She may reconstruct in her mind the hours of labor and wonder if she shouldn't have chosen to have the epidural, thinking maybe that choice is what ultimately led to the C-section because it may have slowed labor. She may feel angry or sad that she couldn't clutch her baby to her chest immediately. She may be reeling from the terrible fright of being rushed into surgery, if it was an emergency and the baby's well-being was in question. All that was true for Daniela.

Settling in back home with her new baby girl, Daniela struggled to make peace with her birth experience. As she sifted through her fear, anger, disappointment, and self-blame, she looked to her husband to bear witness to her feelings. He couldn't. It hurt him too much, I suspect; he just wanted her to feel better, so he encouraged her to "let go" and focus on their beautiful daughter and the fact that everyone was healthy and alive. His inability to be with her in her feelings about the birth became just one of many divides between them in their new lives as parents.

Talking to an acquaintance and mother of three recently, I was forced to pinpoint what, exactly, I believe about the lasting impact of childbirth. This woman has had three uncomplicated vaginal births. She is the picture of the "earth mama," a natural beauty with long blond hair and a baby at her breast, a toddler in an Ergo on her back, and a school-age child holding her hand. She was talking about a friend of hers who had just had a terrible birth experience, and she said, "I just wish she could fast-forward to the time when she won't care about how her baby came into the world. We focus so much on preparing for childbirth, and we don't realize, while we are pregnant, how the birth experience is just one small blip on the screen of motherhood."

On one hand, her words rang true and wise. There was a part of me that stood in wholehearted agreement with the idea that birth itself is nothing compared with the endless stream of challenges that motherhood brings.* And I have seen women with even the roughest birth stories put those stories well behind them, with humor and a sort of "what was I upset about?" attitude now that they are immersed in the un-glorious, unrelenting business of parenting. Whatever is hard and less than ideal about birth, it eventually pales in comparison to what is hard and less than ideal about motherhood.

On the other hand, a part of me resisted my acquaintance's conceptualization. Although, in time, the conscious *memory* of birth usually becomes just a small blip on the screen, the birth experience is anything but insignificant. It is a lived, felt experience that is remembered forever in the body and the psyche. It has real implications for how a woman copes physically and psychologically in the postpartum period, and even how she sees herself long into the future. All these years later, I still draw on my experience of healthy, natural, not-scary deliveries of my sons when I need a reminder of my own strength and competence. The experience of childbirth has stayed with me, and in my case, that's a good thing. But what about when troubling, disappointing, even traumatic birth experiences stay with the women who had them? What about the psychological impact of perceiving yourself as a failure at motherhood—because you "failed" at childbirth—right out of the

---

* I must again express my dismay at how many books there are about pregnancy and childbirth and how few books there are about the complete metamorphosis we undergo once we become parents.

gate? And beyond the repercussions that are consciously apparent to these women—for instance, a blow to self-efficacy or a mistrust of medical professionals—what about the unconscious repercussions? What about what the body remembers?

In his tremendously important book *The Body Keeps the Score*, trauma expert Dr. Bessel van der Kolk shows us that our bodies are living archives of everything we have ever experienced. Even in the absence of conscious mental memories of certain events, the body "remembers" and reacts to new situations based on what it recalls about the past. This is especially so in the realm of trauma. When we have faced horror or prolonged neglect or the threat of death or great harm (to ourselves or someone we love), our bodies never forget. These traumatic experiences leave an indelible mark on our physiology, altering our way of moving through the world as embodied beings.

When I was sixteen years old, I underwent reconstructive jaw surgery to correct a problem with my bite. In the recovery room moments after the surgery was complete and my jaw had been wired shut, my blood oxygen level began to plummet. Due to unexpected swelling in my nasal passages from the removal of my adenoids during the surgery, I could not breathe through my nose, and I could not open my mouth to gasp for desperately needed air. In a panic, the doctors snipped the wires that were supposed to be there for six weeks and manually opened my mouth so I could breathe.

I remember none of this. I was still under anesthesia, and the whole experience was just a story told to me once I was alert enough to listen to the medical team and my parents tell me how things had gone with the surgery. From my conscious first-person perspective, I might as well have been hearing the story of something that had happened to someone else; my reaction was something along the lines of "Wow, that sounds really scary." It took me over twenty years to realize that *my body* was there the whole time, even if my

consciousness was not. My body knows very well that this happened
to me, not someone else. Until reading van der Kolk's *The Body Keeps
the Score*, I never stopped to wonder why I feel a pronounced ache
and tension in my jaw every time I feel anxiety or fear. I don't hold
tension in my jaw in general; stress doesn't cause me to clench my
jaw, I am not a teeth grinder at night, and I'm not prone to head-
aches. But in moments of acute anxiety or fear, suddenly my jaw
clamps shut so tightly, it might as well be wired shut. That's my
body remembering. That's my body associating profound fear and
panic—from being unable to breathe—with immobility in my jaw.

Each of us has a story like this, if not several. The most dramatic
moments of our lives are encapsulated in our bodies. Our bodies
remember long after our minds forget. Our bodies remember even
when we *want* to forget. Our bodies remember even—perhaps
especially—if we never formed a conscious verbal memory of the
experience in the first place. In other words, when those dramatic
moments are also *traumatic*, dissociation is a common reaction. We
cope with the unbearable by removing ourselves psychologically,
and the results are fuzzy, distorted, or even nonexistent memories of
what happened. But it turns out that sometimes the faintest, fuzziest
of memories can have the most impact. In her bestselling memoir
The Liars' Club, Mary Karr writes about her dissociation from her
own childhood trauma:

> *When the truth would be unbearable the mind often just blanks it
> out. But some ghost of an event may stay in your head. Then, like
> the smudge of a bad word quickly wiped off a school blackboard,
> this ghost can call undue attention to itself by its very vagueness.
> You keep studying the dim shape of it, as if the original form will
> magically emerge. This blank spot in my past, then, spoke most
> loudly to me by being blank. It was a hole in my life that I both
> feared and kept coming back to because I couldn't quite fill it in.*[3]

These words bring to mind the relationship many women have with their traumatic birth stories. The worst moments—like when they feared their baby might not survive—are often removed from conscious memory. That is an adaptive coping mechanism; it's too painful to bear, so we just don't bear it. But it is through that removal, that disavowal, that the moments retain such power. We cannot fully forget, and we cannot fully remember.

A similar process unfolds even when the birth experience is not traumatic per se, but just difficult, unexpected, or deeply disappointing. Wishing away the negative emotion, as women so often attempt to do (either of their own accord or at the urging of their loved ones), prevents its resolution. We cannot metabolize the difficult experience and integrate the memory of it into our life narrative if we do not give it room to breathe and be felt in the first place. And without the chance to voice and work through perceptions of failure and inadequacy in childbirth, those feelings might follow women into the rest of motherhood, where there are already countless opportunities to doubt and question ourselves.

This is all the reason we need to give women both the permission and the resources required to attend to their bodies, their minds, and their hearts in order to recover from difficult births. "Permission" means allowing women to be distressed about their distressing birth experiences. It means we stop telling ourselves and one another that the outcome—a healthy baby—somehow negates or justifies the scary, disempowering, or otherwise upsetting birth experience that culminated in that healthy baby. It means we stop assuming that a woman who is fixated on her upsetting birth story must have postpartum depression and should probably take medication. It means partners, husbands, parents, in-laws, nurses, midwives, lactation consultants, coworkers, and friends stop encouraging new mothers to move on from whatever disappointments they have about their birth story, and start encouraging them instead to tell that story as many times as they need to, to as many pairs of supportive ears as they can find.

The stories of Daniela and Natalie highlight what happens when women aren't given time and permission to feel their feelings about bad birth experiences. And difficult, or downright terrible, birth experiences are alarmingly common. Roughly one-third of births in the United States are caesareans.[4] Yet research conducted by the World Health Organization indicates that maternal and child health benefits do not increase as the C-section rate increases beyond the 10 to 15 percent mark. This means that a large proportion of C-sections performed in our country are medically unnecessary. They result from the practice of defensive medicine, and from our "fee for service" health care model in which the more interventions and procedures medical providers use, the more they get paid. Premiums for malpractice insurance are especially high in obstetrics, and the pressures imposed on obstetric providers to practice "legally defensible medicine" often result in medically unnecessary interventions, including C-sections. Among the 1.2 million American women undergoing C-sections every year, there will likely be a range of big, bad feelings about how the birth went, whether the surgery was medically necessary or not.

There Is No Such Thing as "Bouncing Back" After Birth

Regardless of whether the birth itself went well, every woman needs a great deal of practical and emotional support in the early weeks and months of motherhood. Unfortunately, she is unlikely to receive the care she needs. Babies safely ensconced in their arms, new mothers in the United States enter into a postpartum culture of caring and support that can only be described as woefully inadequate.

Elsewhere in the popular and scholarly literature, the sociological, political, and economic aspects of this issue have been explored in depth. My hope is to illuminate the *psychological* repercussions of this inadequate culture of caring for new mothers in the United States. It's bad enough for women's short-term welfare that the childbirth experience itself is so fraught, and that the postpartum window during which rest, recovery, and support are sanctioned is so outrageously brief. But there is also the very real, and poorly understood, longer-term impact. There is a ripple effect in which our uniquely restrictive, high-pressure, low-support culture of birth and postpartum recovery sets women up to struggle in so many ways, both internally and within their relationships.

Seven weeks into my new role as a mother, I wrote:

Today Noah is seven weeks old. Supposedly the official post-partum period ended one week ago, meaning that now my life and my body are supposed to be back to normal. I'd like to know who decided that a woman is only "postpartum" for six weeks. An arbitrary cutoff like this carries with it all sorts of implicit messages like that the hard part is over, that one shouldn't still be on the verge of a nervous breakdown, that one's adjustment to life as a mother should be well under way with only a few minor kinks to work out. So, if a new mom is still struggling on a daily basis and feeling significantly out of sorts, she gets to add to the mix a sense of inadequacy and shame for not being "all better" yet.

I am certainly not "all better" yet. Today has been an ex-tremely challenging, exhausting, nerve-racking day like so many others I've had in the last seven weeks. Noah won't stop crying unless I feed him, and when I feed him, he fusses and then spits up, suggesting he really wasn't hungry and he's just get-ting overly full. My nipples are sore again from this increase in the frequency of his feedings. The house is a mess and I have had the usual experience of adding more tasks to my to-do list instead of crossing any off. I feel fat. Nothing in my regular wardrobe fits me, and my maternity clothes make me look dumpy—not to mention it just feels miserable to still be wearing them when I'm not pregnant anymore. My back aches and I'm carrying so much tension in my body that I'd kill for a massage, but where will I find the time or the money for that?

It was so easy to rattle off this long list of complaints at the seven-week mark, and that's a good indication of just how much I was still struggling at that point. But the real problem was my sense that I should no longer be struggling so much. When you are six weeks postpartum, you visit your midwife or OB-GYN, and assuming all looks well in the parts that were involved in giving birth, you are given the green light to have sex again. *Do what?* It is the rare woman who actually feels like having sex when she is caring for a weeks-old infant,* but I digress. Attached to the six-week mark are so many milestones that imply the adjustment period is over. For most working women, paid maternity leave ends at this point. Day care centers usually accept babies six weeks old but not younger, another suggestion that at this point a mother can begin to "move on" and return to the facets of her life that have been put on hold.

Author Hillary Brenhouse writes,

In the [United] States, a woman is looked after, by herself and by others, only so long as her body is a receptacle for the baby. Attention then transfers to the needs of the infant. To ask for respite is

---

* See Vicki Iovine's *The Girlfriends' Guide to Surviving the First Year of Motherhood* for a hilarious account of navigating sexual intimacy after having a baby. I'll also address the emotional and psychological challenges of new parents' sex lives in subsequent chapters.

to betray not only weakness and helplessness, but selfishness. You should be prepared for the emotional and physical demands of your new motherly role and you should like them, too.[5]

The message being sent to new mothers within this unforgiving postpartum culture is, essentially, "You should be able to handle this yourself and bounce back quickly." When women struggle on either or both fronts—when they find themselves in need of support and/ or they find it's taking them quite a long time to "bounce back"— they figure something must be wrong with them. Brenhouse writes, "For the expectant, we issue reams of proscriptions—more than can reasonably be followed. We tell them what to eat and what not to eat. We ask that they visit the doctor regularly and that they not do any strenuous activity. We give them our seats on the bus. Finally, once they've actually undergone the physical trauma of it, their bodies thoroughly depleted, we beckon them most immediately to rejoin the rest of us."

Most immediately, indeed. Three weeks after giving birth to my first child, I was in the classroom, teaching. Why? Because it was the first day of the semester, of course! At least I had three weeks to recover before I had to show up to work! My timing was even more fabulous with my second son, whose birth was wedged right smack in the middle of a semester. That meant I was grading papers and exchanging emails with students while I held a days-old infant in my arms. I had taken great pains to leave my students in good hands for the couple of weeks I wouldn't be able to physically be in the classroom; I mapped out assignments and activities and exams in advance, and I lined up several of my gracious colleagues to substitute for me as best they could. But when classes are under way and you are the professor for those classes, no amount of advance planning for an absence leaves you truly "off duty." I was still responsible, and I was orchestrating the classes and tracking the details of them

from my computer at home, instead of devoting my attention exclusively to my new baby, my recovering body, and my family.

I want to be sure to convey that I *was* granted generous maternity
leave, and that nobody forced me into the precarious work/newborn
juggling acts I just described. With both of my sons' births, I got
the equivalent of a semester off from teaching. But both times, the
leave time was a complicated, pieced-together arrangement involving teaching at least one class while transitioning to having a new
baby. I would say to people, "I'm only teaching one class this semester
instead of three because I have a brand-new baby" (when Noah was
born), or "I'm teaching two classes this semester instead of three
because I'm going to have a baby halfway through" (when I was
pregnant with Quinn). These are accommodations, to be sure, and
I was grateful for them, but they are a far cry from the ideal picture
of a new mother nestled in at home with her infant, free of work
responsibilities until many months later. I thought I was lucky compared to a lot of other new moms, and in terms of being able to
keep my salary intact, I truly was. Viewed from a different angle,
though, this arrangement stands in direct opposition to the concept
of "leave." I did not leave my work responsibilities behind at all. It
was practically guaranteed that I would fail to take adequate care of
myself in that early postpartum period. And this, I'm afraid, is the
norm in our society.

Ironically, we did a far better job of caring for new mothers in the
past than we do in modern-day America. In colonial times, women
were expected to stay in bed for a minimum of three to four weeks to
recuperate, rest, and bond with their babies during what was known as
the "lying-in" period. Some version of the lie-in still exists across many
parts of Europe, and in Africa, Asia, and the Middle East. In China,
standard practice is thirty days of restful confinement, plus another
week if a woman has had a C-section. In Mexico, it is forty days, or
long enough for the womb to return to its place. Women in Bali are not

allowed to enter the kitchen until the baby's umbilical cord stump has fallen off. Hospital stays after childbirth are a week in France and other European countries, compared to 24 to 48 hours in the United States.

In their book *The Mommy Myth: The Idealization of Motherhood and How It Has Undermined All Women*, Susan Douglas and Meredith Michaels assign the reader a powerful mental exercise in which we are to imagine that when we drop our toddler off at day care, we also drop off our clothes that need laundering or mending, and we ask for our toddler's vaccinations to be administered by the on-site medical staff. When we return at day's end to pick her up, we also pick up a healthy fresh dinner prepared by chefs on-site, and a few armfuls of groceries we ordered at drop-off time. What working mother would not relish such a scenario, in which she is spared time in the kitchen and trips to the pediatrician and grocery store? What a fabulous fantasy!

The shocking moment for the reader occurs when she realizes that in 1945 America, this was not a fantasy. These multipurpose centers were implemented to support mothers who, because of the war, were forced to work outside the home. And did I mention that these government-funded childcare centers were *highly affordable, if not free?* What happened when all the men returned from the war, and working outside the home became a choice (and one that was generally frowned upon) rather than a mandate for mothers? The centers vanished.

What does it say that as a nation, we were doing a better job in 1945 of supporting working mothers than we are today? Evidently, when the concept of women working outside the home was new, it was easier to recognize the hardships inherent in such an arrangement. Public policy reflected that. How could women possibly manage all the tasks of rearing the children, feeding the children, and holding down the fort if they were also working in the factory from nine to five? Clearly, such a feat could only be accomplished with a little help, financial and practical. Today, it is the norm for women to go on working, or even to *start* working (to earn additional income for their growing families), after bearing a child. In this not-so-new normal, there is so little recognition at the policy level of how incredibly difficult this balancing act is that at the individual level, working mothers often don't know why they are struggling so much. They think, *Why am I so exhausted? Why is my fuse so short?*

If we look at parental-leave policies, the story becomes even more bleak. As scholars Carmen Knudson-Martin and Anne Rankin Mahoney write in their book *Couples, Gender, and Power,*

> *U.S. public policies designed to protect mothers and help equalize some of the pressures on women created by their child-bearing capacity lag dramatically behind other high-income countries and even behind many middle- and low-income countries. Out of 173 countries studied, 168 offer guaranteed* paid *leave to women in connection with childbirth, over half of which offered 14 or more weeks. In contrast, the U.S. Family and Medical Leave Act, enacted in 1993 and heralded as a major piece of legislation designed to help families, guarantees 12 weeks* unpaid *leave for family needs. Many family members find it irrelevant because they cannot afford to take it.*[6]

Parental leave for fathers is fraught in its own ways. Only about 14 percent of companies offer paid leave to fathers, and even when paid policies are formally offered, unspoken social norms still heavily influence a new father's choices about how much time to take off work. Writes Claire Cain Miller in the 2014 *New York Times* article "Paternity Leave: The Rewards and the Remaining Stigma," "The challenge . . . is not just persuading employers to offer paternity leave but also persuading men to take it." One study found that while 89 percent of fathers took some time off after their baby's birth, nearly two-thirds of them took less than a week.[7] Every father in my circle of friends, including the one to whom I am married, remained engaged to some degree in work even during that all-too-brief period of staying home right after the baby's birth, whether taking phone calls, answering emails, or even trying to meet deadlines on projects. Men fear the consequences of putting out any signals that their families are more important than their work, even temporarily. Recent studies indicate that just as there is a "motherhood penalty" for women in the labor force—meaning that women who take time off for mothering reduce their earnings potential for the life of their careers—men who take time off to fulfill family responsibilities also suffer negative financial consequences greater than when they take time off for other reasons.[8] The message is clear: as a society, we do not condone paternity leave, and when fathers exercise their right to it, the professional and financial repercussions are not insignificant. These findings become all the more disturbing when juxtaposed with research demonstrating exactly how beneficial paternity leave is to the child, the couple, and the family.

For instance, we know from research that a father's involvement in the care of the baby is of paramount importance to the couple's well-being across the transition to parenthood. It is also a major predictor of a mother's well-being in particular. Even her chances of becoming depressed in the first year after birth are reduced when her mate takes leave from work.[9] One study found that longer paternity leaves are associated with greater father involvement nine months after the leave occurred.[10] While you might assume that fathers who are more inclined to be involved with their children in the first place are the ones opting to take longer leaves, this study actually controlled for that. So, from a statistical standpoint, it is accurate to say that the longer leave *generates* greater long-term father involvement.

Fathers who take leave to care for their infants, especially when they do so upon the mother's return to work, actually describe feeling grateful for having had the opportunity to learn what soothes their babies. Recent neuroscience research reveals that for fathers, the neural pathways that promote optimal caregiving get forged by repeated daily action.[11] In mothers, the brain changes that facilitate nurturance and bonding are more primitive and automatic, prompted by the neurochemical changes triggered in pregnancy, labor, and lactation. But it is through *ongoing, consistent involvement* in the care of their babies across time that fathers' brains become wired for better attunement and caregiving. And yet the stigma against fathers taking more than the tiniest leave from work impedes that ongoing, consistent involvement.

When a father is less involved with care early on, the mother's greater expertise at soothing the baby and reading the baby's signals paves the way for problematic patterns and dynamics. The seeds of resentment and imbalance are sown every time a baby's cries are heard only by Mom, or soothed more quickly by Mom than by Dad. There are basic behavioral principles governing the process in the short term; if Mom's tools (her touch, her voice, her breast, her special way of swaddling, her special way of rocking) work better than Dad's to quickly end the aversive stimulus of baby's cries, of course everyone will prefer that Mom swoop in and do her thing. In the long term, however, the benefits of this swooping in are far surpassed by the costs. Dad is more likely to feel inept as a parent compared to Mom, and Mom is more likely to resent Dad not only for his ineptitude but also for the lesser burden this ensures him. The bond between baby and father is likely to be weaker, and as we will discuss in chapter 7, Dad is more likely to feel displaced and threatened by Mom's strong connection with the baby.

Although it's incredibly difficult to do in the moment, it's important for new parents to make here-and-now choices with long-term ideals in mind. It might take Dad longer to soothe his crying baby, but it's important that he has opportunities to do so. When both parents want to go get some exercise on a Saturday morning, it might be easier for Dad to be the one to go to the gym because the baby might get hungry and might not take a bottle, but what's needed is a creative solution that allows both grown-ups to get their needs met. It might cost the family more money if Dad takes parental leave, but that might be income extremely well "spent" if it is viewed as a kind of insurance policy against developing gendered power imbalances in the relationship, and the marital dissatisfaction that comes with them. As Liza Mundy wrote in a 2013 article in *The Atlantic*,[12] paternity leave is "a brilliant and ambitious form of social engineering: a behavior-modification tool that has been shown to boost male participation in the household, enhance female participation in the labor force, and promote gender equity in both domains." With the far majority of mothers of young children working outside the home, the call for men to contribute more within the home and as parents simply cannot go unanswered.

It Takes a Village, but Where Have All the Villages Gone?

I have no memories of ever having been cared for by a babysitter or childcare professional when I was a child. No teenage girl, no college-age nanny, no day care provider. Growing up, this did not strike me as unusual, if I even noticed it at all. But after I had my first child, I began to marvel at the fact that vast amounts of our income were being devoted to paying others to take care of our son, whereas for my own parents, my existence on the planet seemed not to require anything of the sort. I asked my mother whether my memory was accurate. She confirmed that it was true, and it was true despite the fact that she and my father both had full-time jobs (at least once my brother and I were beyond our toddler years), *and* despite the fact that they performed in a country rock band at weddings, bars, and county fairs nearly every weekend and sometimes on weeknights during the majority of my early childhood. There was no need to hire a babysitter because my maternal grandparents lived a mile and a half down the road, and my paternal grandparents lived about fifteen minutes away. They were fixtures in my life, extensions of my parents who provided nearly as much love, food, discipline, and influence as my parents did.

In contrast, my children's grandparents live three thousand miles away. My sons see most members of their extended family once or twice a year, with the exception of my mom, who uses all her vacation time and all her frequent-flier miles to come stay with us and soak up her grandchildren. When my boys look back on their very early years, they will remember their day care providers and preschool teachers—not their grandparents—as the influential caretakers in their early lives besides me and their dad. When our kids were really little, if ever my husband and I indulged our perpetual craving for a night out alone, it came at one of two costs: an uncomfortable feeling of indebtedness to one of the small handful of good friends we occasionally, reluctantly asked to take our kids off our hands, or a hefty check written out to the babysitter. Most of our peers with small children are in the same boat, far away from their own parents, siblings, aunts, and uncles.

The phenomenon of families scattering geographically is an undeniable one. Couples are embarking on the parenthood journey in an increasingly insular environment, and the potential negative consequences of this, especially for the marriage itself and the well-being of the spouses within it, have been largely overlooked. As psychologist Susan Pinker writes in her bestselling 2014 book *The Village Effect*, "Given that the only person many Americans say they can trust is their spouse, it turns out that many of us are just one person away from having no one at all."[13]

When we place all our trust and dependency eggs in one basket, we create a precarious situation. Though you might expect that the responsibility of guarding a basket of this weight motivates spouses to handle it with greater care, the more likely scenario is that the pressure, fear, and vigilance of being its sole caretaker will wreak havoc on the relationship. If I've got only my husband to carry me through a hard time, and he drops me (so to speak), it's devastating. So I'm watching him carefully, scanning his face for signs that he's growing weary, and I'm checking myself constantly, trying not to be too heavy. This would be a delicate enough situation, difficult enough to sustain, if he were fully resourced and fortified for the journey. But he's *also* having a hard time. The new baby creates a strain for him, too, and without an extended support system nearby, chances are the only person he can lean on is me.

In *The Village Effect*, Pinker details the benefits of face-to-face interaction for our health and happiness. Studies show that engaging with our fellow humans in person—not online, through texts, or over the phone—confers an array of benefits. Those benefits include, to name just a few, slower growth of cancerous tumors, longer lives, stronger learning in children, better mental health, a greater capacity for joy, and—of special significance for new mothers who need so much to feel seen and understood and validated—increased empathy. Even a serious introvert like me cannot deny the evidence that we are better off when we engage with others than when we keep to ourselves. I'll admit it: I'm a person who sometimes looks the other way when I see someone I know at the store, and I've been known to wait in the car while picking my kid up from baseball practice so I don't have to make small talk with other parents. I'd love to justify these choices by citing data that it's only the deeply meaningful, intimate dialogue with close friends and loved ones that matters for our well-being, but I can't. Instead there is overwhelming evidence that encounters with other people in our social circle—even those on the outer borders of that circle—provide not just momentary boosts in well-being but significant long-term health benefits. This means that even if we are raising our children without nearby kin, and even if our closest friends are unavailable, we stand to gain quite a lot just by getting out of the house. Both our health and our immediate well-being and mood will likely get a boost from a walk to the coffee shop or a trip to the library for toddler story time with other parents.

Pinker's book sounds an alarm about the outrageous amount of time we spend on screens, staring at blue light and words and images instead of into the eyes of a flesh-and-blood person. We learn from Pinker's assemblage of research data that emails and texts and online chat rooms are no substitute for spending time in the presence of others. There are echoes of Robert Putnam's warnings fourteen years earlier—well before smartphones became a way of life and an endemic source of social disconnection—in his influential book *Bowling Alone*. Even then, he informed us, "There has been a general decline in social participation over the past twenty-five years, [and in] this same period [we have] witnessed a significant decline in self-reported health, despite tremendous gains in medical diagnosis and treatment. Of course, by many objective measures, including life expectancy, Americans are healthier than ever before, but these self-reports indicate that we are feeling worse."[14]

Both of these important books remind us of one very robust research finding: for our health, happiness, and life satisfaction, the breadth and depth of our social connections are of vital importance. This is true for anyone—male or female, young or old—but it has a direct bearing on women's well-being in the transition to motherhood. In what Pinker calls "the female effect," research suggests that the majority of social support so vital to women's well-being comes from their female friends and family members. Pinker points out that making contact with other women releases oxytocin, a hormone often dubbed the "bonding hormone" because we secrete it during orgasm, childbirth, breastfeeding, and caregiving. But oxytocin doesn't just make us feel connected and fond of each other; it also counters stress and actually makes us physically healthier. Pinker states, "Oxytocin surges through your bloodstream, damping down pain and inflammation, making you feel good in the here and now, and ultimately increasing your chance of survival."[15]

Studies also show that female-female relationships are characterized by the greatest degree of what researchers call "communal responsiveness": the sense of inherent responsibility one person feels for another's well-being and the willingness to attend to that person's needs with no strings attached.[16] This means that two women, whether friends, a mother-daughter dyad, sisters, or a same-sex couple, are likely to care for each other in a way that is arguably deeper and more consistent than any dyad involving a male. This may seem counterintuitive—the notion that reciprocal caring is, or at least *should* be, greatest in our committed romantic partnerships is a widespread one—but it is consistent with abundant research demonstrating that men reap more health benefits from marriage than women do, and that husbands report feeling understood and affirmed by their spouses far more than wives do.[17]

This is just a glimpse into some of the quite compelling research about the unique benefits women can provide to one another, and it brings into focus how much we stand to gain by turning to one another during the transition to parenthood (and during any tough time). But too often, we rely primarily or even exclusively on our (usually male) partners, and we are far removed from our mothers, mothers-in-law, and sisters. Even our neighbors and nearby friends are more likely to send a text that says, "How r u?" than to appear at the door with arms outstretched for a hug, eyes that convey compassion and interest, and maybe a bottle of wine or a casserole in hand.

New mothers are likely to go about their days with no adult companionship, female or otherwise. After an extremely short hospital stay during which nurses and lactation consultants and friends and family may gather around, most women take their newborns home to an isolated daily life, where the innumerable struggles of new motherhood will be endured primarily alone. For the women who return to paid work six weeks or three months later, this may remedy some of the social disconnection that characterized maternity leave, but it also marks the beginning of a perpetual time shortage. Though it may be exactly what they need, time to connect with other women in meaningful ways often feels like an unattainable luxury to working mothers.

The evolutionary psychologist David Buss has proposed that our increased social isolation may be linked to the greater incidence* of depression in women compared to men.[18, 19] Because we tend to live in isolated nuclear families, stripped of the extended kin and other social supports that existed in previous generations (and which still exist in many other cultures), those bearing the brunt of childcare—that is, women—may be particularly taxed by this lack of community. In addition, the same sex differences that promote reproductive success for our species are also thought to make women more susceptible to depression. For instance, women's stronger orientation toward social belonging and greater capacity for attunement with others—propensities that serve us well in child-rearing and many other realms—may make us more sensitive to separation and criticism, which are key features of depression. Whether we develop full-blown cases of depression or not, going it alone sets women up for a difficult experience both practically and emotionally, one in which their thoughts and feelings exist in an echo chamber. And

* Rates of depression are twice as high in women than in men.

it is one reason why new mothers come to see me for therapy. In my own experience sitting in the client seat in psychotherapy with a growing family, some of the most helpful moments were when my therapist spoke these very simple words, *"It is so hard. This is really such a very, very difficult phase of family life."* The "it" to which she was referring was the strain of mothering young children while maintaining a career. Herself a mother, she was a decade or so ahead of me on the same long-term motherhood-psychologist balancing act, and her words were enormously soothing, a balm for my tired head and aching heart. My heart really did ache; it ached for the rosier image of family life that refused, day after trying day, to come to pass. Connecting with someone who understood and validated my frustrations was tremendously important to my healing process. Left to my own devices, it was so easy to get pulled down into the bog of self-critical thoughts, the same ones I recognize in so many of my clients.

Our public policies send an implicit message that it shouldn't be so hard to balance everything. Put that message next to the lack of honest discourse and add social isolation, and what we have is a poisonous combination. Without a truthful cultural narrative that exposes the hardships of mothering and reassures every struggling new mother that her pain is normal, that pain turns quickly to suffering and shame. Without public policies and workplace standards to accommodate the dual-earner households that are now the norm,[*] and without communities to share the burden of work and to provide emotional support, mothers are too quick to assume their inability to achieve "balance" is a reflection of their own flaws. A societal problem gets internalized as an individual problem.

Because these quiet struggles are shrouded in secrecy, nobody

---

[*] According to Pew Center research, as of 2015, in nearly half (46 percent) of all two-parent households, both parents worked full-time. Only 26 percent of households had a mother staying home full-time.

knows the extent to which everyone else is also having a similarly hard time. And so they think, *Maybe I'm not cut out for this motherhood thing.* I wish instead they could all be thinking, *We aren't meant to be doing this motherhood stuff alone. It's really, really hard. And "balancing" motherhood with careers, or anything else, is impossible.* But our social structures and policies would have us believe we can, and should, be able to weave motherhood seamlessly into our lives, with little to no support.

When overwhelmed new moms look around for help, they find slim pickings. As researcher Bonnie Fox puts it, "Given the dearth of social supports to new parents, the weight of their responsibilities is considerable, especially for women who have the ultimate responsibility for their babies' welfare in addition to the responsibilities they already have with respect to their partners and their homes. The help women need must come largely from family."[20] The trouble is, for many women, the word "family" means "partner." We often have no one else. There may not be a village. And when our partners let us down, as they inevitably will, the stakes are high—so much higher than when any one member of our extended support network drops the ball. As the next couple of chapters will show, this puts considerable strain on a relationship already rendered more fragile by the birth of the baby.

6

The Great Divide

While fatherhood remains one option among many, motherhood revokes the whole concept of free will. It is with motherhood that the myths of equal opportunity and shared autonomy bite the behavioral dust.

—SUSAN MAUSHART, *THE MASK OF MOTHERHOOD*

What can I do to help?"

In therapy, Rachael continued to describe to me her mounting frustration with her husband's response to routine scenarios at home (like getting dinner on the table, getting the children ready for bed, getting the family ready for an outing). Instead of simply acting and trying to do the thing that needed doing, Scott routinely asked his wife to identify how he could be helpful.

Scott's question—an all-too-common one voiced between couples in this scenario—speaks volumes about the roles into which Scott and Rachael have fallen since becoming parents. The good news, in this case, is that Scott is not oblivious to his wife's stress, and he does not feel entitled to stand by and do nothing as she carries out these domestic tasks. Some readers might even be thinking, *What a nice husband, offering to help like that!* But

it is the word "help" that frustrates Rachael. Why, she wants
to know, is he in a position of *helping*?* Why is he not equally
in command of what needs to be done? Why must she delegate
tasks to him, and why is she the only one who knows how many
diapers to put in the diaper bag, which soap is the one that won't
irritate their younger child's skin, or which water bottle belongs
to whom? And how, when inside her head she is rehearsing such
aggravating questions, is she going to refrain from lashing out
at him in anger?

Even as we normalize and better understand our own losses and
challenges in motherhood, our appraisal of these changes *in comparison
to our husbands'* presents another set of challenges, and often sets in
motion a troubling marital dynamic. Our husbands seem to have
sacrificed less. Our husbands seem to be carrying on relatively unencumbered. Our husbands are generally faring better. We are not,
in any way, oblivious to our partners' relative well-being, and our
feelings about it are quite complicated.

On one hand, we want our mates to suffer in the same way we
have suffered. That way, at least, we would feel less alone, less
ashamed, less incompetent by comparison. So we hate them a little
bit for being spared the worst of it. On the other hand, we seek
refuge in their perceived stability. We hand off the baby to them
when we have no more nurturance to give. We vent to them about
how hard the day was. We cry on their shoulders about how hard
mothering is. And then we pull away and wipe our eyes and look
into their faces and ask (maybe silently, maybe out loud), "Why
isn't this as hard for *you*?"

Research on gender differences is one of the most prolific areas

---

* A similar issue is when fathers are depicted as "babysitting" their children when
mothers are away. Has any man in the history of the world ever referred to his wife
being alone with the kids as "babysitting"?

of scientific study. We know a tremendous amount about how girls are different from boys, and how women are different from men, across a huge array of arenas: academic performance, social development, emotional intelligence, physical health, career and financial trajectories, and so on. There is no question that differences exist, but the question of what drives these differences is a source of endless debate. Which differences come from the inherent biological factors that distinguish males from females? Which differences result only from the way boys and girls are differently socialized? And which are some mix of the two? The familiar "nature versus nurture" debate will never be resolved, nor does it need to be; the science of gender (and anything else) runs on unanswered questions, and each new piece of knowledge generates more unanswered questions. In science, the asking and wondering are always more interesting than the knowing.

Inside our personal lives, though, we rarely feel like scientists. We have such a stake in the observations we make about ourselves, our children, and our partners that we can hardly be expected to have a stance of objective curiosity about them. We want to get right to the bottom of why something is upsetting to us, and almost always, the mental shortcuts we take lead us nowhere good.

The best—and most damaging (to marital health)—example of this is the mental shortcut of attributing our spouse's upsetting behavior to his or her personality. A concept called the *fundamental attribution error* has been illuminated again and again in psychological research, and it refers to our tendency to interpret the behavior of other people as stemming from stable personality traits. For example, your boss spoke to you in a patronizing way because he is a sexist power-monger. Your friend missed your birthday because she is inconsiderate. Your kid hasn't cleaned her room because she is disrespectful. And your husband did x, y, or z thing—anything that hurt you, disappointed you, or angered you—because he is selfish.*

What if it was you who committed all these egregious acts? To what would you attribute your own behavior? Ah, well, the fundamental attribution error applies only to others. Self-serving creatures that we are, when we behave poorly, we chalk it up to circumstance and not personality. If you spoke in a patronizing way to your employee, it was because he had just spoken to you in a highly disrespectful manner and undermined your authority. You forgot your friend's birthday because you've been so distracted by your mother's hospitalization. You haven't cleaned up after yourself in the bedroom because you're too exhausted and have no time. And all those things you said or did to hurt, disappoint, or anger your husband? You were just having a bad day or, more likely, just reacting to whatever unkind, unreasonable thing *he* did or said.

The reality is this: women and men experience the transition to parenthood differently. As with any other line of research where gender differences emerge, the question of *why* it's not the same for men and women is a matter of debate. The data give us some compelling clues, and I'll speak to those, but ultimately we simply do not yet know. As science continues to inch forward toward greater clarity, we are meanwhile living the gender differences inside the walls of our own homes, and it's aggravating. It's painful. Searching for a way out of the pain, or at least an explanation for it, we're likely to make some of the common cognitive mistakes—like the fundamental attribution error—that plague the human brain. But the

---

* I didn't choose "selfish" for this example in a random fashion. Research has shown that among unhappily married couples, the number one attribution people make for their spouse's bad behavior is selfishness. This is quite important, and I'll come back to it later.

better we can understand these cognitive distortions, the better our chances of getting through challenges with our partnership intact. If we can resist the mental shortcuts, we can begin to appreciate the dynamic complexity of what drives these gender differences, which often have nothing to do with our spouse's character, or our own.

Welcome to the 1950s

New mothers are quite often blindsided by the degree to which the weight of a new baby, literally and figuratively, rests on them. We can attribute this unpleasant surprise in part to the lack of honest social discourse about new mothers' actual experiences; nobody is saying to expectant parents, "Wait until the baby comes! You'll feel like you traveled back to the 1950s in your gender roles!"

But in addition, the fact that this comes as such a surprise to couples has something to do with unrealistic expectations. In chapter 3, we discussed the problematic nature of expectations and how much emotional suffering comes from the gap between whatever tough experience we're having in the realm of parenthood and what we *expected* it would be, or should be, like. There is one particular widespread expectation that throws new mothers for the biggest loop when it goes unmet, and it almost invariably does. It is the expectation that the care of the new baby will be shared more or less equally between mother and father. For a wide, wide majority of heterosexual couples—regardless of age, race, or socioeconomic status, regardless of how progressive-minded they are, and regardless of whether or not both spouses are career-driven and working outside the home—this is simply not the case.

Many progressive couples hold the perfectly reasonable assumption that the egalitarian arrangement they have worked hard to cultivate within their marriage will not fall all to pieces when they have a baby. They might notice that their friend Addie seems to feel trapped at home while her husband, Mark, still gets out a lot, and they might notice that Mark hands the baby over to Addie when a fresh diaper is needed. They think, *We're not going to be like that. We're going to split all the baby responsibilities right down the middle.*

I wish they were right.

But unless they are one of the few exceptions to the rule, they're more likely to be wrong.

Sometimes women from older generations—the ages of our grandmothers and great-grandmothers—observe that it seems to have been easier on the marriage when there was no question that the wife would stay home with the children. The roles were clearly defined; the children, and everything remotely related to them, were the territory of the mother, and there was *no expectation that it would be otherwise.* This, it seems to me, is a key insight in that it speaks to the power of expectations—our assumptions about the future—over our experience of our current reality. Many modern couples, particularly dual-earner couples and those who strive for an egalitarian relationship in which household tasks and decisions are shared, have the expectation that baby care will also be shared. Of course, moms who intend to breastfeed are aware that in the early months, they will devote much more time to feeding than their partners will, and therefore their sleep will be more disrupted. Still, they are usually caught off guard by the extent to which they are immediately and intimately intertwined with their new babies while their husbands remain, at least relatively speaking, unencumbered. They are caught off guard by how everything baby-related is central to their everyday experience and somehow much more peripheral in the experience of their partners.

At best, this disparity creates a temporary rift, a divide that both partners see as an understandable, mostly benign disconnection that will eventually dissipate as the baby becomes a toddler and then a preschooler. At worst, the disparity is a recipe for resentment, and possibly rage, in a new mother whose husband is neither as emotionally changed nor as practically challenged by the arrival of the baby.

There is a correlation here, and it's not a coincidence: the extent to which we are responsible for attending to the new baby's needs is predictive of how destabilized we feel by the baby's existence.[1] That alone offers a key insight into why mothers are typically more destabilized than fathers during the transition to parenthood. But even when fathers are highly involved in the practical aspects of baby care, there remains a significant discrepancy between mother and father in terms of how much the baby occupies mental and emotional space. I have listened to new mothers marvel—and not in the admiring way they might marvel at someone's brilliance or accomplishments—at how their spouses can ignore the cries of their baby in the night, how they can *not* know what time the baby woke up from her nap, how they can return to work two days after the birth *not* angst-ridden about being away from their baby all day long.

None of this is to say that the transition to fatherhood is not a momentous occasion. New fathers, too, undergo significant change on multiple levels. But among most heterosexual couples, the tension lies in the *relative* change for a father compared to a mother. One could argue that there is nothing wrong with this discrepancy in and of itself; the problem is that the discrepancy is contrary to expectations. New mothers naturally, inevitably, engage in a process of comparison, assessing the ways in which they have been affected by their new son or daughter compared with how their mates have been affected. Almost invariably, there is no contest.

For many couples, the divide begins with pregnancy, when a

woman, compared to her partner, is already undergoing consider-able transformation. The experience of pregnancy cannot be truly, fully shared by even the most interested man, because he does not have a baby growing inside him. Often, a woman wants her mate to be as fascinated and consumed (or pained and exhausted) by the pregnancy as she is, but that's virtually impossible. In one of very few comprehensive empirical studies that tracked couples closely across time as they became parents,[2] researchers Carolyn and Philip Cowan at UC Berkeley found that even before the baby is born, pregnant mothers begin to redefine themselves as parents more so than fathers do. The study participants were asked to fill out "iden-tity pie charts" in which terms like mother/father, partner/lover, daughter/son, worker/student, friend, etc., were assigned portion sizes based on how big those aspects of identity felt. During preg-nancy, women's "mother" slices were on average twice as big as men's "father" slices. It could be argued that this is because they really are already mothering, albeit indirectly, by virtue of having a developing baby in their bodies. But this gap does not close once the baby is born. The Cowans found that when the study participants' babies were eighteen months old, a man's identity as a parent was still less than one-third the size of a woman's.

A tremendous amount of research corroborates the findings of the Cowans' landmark longitudinal study; discrepancies in the "identity pie" are only one way to talk about it. Studies show that whether or not women also work outside the home, they continue to bear the responsibility of acting as the primary caretakers of infants,[3] and consequently they report greater parenting strain and stress in the postpartum period,[4] as well as having to make more significant lifestyle changes than their husbands do.[5] Compared to fathers, mothers experience more depression after the birth of a child, and there is much evidence to suggest that this difference is not solely, or even largely, due to physical or hormonal changes.[6]

The notorious decline in marital satisfaction that occurs across the transition to parenthood—which I'll discuss extensively in chapter 7—is also considerably more prominent for women and in some studies is found *only* among the women.[7]

The Cowans' identity pie chart findings lend great insight into why these discrepancies are so problematic. For men, it would be accurate to say that the addition of a "father" identity does not generally squeeze out other aspects of identity. Tracking men's self-reported identity pie charts over time, they found that the men's pie slices devoted to "partner/lover" and "worker/student" did not shrink to nearly the extent that the women's did after becoming parents. This discrepancy was especially pronounced when it came to the "worker" identity, which, for men, remains essentially unchanged and always (on average) larger than the "father" portion of the pie. The reverse is true for women, whose "worker" identity becomes, and remains, eclipsed by their "mother" identity.

One of my good friends is an immensely talented artist who, while pregnant with her first child, completed her master's degree in fine arts. I remember attending the exhibit and artist's talk that constituted her thesis and taking note of the fecundity that permeated the event. Here was a beautiful rosy-cheeked woman with a big belly beneath a vibrant green dress, surrounded by massive artwork of her own making on the walls—paintings of details from the natural world, of bees extracting nectar from the hearts of flowers, of flora and fauna in various stages of decay and regrowth. The symbolism of this is only apparent to me now, as I look back, because five years and one more child later, her art is on hold. Her art studio in the backyard sits unoccupied and in what she describes as a state of neglected disarray. Her creations, for now, are her children.

It's a familiar story for so many of us. Time is slipping away, and we are neither savoring our children as much as we'd like, nor are

we attending sufficiently to the aspects of ourselves distinct from
mothering. Especially during the early years of our children's lives,
creative pursuits are paused, friendships wane, physical fitness
declines, sexuality hibernates, and career goals are abandoned or
delayed. We find that so many interests and endeavors that matter
to us are now, like the vegetation in my friend's paintings, in various
states of decay.

What the Cowans' pie chart data reveal so clearly is that
this is not the straightforward story of a new parent, man or
woman. This is the story of a new *mother*, and it unfolds next to
a father's decidedly different story. As the Cowans explain in
their book *When Partners Become Parents*, "Even when women
work full-time, their sense of self as Mother is more than 50
percent greater than their psychological investment in their
identity as Worker. This sits in bold contrast to their husbands'
experience. Despite men's increasing psychological investment
as fathers, their Worker/Student aspect of self remains virtually unchanged. Even at its height, the Father aspect of men's
sense of self is smaller than the Worker/Student part."

Of course, the role of women in the workplace has continued to
deepen and expand in the years since this study was conducted, and
men's contributions to childcare have increased.[8] It's possible that
if the pie chart aspect of the Cowans' study were to be replicated
today, we would see some slight modifications among both women
and men in the proportions of their identities they devote to parent
versus worker. However, if very recent research on gender differences in "work-family guilt" is any indication, the internal tug-of-
war over these two competing facets of identity remains greater in
women, and comes at a greater emotional cost. A 2014 study reveals
that among parents of toddlers, women feel considerably more guilt
than men about the ways their work responsibilities interfere with

parenting and vice versa, and the possibility that having a career negatively impacts their children.[9]

The Cowans' findings also reveal, very importantly, that the larger the difference in any given couple between the size of his and her "parent slices," the lower the couple's relationship satisfaction. Other recent studies show that it is not the absolute levels of childcare responsibilities, domestic work, or leisure time that matter for marital satisfaction; it is the degree of change on these fronts *within* each partner.[10] One study found that when husbands' amount of leisure time did not change across the first year of parenthood, wives were less happy in the marriage.[11] Another found that the bigger the discrepancy between a couple's ideal level of father involvement in the domestic sphere and his actual involvement, the more stress the mother felt.[12] This all indicates that the notion of marital tension being linked to the discrepancy in how much parenthood changes and taxes moms versus dads is not mere speculation; the research bears this out.

Another conclusion we can draw from research findings like these is that, compared to women, men are more able to adopt a parent identity without giving up other central aspects of self. It's not that mothers *willingly* abandon other parts of their identity because mothering is the only thing that matters to them anymore; the other parts continue to matter, often enormously so. It's that we have little psychological or physical energy to devote to the other parts. At the individual level, this can be a source of great sadness and disappointment. At the level of the couple, it can mean, as the Cowans put it, "moving through potentially hostile territory."[13] Women are understandably resentful about their husbands' intact capacity to pursue non-parenting interests and goals. Men feel shut out by wives who won't have sex with them or go out to dinner with them or engage in stimulating intellectual dialogue with them. Women feel their other identities have been snuffed out by motherhood, and needs like sleep, exercise, and balanced meals might even be going unmet because they are spending all their time making sure those needs are met for another being. In that context, their husbands' requests for "alone time" or "couple time" often register as insensitive and burdensome. Later, we'll look at how these different positions that men and women occupy actually reflect a fundamental state of longing and deprivation for *both* partners. For now, I'm just showing you the indisputable bottom line, which is this: a new baby's arrival ushers in greater change for Mom than for Dad.

I can remember the weight of this disparity during the period when I was breastfeeding a young baby while working full-time. My husband and I have a long commute, which at the time we did together most days of the week, so usually we arrived home as a family. Always, my first priority was to feed the fussy, hungry baby, who had not been happy to be strapped in his car seat for forty-five minutes. I remember sitting immobilized on the couch when I was hungry, too, when I needed to go to the bathroom, when I wanted the simple freedom of getting home from work and standing at the kitchen counter looking through the mail. I remember observing my husband being free to do each of these things. Though I appreciated the moment of stillness with my baby—the opportunity to hold him and look at him and simply be together—often I was distracted by an undertone of resentment that I couldn't help but feel. Sometimes, my lovely husband would bring me something to drink or a snack—a very thoughtful act on his part—but I didn't want to have to eat and drink while nursing. I wanted both of my hands free. I wanted the unencumbered state he was enjoying. My rational mind would fire off thoughts like, *It's not his fault you're stuck here on the couch. He's not guilty of anything right now. At least one of us is able to let the dog out and get dinner going.* Sometimes, those thoughts would nip the resentment in the bud, but not always. It just wasn't fair, and it was easy to feel sorry for myself and to get attached to the totally useless, but very compelling, agenda of making sure my free-as-a-bird husband knew exactly how hard it was to be so tethered to a baby.

When I was teaching my Psychology of Parenthood undergraduate seminar, I had my students read a journal article called "The Formative Years: How Parenthood Creates Gender."[14] One admirably honest student said to me one day, "Professor Millwood, I didn't do the reading. But I can tell from the title that this article must be about how children are shaped into gendered roles by their parents, and that's a fascinating topic!" Well, yes, that is a fascinating topic, but this article, as I told the student, isn't about that. It's about how the experience of parenthood shapes the *parents*—not the child—along gender lines. This concept has a bit of a backward quality at first glance. Don't we establish our gender roles long before we choose to become parents? Don't gender differences and inequalities influence the way we experience parenthood, rather than being produced by parenthood? Indeed, those things are true. Far less intuitive and also true is this: the demands and restrictions of parenting actually *create* gender roles that were far less pronounced before.

Research spanning back to the 1970s, when gender equality issues first became a legitimate topic of scholarly inquiry, tells the following story extremely consistently: for heterosexual couples, the transition to parenthood brings with it a more conventional division of labor.[15] In other words, regardless of how hard a couple works to establish an egalitarian relationship prior to becoming parents, and no matter how progressive or unconventional their pre-baby division of labor may have been, when that first baby comes home, their who-does-what arrangements become more gender stereotypical than they were before. Broadly speaking, this means that Mom takes on more of the domestic and child-rearing duties, even if both Mom and Dad have full-time careers or jobs outside the home. This is not a temporary scenario, referring to a working woman's brief stint as a domestic goddess during her maternity leave when she is home all day with a newborn. A woman's return to work after maternity leave most assuredly does not redistribute the care of the baby; an abundance of research shows that care remains unevenly distributed, even when the number of hours each partner works outside the home is exactly the same. When women are earning more money than their spouses, they still do twice as much domestic work and three times as much caretaking of their children than their husbands do.[16] If you are like me, each of these sentences makes you wince and close your eyes and say, "Make it stop!"

I do have some good news, sort of, but I have to warn you that as soon as I convey it, I will return to more bad news. From 1965 to 2010, the pattern in thirty different industrialized nations has been one of gradual convergence in the amount of time men and women spend on domestic and family tasks. Men's proportional contribution has moved from approximately one-fifth of women's to approximately one-third of women's.[17] In other words, for every hour a man spends in the domestic sphere, a woman spends three. Fifty years ago, for every hour a man spent on domestic duty, a woman spent five hours. In terms of childcare specifically, fathers' hands-on contributions over the past fifty years have tripled, from a little over two hours per week on average to a little over six hours per week.

With these encouraging findings in mind, it would be reasonable to assume that as fathers are doing more, mothers are doing less. Unfortunately, the statistics tell a different story. In that same forty-five-year period (from 1965 to 2010), the time mothers spent in direct hands-on childcare activities *also* increased. When children are under age six, mothers with full-time jobs clock just ten fewer hours per week directly caring for their children than their stay-at-home-mom counterparts,[18] and working moms today spend as much time with their kids as stay-at-home moms did in the 1970s![19]

The inverse relationship between moms' and dads' contributions we might expect—as Dad does more, Mom is able to do less—is simply not there. Of course, this may speak more to the shift in recent decades toward "intensive parenting" than it does to any failure to step up on the part of dads. Despite a clear, if too slow, change toward greater paternal involvement on the domestic front, women face unrelenting pressures to prove to themselves and others that their professional success does not come at the cost of their success as mothers. Men simply do not face similar pressures. It's evident from the research that increased involvement of fathers is not the same as achievement of egalitarian partnerships. More often than not, when couples talk about joint and equal participation in the tasks of raising children and running a home, they are referring to either an illusion or an aspiration, rather than a current reality.

Invisible Male Power and the Myth of Equality

A few years ago, I called a friend of mine the day after her baby was born, to congratulate her and hear her birth story and find out how she was doing. She didn't answer, and when she called me back later, she told me that she had been at the grocery store buying ingredients to make soup for her sick husband. Let me repeat: this was *the day after she gave birth*. I could not fathom how, or why, she found herself anywhere other than in the hospital or in bed, let alone combing the aisles of a supermarket so she could go home and cook a meal for her husband!

This story bears resemblance to a refrain I've heard many times from friends and clients: "I don't want my husband to have to get up with the baby at night when he has to go to work the next day." I can appreciate that they want to protect their husbands from disrupted sleep in the interest of promoting their work efficiency and well-being.

But the women who tell me this are usually in the very early post-partum period, when they are still recovering physically from childbirth (never mind the emotional recovery, and the importance of sleep for emotional well-being). I have to wonder: Why am I not also hearing stories of husbands who say, "I don't want my wife to have to get up with the baby at night when she already has such long days of taking care of him with no help—I can at least help ensure that she faces her next day of mothering with a good night's rest"?

As researcher Bonnie Fox writes of the sample of new mothers she interviewed for one of her studies, "At a time when they needed sleep, men's sleep was a more prominent concern for many women. At a time when they were overwhelmed with trying to figure out their new responsibilities, these women worried about the disruptions in their partners' lives."[20] Among the women in this study, much like the women I've worked with in therapy, there was also a tendency to feel even more dependent on their husbands than they felt before the baby was born. Many new mothers describe feeling that they couldn't handle the demands of parenting without their husbands' instrumental and emotional support, and because of this, they prioritize their husbands' needs and forgo their own. They seem to be saying to themselves, *I need my husband more than ever, so I will tiptoe around and be as careful as possible not to place any additional pressure on him. I need him to be healthy and available.* Though this makes some sense—in the face of stress, we *should* turn to others for support and should at least refrain from behaving in ways that alienate the people who can provide that support—the elements of carefulness and self-sacrifice are very problematic. Women should not feel they must walk on eggshells in order to ensure their husbands' continued support. They should not feel they must preserve and protect their husbands' well-being at the cost of their own.

In one very illuminating study conducted by researchers Carmen

Knudson-Martin and Anne Rankin Mahoney, a small sample of middle-class newlywed couples in southern California were interviewed about their marriages.[21] The researchers were interested above all in questions related to relationship equality and distribution of power: Whose interests shape what happens in the family? Is one partner more likely to organize her or his activities around the other? Do both partners notice and care for the other's feelings and needs? These were not the same questions they overtly asked the participants during the interviews, but they were the questions to which they sought answers in their behind-the-scenes analysis of what the couples shared. All the couples fancied themselves egalitarian; to be eligible for the study, they had to endorse ideals of gender equality and the importance of careers for both wives and husbands. The results were unsettling. Out of twelve couples, only *one* was categorized by the researchers as consciously and actively approaching equality. The majority of the sample—nine couples— were labeled "myth of equality" by the researchers because, despite their egalitarian standards and the portraits they painted of themselves, their relationships were characterized by an imbalance of power that always favored the husband.*

It was not the presence of inequality that surprised the researchers; it was the discrepancy between perception and reality. The couples appeared to be coping with the inequality in their relationships through a complex mix of denial and justification. They engaged in "equality talk," saying things like "We try to understand each other" and "We're each free to be our own person," which, according to the researchers, actually served to obscure and reinforce the underlying inequality. In a kind of smoke-and-mirrors effect, these

---

* If you're curious, the remaining two couples were considered "unacceptable inequality" couples. They espoused egalitarian ideals but were characterized by a great deal of conflict rooted in an overtly unequal distribution of power.

couples spoke of compromise and give-and-take in a way that gave an air of gender equality, while what played out in their daily lives was anything but equal. Wives organized their schedules around their husbands' needs, husbands chose which of the subjects their wives broached were important enough to listen to, and men's career goals were prioritized over women's. Yet nobody was fighting about these issues or complaining about power imbalances in the relationship. These couples were living examples of invisible male power.

In case it appears as though I'm only exposing the naïveté of newlyweds in the 1980s, I want to clarify that this is a phenomenon to which none of us is immune. Though this study was conducted a few decades ago, the phenomenon of self-deception it captured is timeless. It also captures, quite powerfully, how deep the roots of our patriarchal culture run. If we do not even recognize gender inequality when it is playing out inside the walls of our homes and in the dynamics of our marriages, it is because patriarchy has shaped the lens through which we are looking. While we can hope the current rising tide of feminism will alert more couples to the power imbalances in their partnerships, we have a long way to go before the subtler manifestations of those inequities are laid bare. I've shared this research here for the same reason I tell students about it in my classes: it illuminates the uncomfortable fact that our behavior is often out of alignment with our ideals, and shows us how the forces that influence our day-to-day decisions are often operating beneath our awareness.

I could share many, many examples of self-deception and invisible male power from my own life. My husband and I have some pretty unconventional arrangements in terms of gender roles. He does 95 percent of the cooking, and I take care of the bills. He is an extremely involved father and was so from the beginning, and we have had stretches of time during which, because of my work demands, he has spent significantly more time with our children, including not just leisure and play time but actually doing the true work of child-rearing—day care pickup, baths, dinners, schlepping them to soccer games. I have rarely felt inclined to complain about his contributions to the running of our household, and on the contrary I have often felt guilty* that I am not doing my fair share during times when my career demands are more pronounced. Even so, there are moments that reveal his relative power as a man—like when he *tells* me he has a meeting on Thursday night, but I *ask* him if he'd mind if I meet my friend for tea on Saturday morning.

My client Audrey knows that daily exercise is crucial for her well-being. She struggles with depression and anxiety that border on debilitating, and working out keeps her from going over the edge. In order to go to the gym before her husband leaves for work, she must get up at four o'clock in the morning. Already sleep-deprived from bed-sharing with a restless toddler and a nursing baby, she gets up at this ungodly hour to fit exercise into her day. When we discuss whether there might be other ways of finding time to exercise, it becomes clear that she will need to ask her husband. She will need to request that he make a change to his schedule. Though this couple faces some real financial challenges that limit their options for a less restrictive daily schedule, what concerns me is the power imbalance. Her stay-at-home-mom status positions her to need her husband's consent and cooperation in order to fulfill her own basic needs. She organizes her daily life around his, because like any heterosexual woman, she has been socialized to accommodate her partner's needs, readily and often without question. That kind of

---

* My guilt has many sources, but one of them is invisible male power. If I go out for the evening or he spends a day somewhere with the kids while I am home alone, I feel somehow indebted to him. Yet if he is away on a trip or out with a friend or at a meeting during the evening, I feel zero sense that he owes me. I just feel immersed in mothering and being in domestic mode, doing what I am supposed to do.

accommodation is not wrong or bad, except when it's so one-sided. Reciprocity is key to equality, and reciprocity is sorely lacking in Audrey's relationship. In a marriage with a truly equal balance of power, each partner "bends" or changes to accommodate the needs of the other at about the same rate. Unfortunately, research shows that this is not the case in a great majority of heterosexual couples.

A recent experience of Audrey's also exemplifies gender differences in what's been called "uncontaminated free time." A clear finding from the most recent version* of the American Time Use Survey is that women report having less free time than men. An interesting twist from a different research study is that once upon a time (in the 1970s), leisure time reduced tension and the feeling of being rushed for both men and women, but by the year 2000, only men were getting this payoff from leisure time.[22] This is because, additional research shows, women's "free" time is far more likely to involve the presence of her children than men's.[23] Men are likely to vacate the house for the day to pursue leisure activities, leaving their children and their chore lists behind. In contrast, women are more likely to relax with a magazine and a cup of tea in the living room, risking contamination of their leisure time with requests for a PB&J, the buzzer on the dryer indicating the laundry is ready to be folded, or the words "I'm done!" being shouted from the bathroom. Audrey told me she was eagerly anticipating a weekend visit from her parents because they were going to babysit so that both she and her husband could separately pursue some desires they'd been postponing: he wanted to hike with a friend, and she wanted to spend the day shopping. Almost in passing, she mentioned that her parents were only taking her older child for the day, because the baby, of course, was still nursing. So off her husband went without

---

* Bureau of Labor Statistics, 2010.

any children, while her shopping excursion involved diaper changes and a baby who couldn't be put down long enough for Audrey to try on clothes in the fitting room.

Ultimately, we determine our division-of-labor arrangements not by equality but according to whether they best serve the children's needs and whether they make sense in light of what each partner is equipped to offer, both of which are—far more often than we realize—predicated on culturally constructed assumptions about gender roles. Our behaviors reinforce what we believe. For instance, if we believe moms are better at caring for sick children and children want their mommies when they don't feel well, it's Mom who will call in sick to work when their toddler has a fever. Dad will not have the chance to learn what helps his daughter rest comfortably when she's sick, and the next time her temperature spikes, she may well say, "I want Mommy to stay home with me, not Daddy!" A father who believes women naturally know how to soothe fussy babies will pass the fussy baby over to Mom, who, if she successfully quiets the baby, will have "proven" the assumption that Mom's got the magic touch. Rachael once told me that Scott had offered to take their kids out for the day so she could have some much-needed alone time. But because their toddler was in a cranky mood, she imagined that the three of them wouldn't be able to have a good time while out and about, and she opted to keep the toddler home with her. Everybody but Rachael benefited from this revised plan—her husband had one fewer child to look after, her older child got some one-on-one time with his dad, and her toddler's cranky mood was ameliorated by cuddle time with Mama. Rachael justified her decision by explaining that she would not have enjoyed her time home alone because she would've been too worried about her toddler's mood, how it was hampering the outing, and whether Scott would be able to read both kids' emotional signals as well as she could.

It's not that Rachael's decision was wrong, but it does qualify as self-deception, and it preserves a status quo that taxes women more than men. Even with a conscious sense of dissatisfaction about current arrangements ("I'm doing so much more than him, and I'm exhausted"), we typically try to legitimize the status quo ("But he can't breastfeed, and the baby just cries when he tries to soothe her"). Other scholars have referred to this process as "glossing" or buying into "family myths," a process that is almost always easier than attempting to modify the underlying mechanisms that maintain the status quo.[24] In line with this, studies have shown the relationship between division of labor and relationship satisfaction to be quite complex, such that even among couples who hold egalitarian ideals, inequitable divisions of labor do not necessarily translate directly to expressed dissatisfaction.[25] While we do not know for sure why that is, one theory is that we rationalize inequities in order to cope with them, telling ourselves such things as, *I am more involved with the kids than he is even though we both have careers, but it's only natural for mothers to be more attuned to their children's needs. And the kids really prefer Mommy.* As one researcher puts it, women produce babies, but having babies produces "womanly persons."[26] When we become mothers, we claim a distinct kind of maternal consciousness or maternal identity that justifies, and ultimately is cemented by, a gendered division of labor.

More Children, More Inequality

This disintegration of equality, if equality had been achieved in the first place, does not stop sometime after the first child has been assimilated into the family. Often, it erodes with each subsequent child. The greater burden on women is most pronounced when children are under six years old,[27] and during those early years, as families expand, the inequity has an insidious, snowballing quality.

Just yesterday, a client soon to have her third child was describing to me her lack of faith that her partner will take time off work after the baby is born: "He says that's his intention, but I'll believe it when I see it." I asked her if she had an alternate plan for getting support if her partner did, indeed, disappoint her. She told me she did not. I felt an unusual tension between us, in which my wish for her to feel supported and cared for in the immediate days after she gives birth was at odds with her insistence that such a thing was not possible. She was bitterly resigned. Her intention, it seemed, was to do it all herself, out of either spite or an inability to imagine any other possibilities, or both. She anticipated feeling let down by her partner, and while that anticipation is valid, given their history (he has let her down many, many times over), it was her readiness to accept that fate that concerned me. I said something to her along the lines of, "Laura, you may well be right that he isn't going to take much time off work. There may be no avoiding feeling the disappointment of that. But I wonder, could you enlist support from others? Can you take steps to bring about a scenario in which you feel disappointed in him but also buoyed by the love and support of others?"

She had done what she could to communicate to him how important his support was. She had told him she is afraid of how depleted she will feel in the early days and weeks after this baby is born, and had made her request—that he take at least a week off work—clear. On that front, she had done all she could and really had no control over whether he was going to show up for her. But where plenty of control remained—brainstorming with me, for example, about how else she could get support, and making some phone calls to family members and friends to line up that support—she could not exercise it. My sense is that she could not even see it. Too accustomed to her disempowered state, making do with extremely limited resources, bearing alone the burden of caring for her children with minimal practical or emotional support from her partner, Laura is blind to opportunities for creating a different reality. She lives in a world of impossibility, of closed doors and dead ends.

It's hard to talk frankly about power. In this interaction with Laura, I was hovering uncomfortably close to an invalidating stance, the place where even gentle confrontation can feel shaming and can elicit a defensive or wounded "you don't get it" response in the other. I wanted Laura to feel seen and understood in her place of impossibility, but I also had to stand firmly on the side of possibility. After all, if I joined her in her sense that she is doomed to that disappointed, unsupported state, how would that serve her? But the very power differentials I hope to help Laura disrupt in her marriage also lurk within the therapy relationship. There are unspoken comparisons between her and me being made, and perceptions on her part that I have more resources than her. The assumption she makes when she hears me advocating for her to seek support from other people in her life is that I do not find it difficult to advocate for myself to get the support I need. She knows nothing of the conversations I have with my own therapist, who similarly urges me to consider possibilities I don't see and who sometimes points out how, without even realizing it, I take on burdens that are not mine to bear, or refuse to ask favors from others that I would gladly do *for* others. The illusion of others as more competent, more immune to the struggles of motherhood, is such a compelling one.

Divided We Fall, United We Stand

I'm as hopeful as any other working mom about the latest research on men's increased contributions to childcare and domestic responsibilities. Still, a closer look at the discrepancies that remain brings some troubling insights. Despite the choices women make about whether and when to get married, whether and when to have children, and how many children to have, the choices *couples* make once a baby materializes are often not choices at all. Couples find themselves entrenched in gender-stereotyped positions around the care of the baby and the home. They revert to patterns, deeply embedded within our culture, in which men have greater power. What gets negotiated between them, usually without words, are questions no less profound than whose needs matter more and whose wishes come first.

Our reactions to this imbalance are complex and varied, and do not translate neatly into obvious protest or dissatisfaction. We have many ways of distorting, denying, and justifying our unequal arrangements; as I described earlier, we can be quite adept at the legitimizing and self-deception that keep invisible male power alive and well. We may even sabotage our partners' efforts to ease our burdens; who among us has not criticized, at least silently if not out loud, our partners' poor diapering or dishwashing or lunch box–packing skills? Competence in the child-rearing and domestic spheres is an important and valid source of agency, power, and pride for a great many of us. And yet all these factors reinforce and maintain a status quo that ultimately erodes our well-being.

The inequities are real. They are not imagined in the minds of depleted, angry women. What looks like a choice—who will interrupt their career to stay home with the baby, who will leave work early to fetch a sick child from school, whose needs for exercise or creative pursuits or solitude will be met first—is so often not a choice, but instead a mandate driven by hidden power differentials and public policies that continue to privilege men and traditional family arrangements. Only systems-level change that remedies the inequities will bring actual choice to women attempting to balance career and family.

In the meantime, understanding that we are *all* in the grips of this system, men and women alike, can go a long way toward alleviating tensions and sparking change in any given marriage. Uniting with our partner against a common enemy is far preferable to viewing our partner *as* the enemy. As psychologist Martha McMahon states in her book *Engendering Motherhood*, "Whatever its complex source, men and women find themselves trapped in a pattern of gendered interaction they and their partners reproduce on a daily basis."[28] Elsewhere in both scholarly and popular literature, that "complex source" is examined more thoroughly. I've only scratched the surface of it here, because what I am most concerned with is what all this means for the way we feel about our partners as we navigate motherhood. The next chapter brings those feelings into clearer view.

7

Couples Adrift

Having a baby is like throwing a hand grenade into a marriage.
—Nora Ephron

On a walk one morning with a new friend whose second child is in his infancy, we spoke of the marital tensions that arise around efforts to get a baby to fall, and stay, asleep. She was describing the way her baby stirs at the slightest noise, even the cracking of her ankle as she tiptoes away from the crib after laying him down. I remembered that my husband and I used to joke about how making the transfer of a sleeping baby from arms to crib is good training for the bomb squad. Incredible agility is required; one false move, and disaster ensues.

In our conversation, my friend described a recent night in which she had managed the stealthy walk-away, with the noise machine humming and the fan set on high. Quiet as a mouse, she turned on her bedside lamp in the special way she does so that the on-off knob does not click. She silently slid under the covers and began to read her book, careful not to allow the pages, as she turned them, to brush up against the bedspread. Then her husband walked in and, though apparently not completely oblivious to the baby's tenuous asleep status because he addressed his wife in a whisper, proceeded to turn on the bright closet light right next to their baby's crib, switch the fan down to low, and clear his throat heartily a few times as he dropped his slippers onto the hardwood floor from a good eighteen inches above, where his feet were dangling off the end of the bed. *"Are you kidding me??"* she whispered to him. He looked at her blankly, genuinely unaware of what his transgression might be.

Another mother I spoke with told me about a night when her young baby was very congested. She lay awake listening to, and worrying about, his labored breathing. Her spouse, on the other hand, lay sound asleep, entirely oblivious to their baby's sick, restless sleep and his wife's nighttime vigil. In fact, his snoring practically obscured the sounds she strained to hear. Her rage at him was so all-consuming that she genuinely felt for a moment that she wanted to kill him.

These stories highlight how ripe for spousal tension just about any situation can become when there is a new baby in the house. My friend's annoyance with her husband is understandable on many levels. This is not an unhappy couple, nor is her husband an uninvolved father. He is very much supportive and involved. But her world at present is organized almost completely around the baby's needs; she is dialed in, around the clock, to his current state. It is her husband's lack of attunement to the delicacy of the situation, his inability to intuit that his wife was holding her breath, waiting to see if her careful, methodical strategies to get their easily awoken baby to stay asleep in those first touch-and-go moments in his crib were successful, that was an affront to her. Her disbelief that he could be so careless, as evidenced by her choice of words ("Are you kidding me??"), captures the heart of the matter in terms of the tension between them. She thinks, *I can't believe he doesn't get it. He doesn't understand my world right now.* Maybe even, *I am so alone in this.*

This moment represents one of the greatest sources of marital discord in the transition to parenthood. My friend and her husband are inhabiting different worlds, hers with the baby in the center, and his with the baby on the periphery. While tensions arising from this different-worlds situation are highest when a baby is new, they don't ever fully disappear. It is now ingrained in me, even though we are well beyond the napping, rocking chair, bomb-squad-training years, that any time in which my children are asleep is precious time for me, and that every effort must be made to ensure they remain asleep.* Occasionally, I wake up early in the morning before my boys do. I lie in bed fantasizing about the sublime experience of sitting on the couch with a cup of coffee and a magazine, in silence, watching the sun rise. I generate enough hope that this could actually happen that I get out of bed and gingerly, in complete darkness, make my way downstairs. I take silent, carefully executed steps on the bare wood stairs, and do a stealthy ninja lunge to avoid the creaky place in the floor right at the bottom of the stairs. By the dim glow of the pantry light, I discover that there are no ground coffee beans. I take the coffee grinder into the bathroom, wrap it in a towel to muffle the noise, close the door, and say a little prayer before turning it on. I take the kettle off the burner just before it begins to whistle. Feeling victorious, I sit down with my steaming cup of coffee, about to savor it and my solitude, when I am assaulted by the sound of what seems to be a herd of buffalo barreling down the stairs. It's my husband. He woke up before the kids did, too (a true rarity), with apparently *no sense whatsoever* of the precariousness of the situation. Mere seconds later, the first child comes thumping, bleary-eyed, down the stairs, his brother following soon after.

This really has happened. Not just once, but several times. In part, there is an issue here around my husband's sheer inability to

---

* Of course, I am the mother of two kids who act as if we are punishing them when we tell them it's time for bed, and for whom "sleeping in" means sleeping until six fifteen a.m.

tiptoe. He scares all our houseguests with the way he barrels down the stairs (people often wonder what the emergency might be, and I say, "Oh, that's just how Ari traverses the stairway"). He sometimes wants to gaze upon our sleeping children late at night, long after their bedtime and right before ours, and we have decided that he really shouldn't do that unless I come with him to make sure he doesn't step on their noisemaking toys on the floor or sit down on one of their appendages when he decides he wants to perch on the bed for a moment. He is many wonderful things, this man, but light on his feet and careful with his body are not among them.

But when he does not modify his stair treading, from the *house-is-on-fire* quality that is his custom to an at least marginally quiet manner that would suggest he does not want to wreck the precious opportunity to greet the day with some peace and quiet, the issue becomes something greater. We are still, all these years beyond the initial transition to parenthood, inhabiting different worlds. There was nothing ill-intentioned about my husband's disruption of the quiet; I am sure of that. However, I am also sure that he would have made a different choice, and would have at least *tried* to be quiet, if he shared my hopeful vision for at least a few minutes of serenely sipping coffee before the demands of parenting began. Somehow the cumulative exhaustion of parenting is still, in this very differ-ent chapter of our lives in which the caretaking responsibilities are more equal than they used to be, far greater for me. Much of the lost personal freedom I mourned when my babies were new has been restored, but it's as if some part of me doesn't realize or believe it. I often catch myself rushing when I am not actually in a hurry. I spend enormous amounts of mental energy pondering the best use of my alone time when I get it, still relating to it as a precious, limited commodity rather than something I'm now able to access fairly readily.

These shifts weren't experienced in the same way by my husband.

I don't deny that fatherhood has changed him, even in dramatic ways, but his changes are different from mine. Women are taxed, and changed, by parenthood more than men are. This is not my opinion, and it is not a statement based on anecdotal evidence from my particular encounters with clients and friends. It is a statement based on a great deal of scientific evidence, and it is fundamental to understanding the marital distress new parents so often experience. Let's take a look, from a research perspective, at just how pervasive, and pronounced, that marital distress is.

The Story the Research Tells

Among the many myths of parenthood are the notions that childbirth is the happiest event in the new parents' life, that women are naturally equipped to manage the demands of the early postpartum period, and that new babies bring couples closer together. While these myths persist in popular culture, for decades the scientific research has told a different story. In chapter 2, we looked at some of the very large body of research that establishes that the birth of a first child (1) represents a period of increased stress for nearly all women, (2) triggers the onset or exacerbation of depression for many women, and (3) presents a challenge for a majority of couples, during which marital or relationship satisfaction decreases, often dramatically. This decline in marital satisfaction has been well documented in longitudinal studies that examine couples' levels of satisfaction over time, from before the birth of their baby to several months, and sometimes years, afterward. In one large-scale review of the research literature, it was found that for 40 to 70 percent of couples undergoing the transition to parenthood, there is a decline in marital quality, one that is quite steep in the first year of the baby's life.[1] The level of conflict between partners tends to increase by a factor of 9, while the number of positive marital exchanges decreases substantially.[2]

For many couples, the decline in marital quality is temporary, tending to peak at around one year post-birth and improving within the child's second year.[3] However, even if couples recover naturally from this period of relationship dissatisfaction, there is evidence that marital distress has a negative effect on early parenting[4] and even on children's social and cognitive development.[5] In other words, though it's encouraging to know that a lot of couples emerge, without professional help, from the tough spot in which they found themselves as new parents, that doesn't mean there was no residual damage or that it wasn't terribly upsetting for them to be at odds with each other for so long. On top of that, many couples do not recover from the slow decline into marital distress that began when their first baby was born. This happens often enough that having a baby has been identified, statistically, as a risk factor for divorce. Couples without children are, on the whole, more satisfied with their marriages than couples with children, and this remains true long after the children are tiny hand-grenade babies.[6]

Of course, the story the research tells is not the story of every couple. Quantitative empirical research, by definition, deals in averages and trends, obscuring our vision of those who fall outside the norm. Certainly, many couples weather the storm of early parenthood just fine, and some rare couples wouldn't even call it a storm. Certainly, many women are thoroughly happy as they cross the threshold into motherhood, and remain so during their babies' early years. But the empirical fact remains that *most* couples struggle, at least temporarily, and *most* women are rattled—even if they ultimately find their footing again—by the transition to parenthood.

That these two struggles are happening simultaneously—a

woman's overall well-being and a couple's stability both compromised—is not in the least bit coincidental.

As discussed in chapter 2, research on postpartum depression, and depression in women in general, illuminates the connection between marital adjustment and women's well-being. First, marital dissatisfaction is a strong predictor of depression in women. This means that when a woman's marriage is unhappy, her likelihood of being depressed is higher. Second, there is evidence that when a mother is depressed, her husband is also more likely to be depressed. These findings point toward the notion of a distressed or dysfunctional interpersonal *system*, as opposed to a distressed or dysfunctional *person*. Interestingly, depression is being reconceptualized within the mental health field as akin to a fever—as a nonspecific condition that can signal many possible underlying problems. A fever tells us something is wrong within the body, but the "something" could be a virus or bacteria, a mild or serious illness; it could require treatment or just rest; it could be life-threatening or not. In a similar manner, depression tells us something is wrong within a person's life, but the possibilities are many. Maybe it is a role transition or loss or bereavement, maybe it is inflammation or hypothyroid or a chemical imbalance, maybe it is a distressed marriage.

Again, one finding that turns up over and over in the research is that poor social support, *particularly within one's own marriage or primary relationship*, is linked with depression in new mothers. One study even found that the husbands of women who had not just one but two episodes of PPD* were rated by independent observers as

---

* Although this finding emerged out of attempts to understand the factors that contribute to PPD, we must ask ourselves whether the same factors are at play in mothers whose distress does not fit into a neat diagnostic category. As we discussed at length in chapter 1, it is a misconception that women either have PPD or do not have it. Not all distress is clinical, and negative emotion in women is not a form of pathology.

being indifferent toward their wives.[7] It is worth noting that this finding came as a surprise to the researchers, who expected hostility or criticism in husbands, not indifference, would place women at greater risk for PPD. This unexpected finding points precisely to the notion of *loss* we have discussed so much already; the depressed mothers in this study had lost their partners' attunement and responsiveness. As we will soon see, it's quite possible that the husbands had suffered a similar loss.

Findings like this hint at what, exactly, goes awry for couples when they become so unhappy. We've established that most couples aren't having a fabulous time of it when they're adjusting to the new territory of parenthood. We've established that moms aren't, either. We've established that these two things are not a coincidence. The question now becomes, why? What's happening at a deeper level that explains all the turmoil?

If I had only one word to answer that question, it would be this: Attachment.

Within the bond of marriage (or any long-term, committed, monogamous intimate relationship) *there is so much at stake*.

"The good news is that sometimes the bond between a husband and wife is stronger than any damage that can be done to it. The bad news is that no two adults can do each other more damage than husband and wife."[8] These words, written by Judith Viorst, the author best known for *Alexander and the Terrible, Horrible, No Good, Very Bad Day*, may seem to state the obvious. Maybe everybody knows that marriage can either be our salvation or the death of us. What is far less obvious is that sometimes, these two seemingly opposing states can coexist.

My client Tess is in a very difficult place, fairly perpetually, in which she feels outrage at her partner while simultaneously craving his attention and affection. He used to walk through the door each evening and move toward her for a kiss, but not anymore. He's grown tired of his lips landing on her cheek, her eyes looking the other way, in that moment of desire and vulnerability when he attempts a connection. In his view, Tess is too angry to respond to his bids, so now he doesn't even make them. He has no idea that what he perceives as a stony anger in her is infinitely more complex.

Tess and I have discussed that her reaction to psychological pain is not unlike that of an injured animal. Her instinct is to crawl into the woods alone and lick her wounds in a place that feels safe. Her partner, not consciously aware that he has inflicted these wounds, wonders why she seems to snarl at him from her distant position. She is trapped in a tight corner of safety from which she cannot emerge, a self-imposed solitary confinement.

Her wounds are complex, and we have spent much time in therapy trying to better understand them. One thing we have learned is that her most painful wound—the one that aches each day and sends her into hiding—is at its core an attachment injury. Tess's partner has never asked her to be his wife. They have two children and a long history together, but they are not married. He tells her he does not see a need to go through with a ceremony, that his commitment to her should be obvious by their shared life, their children, and his efforts to support their family. She hates that this bothers her. For a long time, she feigned agreement and eschewed the institution of marriage. But she has realized, slowly and much to her dismay, that she was only pretending it didn't matter to her. It matters enormously.

For Tess, as for so many others, the question of marriage is not a religious or legal question. It is not even a question of social pretenses or appearances. It is about what the decision to marry represents at the most fundamental psychological and emotional level. Tess cannot shake the feeling that her partner has not yet truly committed to spending his life with her. She tells herself she is crazy to feel this way, since they have two children and a third on the way and own a home together. The years are ticking by, and they are, in effect, spending their lives together. Nonetheless, her feelings are understandable. Sure, not everybody in her position would feel that way; plenty of lifelong committed couples are happily unmarried, with neither the relationship nor either partner's self-esteem suffering as a result of their choice not to marry. For Tess, though, her partner's reluctance to marry her *even now that he knows how much it would mean to her* is extraordinarily painful. She is not confident in his availability. She cannot get an affirmative answer to the million-dollar question: "Are you there for me?" He is not, therefore, a safe haven for her from the fears and uncertainties of life. In her mind, if he were really, truly, no-holds-barred there for her, he would have no hesitation about getting married. In the attachment terms we are about to discuss in depth, their bond is not secure.

An Attachment Perspective on Adult Love

Let's consider the kinds of questions and remarks we would hear if we were eavesdropping in the homes of new parents:

"Did you really have to work late yet again? You know my days with the baby are so hard!"

"Can't you put the baby to sleep in her crib instead of our bed just this once?"

"I can't go to my Spin class unless you pick up the baby from day care. Can't you just agree to that one day a week?"

"How was I supposed to know you wanted me to go with you to the baby's checkup? You act like you don't want me to be a part of those things."

"I have no idea why he's not sleeping through the night yet. But you don't even have a clue how many times he's waking up, because you get to sleep through it."

The deeper questions being asked are these:

Are you there for me?

Where did you go?

I'm calling for you and I don't know if you hear me.

Can't you see how much I need you?

As a psychotherapist and a professor, not to mention a wife and a mother, I cannot imagine functioning without the framework of attachment theory. I became involved in research on attachment as an undergraduate, and never looked back. It organizes my thinking in all my roles. It helps me understand what I am feeling, what my children are feeling, what my husband is feeling, and what my clients are feeling. Since this lens allows us to make sense of nearly everything about how and why couples struggle during the transition to parenthood, it's worth getting into in some good detail. We'll do this by looking at some of the key principles that define attachment theory.[9]

First, attachment is an innate motivating force. When my students learn about attachment theory, they have no trouble grasping the key concept that babies, because they come into the world so helpless and vulnerable, are biologically wired to seek and maintain close contact with their mothers. Likewise, students understand readily that mothers are also biologically wired to keep their babies in close proximity to ensure their safety and well-being. This just makes sense. But a concept less readily embraced is that this innate motivation to seek closeness with significant others *stays with us across our life-span*. As a culture, we frown upon dependency. We herald autonomy and expect that healthy adults have "outgrown" their dependency needs. Attachment theory suggests a very different view of dependency: it is a lifelong need, a defining feature of the human condition that organizes and motivates behavior "from the cradle to the grave."[10]

I am struck, over and over again, by my students' complex mix of reactions to this concept. On one hand, I sense in them some relief. They recognize their own dependency needs as young adults and are glad to have them sanctioned by a well-established psychological theory. Sometimes there are audible sighs of relief at the realization that the time to cross over from dependency to autonomy is not, after all, growing short. On the other hand, they are a little bit puzzled, a little bit resistant, a little bit argumentative. The cultural narrative is that the farther up the independence ladder we have climbed, the more mature we are. Only babies and small children should need the safe haven of a close other. At best, we concede that adults thrive on close connection, too, but we believe it isn't actually necessary for survival or well-being the way it is for a child. At worst, we pathologize adult dependency, seeing it as a sign of weakness and a symptom of low self-esteem, dysfunctional relationships, and psychological disorders.

Since nobody actually outgrows their dependency needs and the prevailing cultural dictum is that we should, we are in a bit of a bind. We may resolve that bind by denying our dependency needs, even to ourselves. We may acknowledge them in secret but never express them freely. We may express them reluctantly, cautiously, sheepishly, tangled up with shame and self-castigation. Mostly we move through life vaguely aware of how good it feels to know a close, trusted other has our back but not broadcasting how much we hunger for that need to be fulfilled.

Another key principle of attachment theory is that secure dependence complements autonomy. This, too, is an idea that challenges popular notions of what it means to be a healthy, independent adult. From an attachment perspective, the fulfillment of dependency needs is precisely what allows for autonomy. The key insight is that dependence and autonomy are two sides of the same coin[11] and that each fosters the other in ongoing, reciprocal fashion. Attachment theory proposes that the fulfillment of dependency needs *in an enduring manner across the life-span* is actually what allows for continuing self-growth, individuation, and self-assuredness. There is no point at which we have gathered enough strength from close connection to function autonomously, nor is autonomy seen as impeding the possibilities for closeness. Rather, the more we can rest securely in a felt sense of close connection, the more defined our sense of separate and unique self becomes.

When, for instance, a wife feels certain that her husband is interested in understanding her internal world, she can risk divulging increasingly intimate details to him. Rather than being preoccupied with whether he cares or whether he's truly listening, she is freed up to explore her own thoughts and feelings. Her capacity to rely on him—unencumbered by doubts—not only facilitates her own self-understanding but also emboldens her to step into a new arena.

Furthermore, if she falters or falls in that new arena, it is him to whom she will go for comfort. Secure attachment offers an essential safe haven. The eminent attachment scholar and psychotherapist Sue Johnson writes, "The presence of an attachment figure, which usually means parents, children, spouses, and lovers, provides comfort and security, while the perceived inaccessibility of such figures creates distress. Proximity to a loved one tranquilizes the nervous system.[12] *It is the natural antidote to the inevitable anxieties and vulnerabilities of life.*"[13] We all know that life is inherently uncertain and that hard times are unavoidable, but it is easy to lose sight of the restorative power of connection, a reprieve that only a committed, loving other can provide. From the perspective of attachment theory, we are not meant to endure hardships alone. The need to retreat from uncertainty and into the arms of someone who shelters us from it all, even temporarily, is inborn and adaptive. It recalibrates and strengthens us so we can press on.

When my older son emerged from general anesthesia after a tonsillectomy at age five, he was extremely distressed. He felt severe pain in his throat and terrifying disorientation from the anesthesia. He was thrashing about, coughing, screaming, and sobbing all at once. His state was terribly painful for me to witness, but instinctively, I climbed onto his hospital bed and held him close to me and tried to soothe him with my voice and my touch. What he did not know is that I was, myself, in tears. Seeing my little boy in such despair created a state in me from which I also needed relief—and it was my husband who was *my* safe haven. He climbed onto the bed also, putting his arms around me as I had my arms around Noah. He soothed me immediately, in turn improving my capacity to give Noah what he needed. As much as I wish that moment never had to happen, I see it now in my mind's eye as a beautiful image of layered safe havens.

In the parent-child relationship, the safe haven concept is easy to understand; a parent is an almost *literal* haven for a child, cradling a child in her arms when he is tired or afraid, or scooping up a child who is in danger, just in time. In an adult love relationship, our partners may not envelop us in the same literal fashion, but through emotional attunement, they act as havens just as powerfully. Research even shows us that happily married, securely bonded spouses are physiologically soothed in times of stress or uncertainty simply by touching each other or looking into each other's eyes.[14]

There is good reason attachment is best known as a framework for understanding the primary bonds of childhood, more so than one that helps us understand adult love. The quality of the essential connections we make with our primary caregivers when we are young has a profound impact on who we are and how we relate to others. Perhaps most important, those early connections determine lifelong *emotional* skills, which are at the heart of our ability to understand ourselves and connect with those we love. Secure connections early in life allow for more nuanced understandings of our own and others' emotions, as well as more effective ways of coping with them. In the absence of significant strain or stress, a person with insecure tendencies may have only a little bit of occasional trouble naming her own emotions or tuning into those of her partner. But that same person, in the face of some stressful disruption or threatening scenario, is likely to have a lot more trouble handling her own emotions and staying accurately attuned to those of her partner. This has everything to do with how readily we get into an attachment-related "high alert" zone, and how readily we make negative assumptions about whether we can count on the other during hard times.

So what are the ingredients for secure attachment? Emotional accessibility and responsiveness are critical components of creating a healthy bond. The face-to-face, intimate interactions that unfold over and over again between a parent and baby are the raw ingredients for a secure bond. This means a mother's ability to pay attention—the quality of her antennae for detecting her child's emotional signals—is of primary importance. The physical presence or proximity of an attachment figure is important, too, of course, but it is not the foundation of a bond. When an attachment figure is physically present but emotionally absent, this provokes separation distress in the other as reliably, and perhaps even with greater force, as physical absence. Emotional responsiveness from an attachment figure tells us that figure is not just present but *interested*, concerned, and intent on reading our cues. As Johnson states, "In attachment terms, any response (even anger) is better than none. If there is no engagement, no emotional responsiveness, the message from the attachment figure reads as 'Your signals do not matter, and there is no connection between us.'"[15] Remember the study showing that women with repeated episodes of postpartum depression had husbands who were indifferent, not necessarily hostile or critical? Remember Julia, who wasn't sure which was worse, her aggravation toward her husband or her indifference toward him? Viewed from an attachment angle, it's clear which is worse. Anger is a form of protest against unmet needs. When we're angry, we're still in the ring, fighting to get our needs met. Indifference, on the other hand, signals resignation. We've walked out of the ring, convinced there is no point in fighting anymore. The flames of anger have burned out, leaving behind the ashes of apathy.

Viewed from this perspective, it's easy to understand why disconnection is often the presenting complaint among couples entering therapy. They aren't likely to use attachment language, but they do say things like "We've drifted apart" or "We just can't seem to understand each other" or "We don't communicate very well." And it's easy to see why research has identified "stonewalling"—one partner shutting out the other during a discussion of conflict—as so damaging. It's a behavioral emblem of disconnection. The stonewaller is not just missing the partner's signals or lacking in emotional attunement skills; he or she is blatantly unresponsive. Stonewalling has been identified by prominent couples researcher John Gottman as one of the top predictors of relationship demise, and as such is one of his "four horsemen of the apocalypse." When I teach about these "four horsemen" (the other three are criticism, defensiveness, and contempt), I show my students video clips of couples in Gottman's lab engaging in each behavior. Stonewalling is invariably the most painful to watch. Contempt is difficult, to be sure; students become very uncomfortable when viewing members of a couple mocking each other or rolling their eyes in disgust. But even worse are the moments of silence on the videotape in which a partner, having just seen and heard his partner cry, or protest, or plead, says nothing. That silent partner's face betrays no emotion; it is the quintessential poker face. It says to the despairing other, *You have no impact.*

While attachment needs are fundamental, ever-present, and life-long, they are not insistent at all times, asking to be met all day, every day. Rather, we can think of them as being triggered, or activated, by certain situations. During times of fear and uncertainty—such as illness, trauma, loss, or other stressful circumstances—our attachment needs become pronounced. During periods of stability, they may be "quiet" or even lying dormant because all is well. But when all is not well, the mere presence and attention of an attachment figure is a potent source of comfort, and we are inherently motivated to seek out that comfort.

The attachment system may also become activated in the face of some threat, real or perceived, to the attachment relationship. If a partner is perceived to be distant, preoccupied, or otherwise unavailable, this is experienced as an assault on the attachment bond and will give rise to strong emotions and attachment-oriented behavior. We may take steps to reestablish closeness, demanding answers or reassurances from our partner. We may protest in anger. Whatever we do, we do it in response to a perceived threat and in hopes of restoring stability to the attachment relationship.

We can think of "attachment behavior" as any behavior designed to keep or restore closeness with an important other. We won't see the behavior all the time. Sometimes babies are quietly looking out the window instead of crying or squealing or reaching for their mothers. But if, suddenly, Baby looks for Mom and she isn't there, or Baby sees something scary through the window, or Baby is hungry or doesn't feel well, she or he will surely cry out. Sometimes spouses are occupying distant corners of the house, each engaged in his or her own separate task. But if, suddenly, a torrential downpour hits and lightning strikes and the power goes out, those partners will seek each other out in the darkness. That dependency need gets triggered when we feel unwell or unsafe, or when we begin to doubt the other's availability.

During the transition to parenthood, *both types of triggers are likely to be present*. It is a time of stress and compromised physical and emotional functioning, and for most, though perhaps not all, it is a time of direct threat to the attachment bond.* Remember, fear and uncertainty activate attachment needs. I propose that in no other normative, allegedly happy life event is there greater fear and uncertainty, on so many levels, than in the transition to parenthood.

In love, in the bond of marriage, there is so much at stake. So much risk. So much potential. So much yearning. So much hurt, and so much healing. Only in our most intimate relationships is there simultaneously so much to gain and so much to lose.

These dualities are often encapsulated in the act of withdrawal. On the face of it, the behavior of withdrawing seems to say, "I don't want to be near you." But quite often, the person withdrawing is filled with longing and aching: longing to be pursued, understood, soothed. A wife turns her back because she's too scared to let him see the trembling of her lip. A husband turns his back because he feels rejected. He turns his back because it's too painful to look at the disappointment in her eyes. She turns her back because his words sting with truth.

When couples are new to parenthood, withdrawal is likely to make its way into their relationship, if it was not already there. Its manifestations may be many, and it may be mutual or one-sided, but

---

* It may be less obvious why I'm saying this trigger is present in most new parents, but read on.

it will always hurt. And, left unchecked, it has a way of growing. As we will explore in more depth in the next chapter, quite often wives and husbands are feeling equally excluded from each other's worlds, but for different reasons. Witnessing their wives' growing intimate bond with the baby, fathers may feel displaced on some level— even if they have a strong connection with the baby, too, and even if they are genuinely delighting in fatherhood. Many new mothers are resentful of their partners' relatively intact routines and work lives when their own have been disrupted so completely—even if they wouldn't send their babies back for the world. They may have an eagerness to connect with their husbands, only to feel put off by what he chooses to share or how little he seems to know, or wants to know, about her world. Discouraged or annoyed or angered by the disconnect, they feel themselves pulling away from the same person whose company they were craving.

Similarly, more than one client has confessed to me that she has pretended to be asleep when her partner came to bed in the hope that he would not reach out to her sexually, only to cry herself to sleep moments later, feeling so alone. As exhausted mothers, we often resent our husbands for having any interest in sex because it's just one more piece of evidence that they have energy we do not have. Their requests for sex show that they obviously have no clue exactly how drained we are or exactly how uncomfortable and unsexy we feel in our post-childbirth bodies. A fluctuating or nonexistent libido in a new (or even not-so-new) mother is entirely normal, but her partner's expectation that she'll be receptive can send the message that she "should" want it. In this context, our husbands become just one more person placing demands on us, and particularly demands on our bodies, when we are "touched out." In other words, their interest in sex is proof that they aren't with us, don't get us, and don't see where we are, and possibly that they're selfishly pursuing gratification of their own needs. There may well be validity to those interpretations of our husbands' desire for sex, and certainly there is validity to our decreased desire and our need for physical boundaries. But the irony is that sometimes, their sexual overtures may well be their way of saying, *I'm right here. I see you and I want to be with you. I'm reaching for you.*

The irony is that we turn our backs to our partners, attempting to protect ourselves from something—vulnerability, pain, rejection, shame—at the moments we most need to know our partners are there. And our partners, sensing our unavailability, eventually turn away as well. And then there are two lonely people lying in bed next to each other, longing for connection, drifting off to sleep with imagery of a wide and deep chasm between them that cannot be traversed.

Sometimes, quite literally, a baby has come between them. "Honey, something's come between us," said my wryly smiling husband one night when our baby son was snoring in the middle of the bed, each of us on one side of him and wishing that just once, in the last many months, we'd been able to fall asleep in our preferred "spoons" position. In the best of scenarios, a couple can experience a shared sense of loss, longing, and frustration and maybe even have some capacity for a sense of humor about it. More often, though, there are formidable tensions around why, and for how long, and for whose benefit, the baby is sleeping in the bed.

Like so many other parenting decisions, the choice to bed-share or not is an individual one, and I am not here to offer an opinion on the matter. But what is undeniable is that a baby's actual presence in the marital bed, or in the bedroom, is an antiaphrodisiac. Also, I am certain that for some couples, the tangible obstacle of the baby between them is easier to tolerate than the many intangible, perhaps painful, perhaps subconscious reasons they may not be drawn to each other sexually. Almost always, these reasons are rooted in attachment concerns.

Attachment theory gives us a framework for understanding so much of what unfolds within an adult intimate partnership, especially as that partnership adapts to the strain of parenthood. It helps us understand why even the smallest perceived rejection may carry tremendous emotional weight, and why one partner may fight, flee, or freeze when the other is perceived to be unavailable. This "fight-or-flight response" is more commonly known to occur during a brush with some obvious, imminent danger, like a car veering toward us or a bear on the hiking trail, but research tells us that it occurs with regularity in the context of close interpersonal relationships. To be rejected, abandoned, or shut out by an attachment figure is, at a physiological level, akin to facing a life-threatening situation. No wonder people act "crazy" in relationships and go to desperate lengths to restore an attachment bond that has been weakened or broken.

When our attachment needs get activated in a stressful situation, especially a prolonged one like the transition to parenthood, we may find that old wounds feel new again. Early experiences create lasting vulnerabilities that play out in our adult relationships, explaining—if we can bring all this into awareness—the frustrating and sometimes deeply hurtful dynamics in which we become entrenched. My client Tess has probably always struggled with unmet attachment needs, for reasons that extend back to the earliest days of her childhood, growing up with a depressed, emotionally unavailable mother. When Tess and David first got together, their many mutual interests helped them forge a connection that was comfortable, and enough, for them both. They spent a lot of time together and had very little conflict. When she became pregnant with her first child, however, she began to feel painfully lonely. Her world and David's world seemed to veer off in different directions when she became engrossed in the experience of pregnancy and the anticipation of motherhood. David, on the other hand—though certainly not unenthusiastic about impending fatherhood—carried on in his usual mode of immersion in his career as an architect. The seeds of their distress as a couple were planted then, when Tess sensed that he wasn't fully with her as she readied herself for something so monumental. And once the baby was born, those seeds grew into noxious, invasive weeds that are now choking out what was once beautiful in their garden. As Tess faced the full catastrophe of life as a new mother, she turned to her partner over and over, only to perceive that, more often than not, he wasn't there.

What about my friend with the sleep-defying baby and the husband who was just a little too oblivious to how crucial it was for their bedroom to be absolutely silent once the baby was asleep? The questions fueling her distress are essentially the same as Tess's. She feels great aggravation toward her husband because *doesn't he get it?* Does he not understand what her world is like right now, and can she not count on him anymore? I'm sure the gravity of Tess's situation appears greater, and indeed it is: she is a lot further down a desolate path of feeling unseen and unwanted by her partner, and she is in despair. My friend is just plain mad, and a bit incredulous, but not (yet, and hopefully not ever) despairing. Still, for both women the fundamental issue is the same one playing out in the homes of countless new parents. The parents of a newborn are faced with the task not just of developing an attachment bond with their new child, but of doing so *while preserving the existing attachment bond between them.* For a great many couples, the endeavor to integrate a child into their lives is the first opportunity they have to demonstrate—or fail to demonstrate—that they have the capacity to remain connected and responsive to each other under the most trying of circumstances.

8

In the Weeds

The greatest gift a parent has to give a child—and a lover has to give a lover—is emotionally attuned attention and timely responsiveness.
—DR. SUE JOHNSON, *LOVE SENSE*

Sam and Ivy started couples therapy when their daughter was just under a year old and their twin sons were four. I remember a moment during their first session, when Ivy swept a tear-soaked strand of her long red hair away from her eyes while Sam looked away. I thought about how different it would be if Sam were the one gently moving that lock of hair, telling his wife with that one small action that he was listening, concerned, interested. Instead, his averted gaze and his arms folded across his chest seemed to confirm for Ivy what she was describing in that moment: he doesn't listen and he doesn't care. Not the way he once did. Not for a long time.

Earlier in the hour, Sam had spoken of his anger about his wife's endless criticizing of him: "Nothing I do is good enough for her. I'm a good guy, but somehow I wake up every day feeling guilty. I hear Ivy's voice in my head, telling me one more thing I need to do better or more or differently. I'm sick of it."

I listen to the story of how they got here. I listen as Ivy describes how overwhelmed she has felt since the twins were born, and I listen to Sam defend himself against the accusation—unspoken in this

first session but apparently a recurring theme in their arguments—
that Ivy would be less overwhelmed if he did more: "You act like it's
my fault that we had kids. We *both* wanted them, and you were the
one who wanted to try for a daughter. I would've been fine with our
two boys." Sam's words rile Ivy, who, I would later learn, privately
wrestles with a sense of regret about having a third child. She loves
their daughter profoundly, but she does not love who she has become
now that she is the mother of three children. She is, she says, a shell
of her former self. There is no time to attend to her own needs, let
alone to nurture the marriage. "Our relationship has been on the
back burner," she says. "I keep telling myself that eventually I'll
find the energy and motivation to pay more attention to Sam, but it
hasn't happened. And I can't help but feel that it would've happened
by now if Sam had been willing to share more of the burden." Ivy
seems to move among feelings of guilt, sadness, and bitter resentment. She tearfully states, "I miss him, but I'm too tired at the end
of the day to turn to him." Minutes later I hear her say, "If he feels so
ignored, then maybe he's getting a taste of his own medicine. He
has been ignoring my pleas for four years." Sam wonders what pleas
she could possibly be talking about. He has only heard barbs and
insults and endless demands.

   With three children under the age of four, there was no doubt
this couple was, as they say, in the weeds. Though they kissed each
other hello and good-bye and said "I love you" every day, neither
one could remember the last time they really looked at each other.
At best, they were like ships passing in the night, crossing paths
only briefly when he returned from work each evening a half hour
before she left for her nursing shift at the hospital. At worst, they
were embroiled in conflict, arguing about unwashed dishes and late
arrivals and not enough sex. They wound up in my office after a
particularly ugly fight, when Ivy told Sam she'd been happier while

he was away on a business trip: "I was taking care of everything myself, like usual. Only I didn't have to resent you for not helping, because you weren't even here. It felt so good to be out from under all that anger."

Ivy and Sam portrayed so many of the dynamics typical of couples with small children. Though both partners worked full-time outside the home, there was no question—even in Sam's mind—that Ivy took care of far more than 50 percent of the responsibilities on the home front. Their children figured prominently in her mind whether she was with them or not, while Sam acknowledged that when he was at work, he didn't think much about the kids or what needed to be done around the house. Ivy envied him his capacity to concentrate exclusively on his job, especially because she constantly worried she would make a mistake, in her overtired and preoccupied state, at her high-stakes nursing job. Both agreed that Sam's time with the kids in the evenings was a substantial contribution to their shared parenting duties, and also a special time for him and the kids. He enjoyed being on his own with them and felt more competent as a parent when Ivy wasn't around, and the kids loved their "Daddy nights." But this, too, stirred up envy and bitterness in Ivy, who experienced herself as short-tempered and bogged down by unrelenting obligations when she was with her children every day. Often, she eagerly anticipated the handoff to Sam when it was time for her to go to work, only to be distracted, once at the hospital, by guilt about not savoring her time with the kids enough. She wondered what her family was doing at home without her. Longing to connect with them, she'd sometimes call to check in. Sam perceived these check-ins as an attempt to micromanage him, an indication that his wife didn't trust him to take care of their children as well as she could. Ivy would detect the irritation in Sam's voice from the moment he answered the phone, and their calls often ended angrily.

With each recurrence of this exchange, the distance between them increased. Both Sam and Ivy felt increasingly alone, misunderstood, and unappreciated.

As a couples therapist, I often feel like a translator. After ensuring I've accurately understood each partner's internal world, I then go about finding language for each of their experiences that the other can more readily understand. During those difficult initial sessions with Sam and Ivy, I focused on the words they were *not* saying that, once articulated, might allow them to better understand each other. Prominent couples researcher John Gottman states that within every negative emotion, there is a longing or a wish.[1] This is one of those nuggets of wisdom that always guides my work with couples. As the room fills up with angry accusations, defensive retorts, and heavy, despairing silences, I listen for what hasn't been said. I listen for hidden longings. I look for the fundamental emotional states behind the words. I ask myself, *If we could lift the veil of anger (or defensiveness, or stony withdrawal, or whatever the case may be), what would we see?*

With Sam and Ivy, I saw a tremendous amount of pain. Both were longing to know they still mattered to the other. On some level, Sam feared he had been replaced by their children in his wife's priorities and affections; he no longer felt nurtured by his wife, who had once showed him so well, every day, how much she loved him. Ivy felt she was lost at sea, on the verge of drowning, desperately wondering why her husband, nearby in the safety of a lifeboat, would not just paddle over to her and say, "Get in." Both were so distressed that neither could see the other's vulnerable position.

Typically, as a couple becomes more entrenched in a pattern of focusing on their mutually unmet needs, problems with both expressing and listening arise. The signal is distorted *and* the reception is impeded. Feelings that would normally prompt compassion and concern in each other are obscured by negativity. If a husband feels hurt because of something his wife has done (or failed to do) again and again, he is likely to withdraw in silence or conceal that hurt with angry, critical words, much like a tender wound is concealed by the hard edge of a scab. If she's contending with her own wounds from things he has done (or not done), she is not very likely to reach for him when he retreats, or listen neutrally to his critical words while she attempts to decode them and pinpoint an underlying longing. But a third party may well be able to do just that. As a couples therapist, I reach for people who have retreated, and I wager a guess, out loud, about some softer feeling (loss, maybe, or fear or sadness) that may lurk beneath the anger that dominates the dialogue.

In this case, Sam cannot hear or see Ivy's longing for comfort, relief, and support because all he hears are criticisms and complaints. He sees only an unsatisfied, perpetually angry wife and expends his energy in defending himself from a perceived attack. Likewise, Ivy cannot hear or see Sam's longing for affirmation, his need to know he is still special to her and that she desires him. She sees only another needy person placing demands on her. She feels he has no idea how little she has left to give, or how much his lack of support has impacted her connection with him.

How did they get to such an impasse? A cynical, but nonetheless true, answer would be, "They had children." Their marriage was a sturdy, genuinely happy, and loving one before they became parents. Nobody—least of all Sam and Ivy—would have predicted they would end up on a therapist's couch contemplating separation, just six years into their marriage and with three young children in the house. It's probably safe to say that had they chosen not to have kids, there would be far more harmony and closeness between them right now. But what we need to understand is *why* and *how* the transition to parenthood so often equates to the transition to marital distress.

In chapter 7, we discussed the basic tenets of attachment theory, including the fact that attachment needs are lifelong, but not necessarily active or insistent at all times. I described the tenet of attachment theory that says our attachment needs become activated during times of stress or when there is a threat, real or perceived, to the attachment bond. I proposed that *both are true* when partners become parents. It is a time of enormous stress and strain, and the new triad—two parents plus baby—poses a threat to the original dyad. These factors give rise to strong emotions and motivate people to engage in attachment behaviors. Again, any effort a person makes to confirm, strengthen, or restore an attachment bond—regardless of whether the effort pays off or goes over well with the partner—is an attachment behavior. That means that just about anything I say or do in relation to my husband, if it's in the interest of getting some assurance that he's close by and he's got my back and I still matter to him, is an attachment behavior. The theory says that I'll do a lot more of those things, or do them with more fervor, if I'm having a tough time or if there's any indication that maybe he *isn't* there for me like I thought he was. I will start sending signal after signal that I need assurances, I need him, I need evidence that we are close and connected and he is holding me in mind. The question then becomes, will he be emotionally attuned enough to read my signals? If the goal is to stay happily married, the answer really needs to be yes.

How does this emotional tuning-in play out in the everyday life of a marriage? Gottman and his colleagues characterize spousal responses to each other's bids for connection as falling into three categories of behavior: "turning toward," "turning away," or "turning against." For example, if I say, "Pasta sounds good for dinner tonight," and my husband says, "Mmm, yes, it does. Maybe fettuccine with good olive oil and some of those mushrooms we got the other day?" that's turning toward. If my husband says, "Sure, whatever," that's turning away. If he says, "I felt really cranky all day today," and I say, with warmth and eye contact and genuine concern, "Why do you think that is?" that's turning toward. In contrast, if I roll my eyes and say, "What else is new?" that's turning against; I've not only failed to tune in, I've also shamed and alienated him with my sarcastic response. Research suggests that within the context of marriage, each moment of turning toward is like a deposit of intimacy and goodwill in an "emotional bank account." Because those deposits eventually add up to substantial savings, they create a sense of security and protect couples from the damaging effects of occasional, inevitable moments of turning away or even turning against.

Longitudinal studies that closely examine couples' behavior as newlyweds and then track their happiness over time have revealed the important role turning toward plays. In Gottman's research, couples who were divorced within six years had turned toward each other in the lab, as newlyweds, only 33 percent of the time on average, but couples still married six years later had had an average turning-toward rate, as newlyweds, of 86 percent. This is a striking difference. The evidence is clear: misattunement, or a lack of emotional responsiveness in couples, results in sometimes unbridgeable chasms.

Why Attunement Matters

Much has been written, within both the popular press and scholarly literature, about the importance of intimate, face-to-face interaction between parents and babies. Most of us seem to know intuitively, even if we are not familiar with this literature, how much our babies crave and delight in our close attention. Babies need us to respond to their cues, to the signals they give us that they are afraid, hungry, cold, or tired. When we respond to our baby's cry with the voice of concern and a gentle touch, intent on determining what may be wrong and how we can help, not only do we meet the immediate and more concrete need of the child (the need for, say, a fresh diaper or to be rocked to sleep), but we also send a message of immeasurable value to the child: *Your needs matter, and you will not be ignored*.

New mothers, in particular, tend to spend great swaths of their day engaged in such transactions with their infants. As psychologist Daphne de Marneffe points out, "In the seemingly mundane give-and-take of parenting—playing, sharing, connecting, relaxing, enduring boredom, getting mad, cajoling, compromising, and sacrificing—a mother communicates with her child about something no less momentous than what is valuable in life, and about the possibilities and limits of intimate relationships."[2] Though we may (and usually do) lose sight of this deeper meaning behind our day-to-day interactions with our babies, we still know on an intuitive level how much our attunement matters. That's one reason many of us feel so guilty so much of the time: we know our children thrive on our close and careful attention, and yet we cannot give it to them unceasingly.

What is somewhat less intuitive is that as adults, we need this same kind of close attention from the ones we love. And we need it particularly during times of stress. It isn't just a lovely frosting on the cake of life, something we enjoy but could get by without. It is crucial for our well-being. Research on emotional attunement within couples may be relatively new, but it points unmistakably to the crucial role it plays in relationship fulfillment.

Attunement is important in adult intimate relationships for exactly the same reasons it is important to developing babies: attunement allows for the fulfillment of fundamental attachment needs. When our spouses are not attuned to us, they are failing to send us the message so critical for a sense of well-being and felt security (and even, as we will later see, physical health): *Your needs matter and you will not be ignored. I am here for you.*

It's pretty simple, isn't it? We should pay close attention to the human being with whom we've chosen to share a lifetime. We should stay engaged in a call-and-response kind of dance, aware of the ways our partner reaches out to us, and willing, most of the time, to extend a metaphorical hand in response. Nobody's perfect, of course, and even exemplary spouses miss some of each other's bids or just don't always have it in them to respond appropriately. Still, it's a straightforward and seemingly easy concept. Our brains are also wired for connection, and mirror neurons[3]—cells in the brain thought to be associated with empathy*—allow us to feel our way into the heart and mind of another. Why, then, is attunement so challenging for some couples? And how does a couple like Sam and Ivy, once adept at meeting each other's needs, end up at war with each other? It turns out that in a most unfortunate irony, these inbuilt empathy and attunement skills often deteriorate when we need them most. Like when we are afraid and uncertain, for instance. Or when we are stuck in the swamp of prolonged marital conflict. And this is especially true for people who were not securely attached in childhood.

For adults who did not have the advantage of secure, stable attachment relationships with caretakers as children, the neural pathways that signal interpersonal danger are well established, and it takes little to activate them. It's as if there is a paved superhighway

---

* Mirror neurons are so named because they fire in response to what we see *other people* doing or experiencing, but our neural activity looks just like it would if *we* were the ones doing the behavior or having the experience. It's as if our brain activity is mirroring another's circumstances. For instance, if we see an object being thrown at someone else, our brains will light up on an MRI the same way they would if the object were being thrown at us, and physically, we might even flinch. The more closely we are tracking the other, the stronger and more elaborate the mirrored neural activity will be, and the greater the empathy.

to fear and mistrust inside their brains; the on-ramps are abundant, but the off-ramps are few and far between. Once they're traveling down that highway, they could reach the destination ahead with their eyes closed. They've been there so many times before. But they don't want to go. Their hearts are heavy with dread or thumping with panic, and they're looking for an exit. Failing that, they're searching for a way to cope, to calm down while they resign themselves to being, once again, on this familiar journey. Maybe they'll scream and shout and shake the steering wheel, or maybe they'll go numb. But one thing is sure: They have no emotional resources to spare. They're not looking around and wondering how the drivers of the other cars on the road are feeling.

For securely attached people, the path to fear and mistrust is more like a dirt road with weeds popping up along it. It has not been worn smooth by regular travel. Certainly it could get them to the same place as those on the paved highway, but much more slowly, and not without a lot more effort to find the road in the first place.

All of us, regardless of our fortune or misfortune in having our attachment needs met as young children, are biologically wired to seek and maintain close connection with others. All of us are biologically wired to react—to protest or panic or worry or seek reassurance—when our most important close connections are threatened. All of us register cues related to our partner's perceived availability, and all of us react, internally if not also externally, to negative cues. This is what it means to be human. But two factors introduce a great deal of variability in how skillfully we read signals and how we react to them: the quality of our earlier attachment experiences (our "attachment histories"), and our current circumstances.

These factors have powerful effects independent of each other. For instance, even the most fortunate person in terms of early attachment experiences—a highly secure person—will lose access to her customary emotional skillfulness, at least temporarily, when she learns that her spouse is cheating on her or when she is utterly overwhelmed by a baby who hasn't stopped crying for three weeks. Conversely, even during periods of relative stability—say, when a couple has been getting along swimmingly and their stressful jobs are less stressful than usual—an anxious style of attachment in a husband can set him up to misinterpret his wife's cues. She says, "I'm exhausted and need to go to bed early," and he hears, "I'm not interested in being around you right now."

The picture gets exponentially more complicated when these two factors intersect with each other. Our attachment histories actually *determine* how we will perceive and handle our current circumstances. So trying times in a marriage, like bringing home a new baby, are generally a bit less trying if we have the benefit of secure attachment and high emotional skillfulness, and more trying if we do not. Furthermore, there is the obvious but often overlooked fact that just as I bring my attachment history to a relationship, *so does my partner.* The unique pairing of my attachment tendencies with my partner's means that our dynamic might be quite different from the one I had with a previous, differently attached partner. Our unique pairing may serve us perfectly well during times of stability, but may hinder us considerably during periods of stress. This is precisely what happened with Sam and Ivy.

As a girl, Ivy had been very close to her mother. Though her father was often away from home, either for work or to care for his elderly parents in a town two hours away, he was a gentle soul who was generous with affection for both his daughter and his wife. Ivy recalls many evenings alone with her mother, characterized by abundant conversation and shared experiences. Together they prepared and cleaned up after dinner, did crafts, and picked out seeds from gardening catalogs, dreaming of summer when her father would be home more often and the three of them would spend time in the garden. An only child, Ivy felt treasured and supported and understood. When Ivy's best friend was killed in a car accident at age twelve, Ivy's father took time off work to be home with her. She remembers that her parents encouraged her to stay home from school for a week, and during that time all three of them passed the hours together. Her father didn't know what to say, but his decision to stay home with her spoke volumes and soothed Ivy more than any words could have.

Sam's childhood memories carried a different tone, one of isolation and rejection and fear. His mother was volatile, moving between episodes of quiet depression and periods of rage. Though her rage was typically directed at Sam's father, occasionally she blew up at Sam and his brothers. On any given day, Sam might encounter a withdrawn, emotionally distant mother or an aggressive, threatening mother. He learned early on that his best strategy was to keep his distance. He spent most of his after-school hours outside with his brothers, steering clear of the house and the ugly fights that erupted regularly between his parents. After dinner each night, the three siblings beat a hasty retreat to their bedrooms. In one another, they sometimes found comfort and companionship, but as they grew older, they spent more time apart, each coping separately with the fragility of their parents' marriage and the constant threat of their mother's rage. She seemed to single out Sam, especially, accusing him of possessing the same unsavory traits as his father. Sam compensated by excelling in school, but no matter how many straight-A report cards or academic awards he brought home, his mother's approval and admiration remained elusive.

Sam's gentle, quiet way and his dedicated work ethic were qualities that reminded Ivy of her father. In Ivy, Sam found the kind of affirmation he never got from his mother; Ivy freely expressed affection, respect, and admiration for him, and he felt valued in a way he never had before. In addition, all those years spent trying to read his mother's face to determine her mood amounted to an attentiveness in Sam that Ivy appreciated; he was adept at sensing her feelings, and seemed eager to please her. They fit well together, and the early years of their marriage were very happy ones.

When their twins were born, things began to change. Part of the problem was that Ivy felt the strain far more than Sam, and in that respect they were like just about every other heterosexual couple in the throes of early parenthood. But their unique histories also played a role in the unfolding drama of their marital unhappiness. Sam's decision not to take time off work when the babies were born stood in stark contrast to her father's choice to be near Ivy during a previous time of need, and set in motion a train of thought in Ivy that perhaps Sam was not as reliable or available as she had assumed. Ivy's irritable mood, once rare but now the norm, thanks to the stress of mothering three small children, signaled to Sam that she— just like his mother—might blow at any time. Her requests that Sam do more to help with the kids and around the house stirred up in him the familiar feeling of never being good enough.

Before they had children, none of these wires had been tripped in their marriage. They had been relatively lucky in terms of encountering any major stressors together. Ivy brought a fundamental attachment security to the relationship that Sam was able to "borrow," but once they were parents, that changed. Ivy felt far less secure in this new phase of her life, overwhelmed and lacking both the quality and quantity of support she needed from Sam. The anger she directed at him was her way of protesting this new state of affairs, but in Sam, it set off his old familiar way of coping by withdrawing and retreating. His withdrawal left Ivy feeling even more alone and more unsure that he could, and would, be there for her when she most needed him. What began as an unfamiliar dirt road for Ivy eventually became a well-worn path, though still not the paved superhighway that transports Sam so efficiently to a place of panic and fear. Both endured the daily pain of the perception that the other was slipping away.

Sam and Ivy's story offers a powerful example of the ways in which times of uncertainty and change can activate primitive attachment needs. The transition to parenthood, and even the welcoming of another (second, or third) child into an existing family system, is without question one of the greatest periods of change and disruption. Other scholars have pointed out that a couple adjusting to the birth of a child is essentially undergoing a test of their capacity to provide a secure base for each other under stressful circumstances, and for perhaps the first time, those stressful circumstances are not external or fleeting. They are the "new normal," and they directly threaten attachment security.[4] The parents of a newborn are faced with the task not just of developing an attachment bond with their new child, but of doing so while preserving the existing attachment bond between themselves. In the most basic way, they are moving from a period of focusing on each other to focusing together on someone else. While this is a perfectly natural phase in the developmental trajectory of a marriage, *natural* is not the equivalent of *easy*. A felt sense of attachment security within the couple will position them to navigate this shift more easily, but it will not exempt them from the innate responses in our brains and bodies that say, *Am I still safe here with you? Do you still have my back?*

What is so helpful about this attachment view of a couple's evolution from non-parents to parents is that it shines the light on the fundamental, perfectly reasonable, and ultimately *essential* needs that are so difficult to fulfill during this phase. Couples navigating the transition to parenthood often feel crazy and irrational when they are, in fact, following the exquisite order of the human condition. They are reacting to a decrease in their felt security, saying in one way or another, "This is not okay."

Despite this common denominator of decreased security, these attachment concerns are usually experienced differently by mothers and fathers. Generally, a new mother is primarily concerned with getting adequate support in caring for the baby, and a new father is primarily concerned—though perhaps less consciously—with the fear that he has been usurped by the baby.* Indeed, the feeling new fathers often have in relation to their wives is one of being *irrelevant*, or at least less relevant than they used to be, and this is typically a very painful feeling to bear. The irony is that though their wives appear to be consumed with the baby, they are actually *more*, not less, in need of the attentive support of their husbands. At the end of the day, both partners are asking, "Where did you go?" They are both rightfully concerned with preserving the bond on which their well-being rests. That's the good news. The bad news is that the tactics they employ—the particular ways they say, "This is not okay"— often do the opposite of restoring security. In marriage, the things we say and do can be corrosive to the bond we seek to preserve, and the things we *don't* say and *don't* do can be erosive.

In my therapy with couples, something remarkable happens when partners begin to see the attachment longings behind their dreadful conflicts. The behaviors that make it hard to tune into each other, like critical and angry words or stonewalling, fall away. I don't teach constructive communication skills or admonish couples not to engage in those behaviors (though I do try to nip them in the bud, of course, when they occur in the room with me), because actually they tend to disappear when the real feelings find

---

* It is important to note that this difference in men and women is directly linked to the issues of gender inequality—and the tendency for heterosexual couples to revert to more traditional gender roles when they have a baby—discussed at length earlier. As long as the burdens of caretaking fall unevenly in a two-parent household, with mothers doing more than fathers, the immediate attachment concerns will look different for each partner. Mothers are looking for more support, both practical and emotional, and fathers are wondering where they fit into this new equation.

a voice. The real feelings almost always elicit greater compassion. At a minimum, they invite the partner to lean in and listen. When spouses speak words like "I'm so afraid you've lost interest in me" or "I'm feeling so overwhelmed and alone, and I can't seem to trust that you're really there for me," there is a vulnerability and a tenderness that emerges in the space between them. The room gets quieter, the signal becomes clearer, and, consequently, the response changes. As Sam began to express his feeling of irrelevance, and his sadness about feeling disconnected from Ivy, Ivy was far less irritated and critical about his desire to make love to her. The voice in her head when he moved closer to her in bed and began to kiss her had changed from *I can't believe he expects me to want sex when I'm so exhausted* to *He knows I'm tired, and he's tired, too. He's reaching out to me. He just wants to restore some of the connection between us.* With that different internal narrative, there is less frustration about their being on such different pages, and more room for her to discern and directly voice her own needs. She could say to him, "I get that sex appeals to you right now as a way for us to feel connected. I want connection, too, but physically I just need a little space, and sleep is my top priority right now. I need to listen to my body, and I need you to trust that taking care of myself will help us connect in the long run." When the phone rings at night during Sam's time at home with the kids, he picks it up saying, "Hi, honey, we are missing you, too." When she mentions there is laundry in the dryer, he registers her need for support rather than feeling micromanaged. He says, "I might not get the laundry folded tonight, Ivy, but I know it's there and I don't want you to feel alone with all the mounting housework. We'll tackle it together this weekend."

In exchanges like these about the ordinary stuff of domestic family life, couples are quite often communicating about that million-dollar question: *Are you there for me?* When they're trudging through the thick and tall and thorny weeds, it can be so hard to hear the question in the first place, let alone extend a metaphorical hand and say, "Yes. I am right here."

The Hardest Job on Earth

While the paradigm of attachment is tremendously helpful for understanding marital tension, I don't want to insinuate that *everything* about the tension couples experience during the transition to parenthood can be traced back to fundamental attachment concerns. There is at least one other explanation, and it is this:

Parenting is really hard.

I know, this may win the prize for Most Obvious Statement Ever, but it is critically important to acknowledge this fact. It is a big piece of the puzzle of why the transition to parenthood is so emotionally complicated for us as women. By this I mean that not only does parenthood bring so many losses and changes to the lives we once knew, but the stuff of parenting can also be crazy-making. And the sheer difficulty of it helps explain why conflict and animosity become more abundant in our marriages once we become parents.

Think about it: getting along well with our spouses can be challenging enough when life is humming along smoothly. Engaged in something fairly easy, like, say, a stroll through the neighborhood after dinner or washing the dishes together, we have pretty decent chances of having fond feelings toward our partner. But even then, we might feel irritable and nitpicky and spend the whole walk bickering just because that's par for the course in a shared life together. Take things up a few notches to more difficult terrain—say, trying to figure out how to get a child to sleep through the night or trying to stretch a limited income or trying to agree on where and with whose family to spend the holidays—and opportunities for tension abound. Physically demanding experiences, like carrying a baby in the womb or bouncing a colicky baby for six hours on an exercise ball or carrying a heavy toddler around while trying to cook dinner, are ripe with such opportunities, too.

I remember that when Ari and I were first getting accustomed to each other as companions on strenuous bike rides and cross-country-skiing excursions as a young and childless couple, it took very little to annoy me during an outdoor adventure. I'd be huffing and puffing behind him on an uphill climb and he'd look back, cheerful and breathing freely, and say, "Almost to the top!" and I would want to kill him. I was in physically difficult territory, and though it was utterly illogical, I perceived that to be *his* fault, and I didn't even want him to look at me, let alone offer me support and encouragement. Because I was engaged in something so challenging, I was poised to interpret his every move in a negative way, and I felt a chasm between us. Invariably, the chasm would close once I caught my breath and the path was easier again; then I was all rosy and full of gratitude for the excellent workout and the beauty of our surroundings, brought to me by the same jerk responsible for my brush with death ten minutes earlier when I was about to collapse on the trail.

Parenting is one of the most difficult challenges we will face in our lives. It is way, *way* harder than pedaling a bike up a steep hill. We never know when the terrain will level out, and when it does, it doesn't stay level for long. Sometimes we've only just caught our breath and then we must embark again, without choice, on the next climb of indeterminate length. Sometimes, there isn't a long enough rest period for the fond feelings toward our coparent to return, or for us to take in the sweeping vista. Instead we are mired in negative feelings, with righteousness and confusion and helplessness and worries and exhaustion obscuring our view of the bigger picture.

Some of the greatest tensions in my marriage have arisen around the difficult or "problem" behavior of our children. We do not always agree about how to address such behavior, often because we also do not always agree about the origins and function of the behavior. For instance, Ari once said to me, "Quinn is not sensitive to consequences, so we have to make the consequences even more severe." I disagreed completely. I see our son as being sometimes quite devastated by a negative consequence, even one of small magnitude. Why, then, does he still do the "bad thing" that we warned would have a negative consequence? My conceptualization is that the temptation is too great. He is working hard to have greater impulse control, and this comes more easily for some children than for others. Because it came easily to our first child, Ari and I never had the opportunity to be at odds with each other about this matter. But with Quinn, we find ourselves continually on different pages about what may be going on with him and how to handle it.

There is no question that Quinn's emotional reactivity is a challenge for our family. He has emotion regulation problems. This isn't pathological or indicative of a clinical diagnosis in his future; all toddlers have emotion regulation problems. Nobody is born with the inherent capacity to regulate his or her emotions. Rather, it is a skill we develop during early childhood. However, it is also a skill that develops more easily for some children than for others because of inherent differences in temperament. Quinn came into the world wired to feel things intensely, and so our parental job of teaching and modeling emotion regulation skills for him is a challenging one. He is highly reactive, and when he reacts—when he feels an emotion, often anger or frustration or disappointment from being thwarted or given what he considers to be bad news—he does so with great gusto. He stomps, he shouts, he flings his body around, he may throw things. It is very unpleasant for everyone, and we want him to knock it off, of course. But it is exceedingly difficult for him *not* to do it. So when we tell him, "Quinn, if there is any more shouting or kicking and screaming about the game you are trying to play with Noah, then we will have to stop the game," he gets it, and he wants very much to keep playing the game. But seconds later, when he perceives some injustice in the way Noah is engaging with him, he is shouting and veins are popping out of his neck and he is jumping up and down in fury. He can't help it. He needs to learn how, but he's not there yet, and in my mind, the solution is not to increase the negative consequences. The solution is to stay close, to help him identify his feelings, to tell him for the seven hundredth time that it is okay to feel angry but not okay to shout and kick, to offer him some ideas for how he could resolve this problem with respectfully spoken words. And take a deep breath ourselves, and trust that maybe the seven hundred and first time, it will stick.

It would be comfortable for me to rest in that conclusion, having gotten there by means of my own theory about my child's behavior and my own values about parenting. The thing is, my opinion isn't the only one in the conversation, and it is not the only one that matters. So there's no satisfying part where I say, leaning back in my chair, resting my head in my outstretched arms, "Yup. That's what's going on with Quinn, and that's how we need to deal with it." There is only ongoing discussion and tension, each of us believing our own view is right but trying our best to be open to the other's.

As these struggles illustrate, the hard work of raising children provides couples with countless points of contention. Way back in 1969, the eminent family therapist Jay Haley wrote in his fabulously tongue-in-cheek book chapter "How to Have an Awful Marriage": "There is a risk, of course, that a child might improve the marriage. However, the odds are that the birth of a child provides a symphony of new opportunities for the couple to make difficulty with each other." I shared my story of our struggle to agree on the right approach to dealing with Quinn's emotional outbursts only because it was the first issue that sprang to mind; of course, I could've chosen one of the hundreds of other ways Ari and I have disagreed in our approaches to parenting. It's easier to navigate these disagreements now that our kids are a bit older and we're not perpetually sleep-deprived or feeling adrift because of the fundamental attachment concerns all couples face when they first become parents. But during the upheaval of early parenthood, disagreements about anything from sleep training to what was causing rashes or fussiness could lead us into more dangerous territory. In fact, for many couples, these kinds of disagreements can lead to real despair.

My client Maria tends toward what has been labeled "attachment parenting." Though not particularly extreme about it, she believes her baby daughter is better off in her arms or in an Ergo on her back than alone in her crib or stroller. She is not comfortable with most parenting strategies that are designed to teach self-soothing (such as the "cry it out" method). She trusts her baby to let her know when she is ready to stop nursing rather than imposing the weaning process at a time proscribed by books and experts. Maria's husband, on the other hand, does not have the same leanings. He is vocal about his disapproval of the fact that their sixteen-month-old daughter has never slept in her own room, and makes clear to Maria that he thinks breastfeeding should have stopped some time ago. He wants Maria to be more available to him sexually, and he wants to be able to take their daughter on long excursions instead of short outings that end in a rush home to Maria so the baby can nurse.

Maria's choices to continue breastfeeding and bed-sharing are occurring in the context of her husband's disapproval. Though his consent is not actually required in any true sense[5]—as the primary caregiver, she can do what she wants with her baby—in the absence of his consent and support she must contend with much that is unpleasant, both internally and within the marriage. Internally, she is becoming far less confident about her natural inclinations as a mother because she is being criticized for them by her partner.

She wonders if she ought to be more flexible in terms of allowing the baby to take a bottle of formula every now and then, or if she may be fostering unhealthy sleeping habits in the baby by allowing her to sleep beside her and nurse throughout the night. In the space between her and her husband, tensions are thick. They argue and yell. He resents her for discounting his concerns and ignoring his wishes about how to parent their daughter. She resents him for his failure to grasp exactly how taxed she is from caring for their baby around the clock, and feels that if he wants his preferences about parenting to prevail, then *he* should be the one staying home with her. He thinks she would have more energy for other things if she just put the baby down sometimes instead of attending immediately to her every need. It's a tangled web of accusations and resentments.

Unfortunately, faced with all of what's so damned hard about parenting, we aren't likely to smile in our partner's general direction and say, "This is really hard, isn't it, darling?" We are much more likely to scowl, or use the hardship as license to be irritable with each other, or even overtly blame each other for how hard it is. We are more likely to be defensive about our choices when we are already feeling unsure, and when parenting is new, we are unsure almost all the time. Whatever internal resources we might ordinarily have available to use for fending off pointless, superficial fights and generating creative solutions to daily problems vanished after the first few weeks of sleep deprivation. We simply aren't our best selves during this phase. After all, we often don't feel like ourselves, either. Babies have a way of steering life into the weeds.

9

Live-In Buddhas

Every person must choose how much truth [s]he can stand.
—IRVIN YALOM, *WHEN NIETZSCHE WEPT*

As I began to sing to a four-year-old Quinn at bedtime one night, he said, "Mommy, do you know the one thing that would really help me to fall asleep? If you lie down with me for ten minutes." Though my habit was to say no (with justifications in my head like *I'm depleted, the dinner dishes are still in the sink, I want him to be able to soothe himself and be his own guide on the journey into sleep*), this time I said yes. Feeling his warm hand in mine, his tiny arm across my belly, and his twitching as he fell asleep, I knew I had made the right choice. I experienced his falling asleep nestled up against me as a gift. These moments of quiet connection with my children are precious. I crave them so much, and yet I realize I am sometimes the one who prevents them from happening. If I say yes, slow down, and lean in, they are there for the taking.

This was a nice moment of enlightenment, until the shadow of guilt crept over it. *You turn away from your children so often,* said the voice of guilt. *You say they're noisy and in constant motion and you just want them to hold still so you can savor them, but when they hold still and call your name, you don't always answer.*

As I lay there reflecting on Quinn's customary ways of being and the reasons he wears me out so much—he is a contrarian, he is insistent and fervent, he is emotionally reactive, he is stubborn, the wheels of his mind are turning a thousand miles a minute—I thought, *At least he has his emotional freedom.* I am truly so glad for this, because the freedom to have and express my emotions was not a defining feature of my childhood. Or adolescence. Or early adulthood. This, too, was a nice moment of enlightenment, and then, somehow, I felt a little down. Guilt had slipped in again, quietly and through the back door, so I didn't even notice at first. *You're limiting his emotional freedom when you tell him to quiet down and pull himself together. Maybe you're envious.*

In just this one scenario, I was faced with one truth after another after another. They were like waves crashing over me, and just as I began to catch my breath, another one would come. It was a little overwhelming.

In their book *Everyday Blessings: The Inner Work of Mindful Parenting*, Jon and Myla Kabat-Zinn liken children to little Buddhas who live with us, offering the possibility of great wisdom if only we can get in touch with what they are teaching us. The Kabat-Zinns and others have noted that our children act as mirrors, forcing us to see ourselves more fully and realistically than we ever have before and to discover facets of self, both pleasant and unpleasant, not previously acknowledged. Psychologist Harriet Lerner said it well when she wrote that having children will "teach you that you are capable of deep compassion, and also that you are definitely not the nice, calm, competent, clear-thinking, highly evolved person you fancied yourself to be before you became a mother."[1]

My children have taught me that I am a terrible multitasker, that my tolerance for noise and stimulation is abnormally low, and that my need for order and organization is abnormally high. They have taught me that although I have a keen radar for their emotional states and a virtually bottomless reservoir of compassion for their fear and sadness, I have a lot more work to do on my ability to sit with their anger and frustration. They have taught me that I am a natural at cuddling, comforting, and reading tall piles of books, but that it does not come easily to engage in creative, imaginative play. My older son has taught me that I can be quite invalidating when he fails to persist at a task or makes disparaging remarks about himself when he finds he is not automatically good at something. When Noah throws down his pencil with a growl after realizing he has messed up his math homework, the fantasy version of me says, "I see you're feeling quite frustrated right now about not being able to solve this problem. Sometimes I get upset when I keep making mistakes at something, too, especially when I tell myself I should already know how to do it well." The real-life version of me says, in a tone that reveals my significant annoyance, "Oh, *come on*, Noah. You've been working at this problem for all of one minute. Stop being so impatient." Later that same evening, I sit down at the piano to try to work out the notes for a song that has been stuck in my head. I can't find them in the first two minutes that my fingers explore the keys, so I heave a heavy sigh of frustration, get up, and walk away.

Our children show us what we like least about ourselves. And most of the time, this is happening beneath our awareness.

In my therapy office, I listen as Jasmine confesses her latest perceived crime with her children. "I really lost it this time," she says. She describes how she grabbed her toddler by the shoulders and angrily held him in her grasp, gritting her teeth, growling shaming words about his intolerable behavior. Her guilt is palpable in the room. I get it, and not just because I'm an empathic therapist. She tells me how she can hardly stand to recount this story because she never imagined herself capable of such intense fury toward her own child. I think, *This is so familiar.* It's familiar because I have heard it from so many other clients, and because I have lived it. It is the worst kind of guilt, because it is attached not only to a

particular transgression we wish we had not made, but also to a picture of ourselves we wish we did not have to see. These are pictures
of ourselves we do not recognize, distortions of self in which we are
rendered ugly with rage or intolerance. Myla and Jon Kabat-Zinn
were right: there are Buddhas in the house, and the learning is hard.

In his book *The Examined Life*, psychoanalyst Stephen Grosz tells
of a patient of his, whom he calls Jessica, and one of her painful real-
izations on the therapy couch.[2] She said to him, "I always thought I
was a nice person, until I had a baby." A woman who derived much
of her self-worth from exuding competence and composure, Jessica
was troubled by her inability to soothe her daughter's every cry.
More than that, she was deeply troubled by feelings of rage toward
her baby girl, so much so that she began to displace them onto her
husband. "I thought I'd find a kind of love with my baby that I'd
never known before," she said. "A shared warmth, an understanding.
And I did—but I didn't know a tiny baby could also make me
feel so angry." Grosz relays a story that Jessica told him about
one especially bad night, when the baby would not stop crying and
she and her husband, Paul, disagreed about the solution. Weary
of round-the-clock breastfeeding, Jessica wanted the baby to cry
it out so she could learn to self-soothe. Certain their daughter was
hungry, Paul wanted Jessica to feed her. Gridlock ensued. Finally
feeding the baby himself with breast milk from the freezer, Paul
emerged victorious; their daughter *had* been hungry, and fell into
a deep sleep once her belly was full. As Jessica lay sleepless some
time later and began to cry, Paul did not hold her close and console
her as she wanted and expected. When she asked him why, he stung
her with his reply: "I thought you should self-soothe."

In processing this awful night with her therapist, Jessica came
to understand that her husband's biting remark was a response to
months of mounting tension between them, tension created in part
by Jessica's relentless blaming of Paul for the unhappiness she had

felt since their daughter was born. Unable to name (let alone accept) her intense anger at her baby for disrupting her life and her comfortable, false notions of herself, Jessica searched for some other reason why she felt so ill at ease, and landed on Paul.

I think every woman I've worked with in therapy would recognize something of herself in Jessica. In the trenches of early parenthood, we may find ourselves full of hostility for both our babies and our partners, and one of these is far less socially acceptable than the other. We didn't sign up for these emotions, and experiencing them leaves us prone to self-deception; we must bury our resentment for the baby we love, and we must bury our anger at the spouse we love (and need, now more than ever). But feelings find their way to the surface, even if they are disguised. Displacement is a classic defense mechanism that resonates with all of us, whether we're psychoanalytic thinkers or not. When it's not safe to feel or express a feeling in its original context, we find some other context and transfer the feeling there. You can't yell at your boss for fear you'll get fired, so you go home and yell at your child instead. You can't blame your helpless, tiny baby for your rage, so you rage at your husband instead.

The real trouble is that for couples under the strain of new parenthood, displacement creates a double whammy for the relationship. On top of the often justifiable resentment new parents feel toward their partners for various reasons—they let each other down, they make demands on each other that cannot be met, they feel ignored or replaced or marginalized or taken for granted or put upon—there is all of what they cannot permit themselves to feel toward their babies. A husband thus bears the brunt of his wife's anger and grief about the losses brought on by their baby, and a husband redirects at his wife his own discomfort, frustrations, and feelings of inadequacy in the unfamiliar terrain of fatherhood.

The particular needs and personalities of our little Buddha children also shape our identities as parents. Sometimes they push us outside our comfort zones with positive results, allowing us to stretch and grow and willingly take on roles and identities we'd never imagined for ourselves. Other times, they illuminate our limitations; they show us who we *aren't*, who we are unwilling or unable to be. My client Jasmine is the mother of two young boys. Jasmine is quite petite, and is married to a man who is six foot five. Their two children are all rough and tumble, at their happiest when rolling around on the floor, limbs entangled, risk of bodily harm to one or the other imminent. Typically, Jasmine wants nothing to do with that scene and steers clear of the physical chaos. One evening, wanting to engage with her children, she joined them on the floor. Within moments, she'd been whacked in the face and was wincing in pain. The son who accidentally injured her said, sincerely, "I'm sorry, Mommy. When is Daddy coming home?"

Envisioning this scene while my client described it to me took no effort at all, because I know it well. I identify with her probably far more than she realizes, and she does not need to explain to me the sting of her child's question. What rises up to a lump in her throat when her son communicates to her his preference for Daddy as a playmate is a mix of sadness, injured pride, and resignation. Daddy is tougher, stronger, and more fun. Jasmine has been displaced as her boys have grown older, and she struggles to find her footing in this new phase of motherhood. Her babies are gone, and now she has little boys instead, little boys who are increasingly capable of hurting her, increasingly difficult to pick up and carry, increasingly disinterested in her bids for connection through quiet games or Play-Doh or coloring. They want to roughhouse and torment each other and scale the walls with their little monkey-boy limbs. And they admire their father. "As they should," says Jasmine, with the peculiar smile-frown I've come to recognize in her when she's attempting to keep unwanted feelings at bay. She is genuinely happy to witness the deepening bond between her husband and each of their sons. And she also envies him his capacity to relate to their children in a way she cannot. His connection with their boys is only just blossoming, while hers feels worn out and weaker than it once was. I'm not surprised when the rest of the therapy hour is spent discussing a list of grievances about her husband's habits and her lack of sexual interest in him.

When my own sons were babies, it never occurred to me that I would one day wonder what my place was in their lives. Maybe I knew that once they became teenagers, and went off to college, and had families of their own, I would be far less central in their lives. But that seemed like such a far-off, abstract concept. During their infancy and well into toddlerhood, we seemed to exist in an impermeable bubble of mother-child unity, one in which there was no question whose companionship they preferred. When Noah was a toddler, he said to me one summer evening as we sat by the fire pit at the top of our property, "Mommy? I just love to lay my head back on your chest and look at the view." We were the center of each other's universes, and this seemed the natural, immutable state of affairs. The same was true of Quinn's first few years of life. I had no idea how soon my connection to them would change, or how much I would struggle to find ways of feeling close to them once they didn't need me—or prefer me—as much.

It's not lost on me that the sense of disenfranchisement I'm describing, and the search for ways to connect with my children, are experiences much like what my husband had when I was in that bubble with our babies. He could sometimes get inside the bubble, too, of course, and he had countless moments of intimate connection with our sons when they were little. But I know he felt he was on the margins early on, just like so many other new fathers do. He was brave and good about it, saying with sincerity what a beautiful thing it was for him to witness the affection and connection between me and our babies. In a similar way, one might say I'm being brave and good about the changing tides in our family dynamic; our two not-so-little boys very clearly adore their time with their dad in a way they once did not, and I can say with sincerity it is a beautiful thing to behold. I also cannot deny that it is fabulously liberating to no longer be the go-to parent for all needs and wants. It used to be that I would utter the words, "Ask Daddy! He's right there!" about fifty times a day in response to questions like, "Can I have a snack? Will you help me with this? Will you play with me?" Daddy sometimes seemed to be the invisible man, and the children needed constant reminding that they had *two* capable, available parents.

It also goes without saying that it's because these are *boy* children that they gravitate so much toward their father now. They identify with him, and they crave the highly physical, bordering-on-violent playtime with him* that they know I don't offer. Like Jasmine acknowledged, this is as it should be. But that doesn't mean it doesn't hurt sometimes. More than once in the past couple of years, I've spent the weekend or the better part of a week with my boys while their dad was away, and I've had the unsavory taste of jealousy in my mouth when he returns home and they seem to come to life. Were they bored the whole time he was away? Are things that much more exciting when Dad is around? Didn't we have a good time? Somewhere inside me a voice offers, *Their faces would probably light up that way if* you *came home from a weekend away, too.* But I'm not convinced. I feel a difficult truth in my gut, which is that he's a lot better at showing them a good time these days than I am.

As coparents of two boys, we've developed roles that have become more and more defined over the years. He is the adventurous

---

* Affectionately known in our household as "The Abusement of the Daddy."

parent, the one who facilitates play and plans new learning experiences and fun activities and excursions. I am the stabilizing parent, the one who represents home and comfort and calm and attends to everyone's fundamental needs and emotions. My feelings about this arrangement vary. Sometimes it strikes me as more or less inevitable. As their mother, I have always been more closely attuned to their emotions than their father has—which, of course, doesn't mean he is not attuned at all (he very much is). Our roles are also informed by our inherent personalities and dispositions. My husband has energy far surpassing that of most adult humans, and has an almost insatiable appetite for outings and socializing. I am a solitude-seeking, easily overstimulated introvert. If Ari opted out of an excursion to stay home alone, or if I proposed that we cram one more canoe camping trip into our busy summer, the kids would stare blankly at us and wonder what sort of twilight zone they had entered. Why go against the grain? Often I'm even inclined to think we complement each other in ways that benefit the kids; different needs are met by each of their parents, and they get the best of both worlds. *We're a great team*, I say to myself. *We temper each other's extremes and land somewhere in the middle. We are a well-rounded family.*

Except I don't always feel so enlightened. Sometimes it's not pride or contentment I feel about my role as their mother, or confidence that our complementary roles contribute to the kids' well-being and our own. Sometimes it's guilt instead. The Buddha opportunity here is that when I see my children's faces light up at the arrival of their father, and I don't recall seeing similar brightness in their eyes when I've walked in the door anytime recently, I am invited (if not forced) to look at myself and my habitual ways of being. If it's my perception that's off—if their faces *do* light up just the same when they reunite with me—then what is it that prevents me from seeing that and delighting in it? Am I such an incubator for unfounded mommy guilt that I discount all the evidence that I am there enough for my children? Alternatively, if my perception is accurate, what does that say about the role I'm usually in with them? Am I okay with staying inside to finish the last of the dishes while everyone else plays some post-dinner baseball in the yard? Am I okay with saying, approximately nineteen times per day, "No, I will not stop what I'm doing to go upstairs and watch you shoot the missiles out of your LEGO spaceship"? Will my children sit on a therapist's couch someday, saying, "My mom was always too busy to play with me"? Or will they one day attribute their fulfilling, solid marriages to their extraordinary emotional attunement skills, which they got from their exceptionally observant and attentive mother? Either fantasy version of the future can seem perfectly reasonable, depending on the day.

Looking at Guilt Through Buddha Eyes

It's no newsflash that the culture of mothering is dominated by notions of perfection and sacrifice, though it does bear repeating that these standards contribute to the relentless guilt experienced by many of us. In *Perfect Madness: Motherhood in the Age of Anxiety*, Judith Warner writes that "the potential to do damage, to cause one's child unbearable and lifelong pain, [has become] part of the very definition of motherhood."[3] Indeed, the imperative to "be there" for our children, more than our own mothers were there for us, is now firmly embedded in contemporary notions of what it means to be a mother.

The idea of "being there" is not just about being physically there, by our children's sides, spending as much time with them as possible. It is also about emotional attunement. Witnessing. Imagining our children's inner lives with all the attendant fears and vulnerabilities. Anticipating their needs. Doing our best to prevent emotional wounds. All these are tasks that represent some of the central-most values I hold as a mother, but they are also impossible tasks to carry out perfectly and at all times. We fail, as parents, over and over again. No matter how high a premium we place on understanding our children's worlds, there are lapses in our attunement. The question is how to bypass—or at least learn to get out from under—the guilt and anxiety* that these inevitable lapses bring.

I spend a good deal of my time as a therapist looking at guilt with my clients, helping them wrangle it when it's an unwieldy and insistent presence in their lives. I'm confident that if I had a predominantly male clientele, I would not say the same thing. It's not just that *motherhood* is saturated with guilt; it's that *being a woman* means being more susceptible to guilt. Especially when it comes to what researchers call habitual guilt—which is arguably closer to a personality characteristic than a momentary emotion prompted by a specific behavior—studies consistently indicate that women experience more guilt than men.[4] The realm of parenthood is no exception, and for many couples, this guilt differential quickly becomes one more manifestation of the great divide.

While no doubt rooted in the socialization of females as caretakers who learn early on to take responsibility for the physical and emotional well-being of others, there is evidence that the gender difference in guilt has biological underpinnings, as well. As we saw in

---

* In motherhood, guilt and anxiety tend to travel together. Guilty feelings about perceived failures or inadequacies often generate concerns about whether we have somehow damaged or endangered our child. Those concerns can be very compelling and can translate to persistent anxiety about our child's well-being. It can also work in the other direction: the anxious worries we are certain to have during early motherhood can leave us feeling vaguely guilty about what we might not be doing right. Here my primary focus is on the construct of guilt and the importance of curbing it.

chapter 6, the female brain is wired to promote optimal caregiving in offspring, which means it is wired for empathy and attunement. In the same way that this neural circuitry is thought to contribute to women's higher susceptibility to depression, it may also partly explain their greater levels of guilt.[*] An empathic brain is a brain sensitive to feedback that we have somehow failed in our interpersonal worlds, and that kind of feedback can promote guilt. Interestingly, research has found that the gender difference in guilt is less pronounced in midlife than it is in adolescence and early adulthood.[5] Since testosterone levels decrease and oxytocin increases as men age and "settle down," one theory is that the gender difference in guilt-proneness has a hormonal basis.

And chronic or excessive guilt takes a toll. Beyond the obvious psychological toll—it feels bad to feel guilty, and guilt pulls us away from otherwise enjoyable moments—research has linked guilt with lower immune functioning, higher risk of cardio-vascular disease, gastrointestinal problems, and an array of other health symptoms.[6]

Thus the work of dismantling guilt—much like the work of dismantling shame that was discussed in earlier chapters—is of crucial importance for women's health and well-being. One major challenge in this endeavor is that it is very difficult to draw a clear line between valid guilt—the informative, constructive kind that signals to us that we're behaving in a way that is out of alignment with our values and intentions—and unfounded guilt. Unfounded guilt arises from perfectionism or low self-worth or any number of other unrealistic measurements or standards we've internalized. Unfounded guilt shouldn't get any more of our attention or emotional

---

[*] Also note that "excessive or inappropriate guilt" is one of the diagnostic criteria for major depressive disorder.

energy than an errant fly; we need do nothing more with it than notice it, maybe swat it out of our way, and then carry on.

Sorting out unfounded guilt from constructive guilt is an endless task. We cannot ever land in a fully enlightened place in which the two are never confused. The best we can do is stay committed to the process. That, in itself, is a tremendously valuable gift, because once we can identify the distinction, we can protect ourselves from being automatically hijacked by the negative emotional valence of guilt and the cascade of anxious worries and self-critical thoughts that come with it. With practice, we can learn to quiet the voice of unfounded guilt and listen to the wisdom of valid guilt.

How do we go about sorting out the two types of guilt? We begin by claiming the guilt—registering its existence instead of trying to ignore it or push it away. If guilt is a shadow, then taking this essential first step is like suddenly turning around to face the shadow and saying, "I see you. What do you want? Why are you here?" If we can do this, rather than continuing to move along, aware the shadow is trailing us but never stopping to confront it, then we stand a chance of identifying guilt's origins. A lot of women describe feeling vaguely guilty almost all the time, so we must move from vague to specific: To what is the guilt linked? Maybe it is prompted by certain contexts, like only when we are alone with our baby or only when we are away from our baby. Maybe it feels connected to a certain characteristic we think we possess, like impatience, or a short temper. Perhaps it seems to come mostly from a decision we made, like to stop nursing or to hire a nanny or to have another child. Maybe the emotion of guilt piggybacks predictably on some other emotion, like anger.

Whatever we discover in looking squarely at the guilt, it will bring us closer to the critical question of whether it is valid. If I discover through this kind of self-assessment that my guilt is most associated with half-listening to my children when they're talking, I feel in my gut that half-listening goes against my core values and that my children deserve better. I see that it's my habit of mindlessly scrolling through my iPhone that most interferes with listening fully, and I decide I really must commit to turning off my phone when I first get home in the evenings. The guilt was valid—it signaled to me that my behavior was incongruent with my values, not just for a minute but in an ongoing way. In contrast, if turning to look at the shadow of guilt causes recent fleeting moments of anger to flash through my mind, then I ask myself, *Should I feel guilty for getting angry with my children? Isn't anger par for the course in parenthood? Didn't I express that anger appropriately?* In this case, I am in the realm of unfounded guilt, realizing I need to permit myself to be angry sometimes and let go of feeling bad about it.

With inquiry and consideration, we can determine a good course of action in response to guilt. If it's valid, we can offer an apology, correct a mistake, work toward a gradual change in our habits. If it's unfounded, our response can be less action-oriented and more about emotional liberation—freeing ourselves from the mandates that would have us believe our feelings and desires and choices are wrong when they're perfectly right.

Recently one of my long-term clients, Audrey, began our session with a concern about one of her children. She said that her son, age three, had caught his reflection in the mirror and said, "Something's wrong with my face." This was the second day in a row that Henry had expressed this feeling; the day before he had said, simply, "I don't like my face." This would be a tough thing for any parent to witness; I felt empathy both for Audrey and for her little boy, so young to be critical of his own reflected image. Together, Audrey and I explored some theories about why Henry might be saying such things. One possibility, Audrey thought, was that Henry spent most of his day dressed up like a princess, or wearing scarves and jewelry and other feminine embellishments, so perhaps his little boy face was impeding his efforts to look like a princess or a beautiful grown-up woman. I thought this was a pretty good theory, and because on the surface it sounded entirely disconnected from anything Audrey may or may not be doing as a mother—the source of her rushing river of guilt—I wondered about her choice to open the session in this way. What was the underlying significance for her? She said that her response had been to ask, gently, about his experience of his face and to say something affirming: "Why do you say that, buddy? I think your face is perfect and beautiful!" So far, so good.

But for Audrey, like so many other mothers, all roads lead to guilt. I had a feeling our discussion would eventually illuminate how her son's discomfort in his own skin was, in her perception, her fault. We went on to discuss her concerns more broadly about her son. He does not eat enough, or eat well. He does not sleep enough, or sleep well. He is constipated, and cranky, and recoils from her attempts to hug and cuddle him. He whines constantly. I knew these concerns were not new; Audrey had shared many times her sense that Henry was just not comfortable, her worry that something was physically wrong with him, and her fear that maybe he had inherited her proneness to anxiety and depression. And because these worrisome behaviors seemed to be mounting, I thought it might make good sense for her to schedule a visit with Henry's pediatrician. For the moment, I didn't say so; I just listened, fed back what I was hearing, and made my empathy known. "Daily life with Henry sounds really, really hard," I said. "You seem to be describing a gut feeling that something just isn't right with him, and despite your best efforts, you haven't been able to figure out what it is." It was within that last piece of feedback that the guilt was unleashed. Audrey corrected me. Her efforts as a parent are never her best. She has not attended to Henry's discomfort sufficiently or in a loving manner. She has felt irritated with him, and overwhelmed, and mostly

unmotivated to engage with him enough to determine the source
of his distress. His comments about his face had thrown her off this
usual track; they pained her and inspired her to pay more attention
and offer him more comfort. But before that she had been on autopilot, just trying to survive. Tuning out the sound of his whining
voice, which she equates with fingernails on a chalkboard.

Audrey's disclosures were not surprising; this was terrain in
which she had been stuck for quite some time. She is chronically
depleted, chronically depressed, and unable to find fulfillment in her
role as a stay-at-home mother. She cannot see, let alone take pride
in, what she does well as a mother. Her depression shapes her view
of herself and her children. "It's the same thing I feel when I look in
the mirror," says Audrey. "I don't like my face, either. I see all flaws
and aging."

If contending with maternal guilt is an inevitable and difficult
process for everyone, for women like Audrey, it is even more complex. Her depression is on the severe end of the continuum, and it
impedes her ability to distinguish between valid and unfounded
guilt. Depression has a way of both breeding guilt and obscuring
the pathway out of it.

Unfortunately for Audrey, and for so many women, marital distress
does the same thing. It's as if marital tensions make the river of
mothering guilt rush even faster. In light of Henry's remarks about
disliking his face, Audrey asked for her husband's help in attending to their son more fully. She expressed to him how troubled she
was and how she was at her wit's end, and how much she needed
his support. His response was, "If you are this concerned, maybe
we should take him to see a psychologist. Or a sleep specialist.
Or both." In a previous session, Audrey had told me how much it
bothers her that her rarely home husband has his phone with him
as he carries out his one childcare duty, which is to put the kids
to bed. He does this one thing only, upon arriving home from his

twelve-hour workday, and he is only half-focused on the task as he does it. When he suggested that a call to a specialist might be the solution to their son's problem, Audrey was incensed. She wanted *him* to step up to the plate and make the situation better, instead of delegating the responsibility to someone else and being only tangentially involved.

Certainly, I could sympathize with Audrey's anger. The trouble was, it was at least partly fueled by guilt about her own parenting. Because she takes care of the children all day long, she is sometimes distracted. Nobody can sustain a state of undivided attention to their children every minute of every hour, but Audrey cannot identify her guilt as unfounded. She feels perpetually guilty about the autopilot mode she sometimes slips into, the preoccupied and checked-out mental state in which she finds herself on many days. So she criticizes her husband for engaging in the same kind of distracted, mindless behavior. Her criticism feels justified because he has such a brief window of opportunity to engage with his children; he ought to be approaching that opportunity wholeheartedly. And he certainly ought to compensate for his minimal involvement at home by figuring out what was wrong with their son instead of farming out the task to a professional. When Audrey told me she had no intention of calling a psychologist or specialist, it became clear she was letting her resentment toward her husband, and her pursuit of fairness and justice in terms of sharing childcare responsibilities, get in the way of doing something that could help her son and put her own mind at ease.

Here was another one of those complicated jumbles of blame and shame and guilt and resentment. Audrey had brought into my office a metaphorical suitcase stuffed with marital and maternal woes, all tangled up together. As we did the work of unpacking and sorting, I asked Audrey, "Do you think you're angry with your husband because he doesn't feel guilty? Because he doesn't think your son's troubles have anything to do with him?" She sighed with the relief of being understood. For Audrey, her inadequacies as a mother feel so great that she can't even look at herself in the mirror. When she sees her toddler feeling uncomfortable in his own skin, she assumes it's a reflection on her. Her child's symptoms feed right into her river of guilt. Her husband, on the other hand, has no such river. Once he learned of his wife's concern about their son, his response was completely lacking in self-blame or uncertainty or angst. He listened to the list of symptoms and said, simply, "Call a doctor."

Our husbands' freedom from guilt—or at least their *relative* freedom compared to ours—is just another reason to perceive them as so annoyingly unencumbered by the demands of parenthood. One night some friends with a newish baby and a toddler were over for dinner. They were describing how they had spent the afternoon doing the forty-five-minute drive, each way, to and from Burlington (the "big" city nearest our little town in Vermont) and going to a couple of stores to do errands. The wife then said, "The thing is, we didn't need to do those errands today. But sometimes we just have to go somewhere. Sometimes we just need to be in the car, driving, where the kids are contained and still, and we can talk to each other and listen to music." I related to this completely, because many times when our boys were younger we did the exact same thing, for the exact same reason. Then she said, "But I feel so guilty doing that. I feel guilty about wasting gas and wasting time. Most of all, I feel guilty about putting the kids in the car when we should be playing with them or providing them with some enriching experience instead." Her husband, listening to all this, shrugged and said, "I don't feel guilty!" There it was, plain to see. Wife angsty, struggling to feel at ease with herself and her choices around mothering. Husband completely at ease, wondering what the problem could be. It's a familiar dynamic. Paternal Guilt is no match for Maternal Guilt. As psychoanalyst Barbara Almond put it, "Although men struggle with wishes to have or not have children, and with issues of good fathering, they do not hold themselves so thoroughly responsible for the emotional care of their offspring. While those concerns can be deep and terribly troubling, striking at the heart of what it means to be a man and manly, the emotional well-being of the family is generally laid at the mother's doorstep."[7]

Ari and I exchanged a knowing look in response to our friends' story, because a week or so before, the very same dynamic had cropped up when he and I were in the kitchen having our Friday Night Date Night cocktail. This is a tradition* we had recently instituted at the time, when Quinn was about three years old—old enough to start watching kids' movies with his big brother in the basement while we did our own thing upstairs. No babysitter required. Kid food for the kids, delivered to them downstairs, and a simple but very much *adult* meal for us upstairs. On this particular Friday night, early on in the tradition, lovely conversation was flowing between Ari and me, and the kids were contentedly watching their movie in the basement.† Suddenly the words falling out of my mouth were, "I feel guilty." The pure loveliness of this moment—drinking a delicious adult beverage, engaging in uninterrupted conversation with my husband, hearing the giggles of my boys from downstairs as they watched a funny movie—was suddenly tainted by the feeling of guilt. I felt it wasn't right to be occupying a separate space from the boys, having our own kind of enjoyable time apart

---

* Now known as "Friday Night Terdishons," as Quinn referred to it in a note he wrote us one day when he was five or six.

† I feel obliged to point out that this is a fully finished, very comfortable basement with a big-screen TV and a pool table. The boys love to hang out down there. Just in case you thought it was some other kind of basement, the kind with nothing but an overflowing kitty-litter box, a broken-down 1970s stationary bike, and old musty cardboard boxes full of broken Christmas ornaments. Because then you'd probably be thinking, *She* should *be feeling guilty!*

from them. We should all be together instead. We should be watching their funny movie with them, or maybe playing a board game. Ari looked at me, baffled, and said, "Are you kidding? We have *earned* this. We've put in some hard years with these kids. Things are easier now. We deserve these moments. They're happy right now, we're happy, everybody's happy!" Right. All that sounded true enough. But in my bones I still felt guilty.

As I've already made abundantly clear, I'm on the high end of the Maternal Guilt scale. I examine the phenomenon of my persistent guilt nearly every day, often quite carefully and extensively. I do not try to sweep it under the rug. I hold it up to the light and turn it over and around, again and again, studying it from every angle, trying to understand its essential nature. I haven't yet figured out if it is largely that unfounded kind of guilt I defined earlier; on good days, I'm inclined to think so, and I try to ignore it. But ultimately, even with all this exploring and confronting of my guilt, I remain without answers. And it retains some of its power to undermine, not always, but still more often than I'd like, the good times I'm having as a mother, a wife, a woman.

One recent morning, Quinn and I were cuddling on the couch as I sipped the last bit of coffee from my cup. I had one hand on his sleepy head, gently running my fingers through his hair, while the other hand ran a pencil across the page, putting a few more words in my journal before the busy phase of the morning began. Most mornings, some version of this scene plays out; it seems Quinn has learned to let me finish my ritual, because he isn't being a chatterbox or asking immediately for breakfast. I'd like to say the scene is all ease and peaceful coexistence, but the reality is that I am working hard, internally, to fight off guilt. *What's it like for him to come downstairs and find me always writing, absorbed in a task and not yet ready to give him my full attention? Does he feel like my journal is more important than him? Should I be getting up earlier so I'm done with my solitary morning ritual by the time he wakes up?* On this particular morning, I asked him, "Do you know why you always find me sitting here alone early in the morning, with my notebook? You know that I am trying to take good care of myself so that I can be a good mom to you, right?" He replied, *"You're already the best any mama could ever be."*

It wasn't just the words that got me. Something about his tone—the plain and simple quality of his declaration, as if it were indisputable fact—pierced through my ever-present guilt, at least for a moment. That is his subjective truth. He sees no room for improvement. The innocence of his perception somehow makes it more accurate than mine, instead of the other way around. I wasn't thinking, *Oh, how sweet and naive you are. If only you knew all the ways I am failing you. One day you will.* I was thinking something more along the lines of, *If he thinks so, maybe it's true.* Much like beauty is in the eye of the beholder, maybe mothering adequacy is in the eye of the mothered. I think of a bumper sticker I've seen that says, "I wish I was the person my dog thinks I am." That morning on the couch, I didn't wish I was the mother my son thinks I am. I *was* the mother my son thinks I am, at least for a moment. Maybe I can be her more often. Maybe we all can.

Reparenting and Repair

More often than we realize, our uneasy and guilty feelings as mothers originate at least in part from needs of our own that went unmet when we were children. I turn again to Judith Warner's wise words in *Perfect Madness*: "All around me, in recent years, I've seen women living motherhood as an exercise in correction, trying to heal the wounds of their childhoods, and, prophylactically, to seal their children against future pain."[8] As Warner points out, it is *our own* unmet needs, our own fears, our own longings—and not those of our children—that sometimes influence most powerfully the choices we make as parents.

My client Lucy recently focused much of our hour-long session on her concern that her child is not well liked at school. After she wondered aloud whether he had enough friends and whether enough of his peers had RSVP'd "yes" to his birthday party, I asked her, "How does *he* seem to feel about his social life at school?" The question seemed to catch her off guard. When she responded, "He's such a happy kid, both at school and at home," I could see the lightbulb turn on in her head. She paused and said, "I guess I should be giving that a lot more weight." "Right," I said. "If he is not in distress about his friendships, then should you be?"

Lucy was a sensitive child who struggled with being excluded and teased at school. As an adult, she continues to be sensitive, understandably, about her relationships with friends and coworkers. What came into view in that moment during therapy was that Lucy's persistent longing to feel connected and liked fuels her concerns about her son's social acceptance.

Sometimes the power of our unmet needs is triggered by major life decisions or family conflicts—like the mother who gave up her career to stay home with her baby and becomes depressed when her daughter postpones graduate school after becoming pregnant, or the father who grew up too poor to attend an Ivy League school and rails against his son's wish to attend a community college. But subtler, everyday iterations of this phenomenon abound if we look closely. Our own unmet needs may be behind the choices we make about where the baby sleeps, where the seven-year-old sleeps, how long to breastfeed, whether to breastfeed, whether to work late, whom to turn to for help with childcare, or whether to ask for help at all. Warner's point is that "much of what we do in the name of perfect motherhood is really about 'reparenting' ourselves. It's about compensating for the various forms of lack or want or need or loneliness that we remember from our childhood." I agree with her, and I agree that it can be quite problematic. We don't need even more reasons for the stakes to feel so high in parenting, and nobody benefits when there is confusion about whose needs belong to whom. But I also think it's only natural, and that if we bring awareness to it, we can reduce much of what's problematic about it.

When we are not aware that we are acting on our own unmet needs, we are parenting not the small child in front of us but the one inside us. These are, quite obviously, two different people, so the problem is that what we are giving to our actual child and what he or she needs may be out of sync. Lucy's son, for example, was eagerly anticipating his upcoming birthday party and hadn't even asked how many kids were coming, while Lucy was hiding in her bedroom making phone calls to try to round up more kids to attend. She wasn't aware of what was driving her motivation to do so until we talked. But when we are aware of what motivates our actions as parents, it becomes possible to parent our actual child and our own "inner child" simultaneously. Nobody tells an expectant mother with a toddler in tow, "Uh-oh. You can't mother two different children at the same time." Of course she can, and she will, and many of us are quite masterful at meeting the immediate needs of many different human beings, big and small, all at once. So what's so crazy about the idea that we can attend to some of our own unmet needs while we also attend to the needs of our children? There is actually a powerful opportunity here, but it is one that requires being willing to look, and look deeply, at what our children's needs and behaviors are stirring up in us.

My client Anna, whom you met in chapter 1, experienced the tension between mothering herself and mothering her baby girl as she attempted to implement the "cry it out" sleep method. Though she bought into the strategy on an intellectual level—if you don't reward your baby for crying out in the night by going to her immediately and cuddling or feeding her, eventually she'll stop crying out in the night—she found that implementing it was unbearably painful. Her understanding of the behavioral principles involved in the strategy was no match for the primal pull to answer her baby's cries. Those cries conjured, for her, memories of crying alone in her room as a little girl and wishing her parents would stop fighting long enough to hear her and go to her. Anna's husband, Pete, was very much in favor of letting baby Gracie cry it out so they could all get a better night's sleep. The conflict between them about how to proceed was not easy to navigate, but Anna stood her ground. She relayed to me what it felt like to go to Gracie after one grueling forty-minute attempt to let her cry it out. In the dark nursery, Anna rocked her baby girl, whispering, "I'm here, I'm here." As she wiped the tears from Gracie's cheeks, she let her own tears fall, and felt a release of long-held grief about how alone she had felt as a young girl. In that poignant moment, she was meeting her baby's needs *and* her own, and it was her awareness of that that made all the difference. We cannot *undo* the past, but in doing things differently with our own children—giving them what was not sufficiently given to us—we can change our *relationship* to the past.

One weekend a few years ago, some visitors of ours had grown weary of the behavior of their four-year-old son, who had thrown multiple tantrums over the course of a morning. When this little boy's mother sent him outside and then proceeded to lock all the doors of our house so he could not get back in, I watched in disbelief. I was doing my best to keep my judgments in check, but in truth I was appalled; I found it so cruel to shut out a small child like that, especially in an unfamiliar setting, far from home. My internal judging voice was saying to the boy's mother, *I totally get the frustration and the being at your wit's end, but wow. I would never shut my child out like that. I'd never want to make him feel he didn't have access to me if he needed me.* It would be a long time before I realized why I was so distressed by what unfolded at our house that morning, and why I was so quick to judge the parenting as wrong and damaging. Everyone else seemed to think it was no big deal, and maybe even a little funny. The little boy was seemingly unfazed by the doors being locked and soon enough found something to do outside that entertained him, but that concerned me all the more; had this happened so many times before at his own house that he'd grown accustomed to being shut out? Had the fire of protest died down to ashes of resignation? All I knew then was how much it bothered me, but that I didn't feel it was my place to confront our company—friends we didn't know all that well—about their parenting.

Two years later, I awoke from a nightmare about Quinn, something to do with him being held down by someone else and looking at me with pleading eyes, begging me to free him. In my semi-awake state, I first flashed on the face of the little boy who had been locked out of our house, and then his face morphed into Quinn's, much younger, in his high chair. Suddenly I was in touch with a long-forgotten memory, one much more upsetting than the memory of some other person's child being locked outside. Because it was my child, and I was the one who had shut him out.

Quinn was maybe about two and a half, and it was an ordinary evening except that I was parenting alone, slogging through the trials and tribulations of dinnertime with a toddler and a first-grader. I don't even remember the details of why I was so irritated or what was exhausting my supply of patience, and the fuzziness of my recollection is not surprising. This is one of those memories I wish I could wipe away, and to a great degree I did. What I do remember is that when my frustration toward Quinn reached a crescendo, I picked up his entire high chair, with him in it, and placed it on the other side of the door to the garage. I picked up my intensely aggravating, disobedient, but ultimately helpless and strapped-down child, and I shouted at him as I hoisted him across the kitchen, and I shut him in the garage.

I'm pretty sure I had the decency to turn on the light out there, and I probably told him that when he stopped doing whatever "wrong" thing he was doing, I would let him back in. But that hardly lessens the blow of this assault on my ego, this most unwelcome memory. I remember how hard he was wailing when I slammed the door and walked back into the kitchen without him. I remember how quickly I went back out there and released him from his chair and held him tight, apologizing, tears streaming down both our cheeks. It was a truly awful moment for which I feel absolute remorse. What could he possibly have been doing to ignite such fury in me, especially while strapped into his high chair at the age of two?

I'll probably never know, but I do now understand the round-about way in which this memory came back to me, and the multiple layers of meaning in that sequence of events with Quinn in his high chair that night. I had the nightmare when I did because of a deepening awareness at the time of the ways in which I, as a child, didn't have enough access to my own mom and dad. Despite their good intentions and their best efforts as parents, they were young and preoccupied, and I learned self-sufficiency—especially in managing my distress—at an early age. The nightmare, in which I see my child pleading with me to come to his aid, put me in touch with a memory I had tried to bury. I didn't want to see myself as a parent capable of slamming a door in her small child's face. But in remembering what there was to remember, a powerful process of integration occurred. I realized that yes, I was capable of that kind of shutting-out, as we all are, and I remembered that *I also made a swift and heartfelt repair* with my child. When we cried together cheek to cheek on the same side of the door I had slammed seconds before, there was a here-and-now repair of the momentary rupture in our relationship. And in giving my son what I had not myself gotten earlier in life, at least not enough, something in me was being repaired, too.

As has likely become obvious by now, Quinn is a powerhouse of emotion. It takes little to provoke feeling in him, and once provoked, the feeling is not mild in intensity or shy about making its presence known. It's kind of like a tornado that comes without warning, sends everything swirling and tumbling in the air, and then it all drops back down again exactly as it was. I don't relate to any of this. My older son's emotional processing system is wired differently, and much more like mine. Like his brother, Noah is sensitive, and he feels things deeply. He is also highly attuned to the emotional needs of the people around him, but other people often have no idea what *he* is feeling. I see him putting energy into impression management and emotional containment. He tries not to cry, he tries to disguise a moment of embarrassment or surprise as something he meant to do or knew was coming, he seems brave and confident when he's really uncertain or afraid. He wants to appear as if he is in control and unfazed, even though I see that he is most definitely fazed. When he gets upset, he stays upset for a good long while. He broods and ruminates and holds grudges.

I am parenting both of these boys in ways that are, without a doubt, influenced by my own emotional history. I am jarred over and over again by the intensity and sudden onset of Quinn's emotions, and because I am a flawed human, I am tempted sometimes to shame him for his outbursts. "You are six years old now, Quinn," I might say. "You're not a toddler. Get up off the floor and use words to tell us what's going on." But always there is a part of me rejoicing in his emotional freedom, and that part of me usually (not always!) steps forward when he is upset and defines a space for him in which he can have and show his emotions. He is entitled, completely and totally, to feel what he feels. I love him no matter what he is feeling, and I sure hope he knows that. I wish I had had that certainty when

I was little. I wish I hadn't operated under some unspoken mandate that it is crucial to keep emotions in check and that big emotions are meant to be experienced in private. I'm still figuring out how to undo that learning. When I tell Quinn that it's okay to feel quite a lot and to show it, I'm talking to *my* inner child, too.

Without these two children—one whose emotional habits are alien to me and one whose are uncomfortably reminiscent of mine as a child—I would not have developed the same level of awareness about who I am as an emotional being. I fancied myself an extremely self-aware person before I had kids, especially because I am a psychologist. Sitting in the therapist seat, tracking other people's emotions and the nuances of my own responses to whatever they bring into the room, most certainly has taught me a great deal about myself. But nothing compares to the reality check our children foist upon us. Nobody shows us our true nature—all we are capable of in both good and bad ways—like our children do.

Except maybe our spouses.

Married to the Buddha

When my husband and I were a couple of years into our relationship, we had a pretty intense argument about a subject I no longer remember. What I remember is that after we had parted ways angrily and I had ruminated for several hours or a day, I wrote him a big fat letter. The letter detailed all of what I was feeling, and why, and what my point of view was, and how I hoped we would resolve the argument. I left it for him to find somewhere in the house while I continued brooding off in a solitary corner (and claiming a corner like that was not easy in our shoebox-sized first house). After he read the letter, he sought me out and put his arms around me and thanked me for expressing myself so articulately. When he pulled away from the embrace, he had a sincerely puzzled look in his eyes and said, "But I have a question. Why did you write me this letter? Why didn't you just talk to me?"

You know how whatever kids experience inside the walls of their childhood home is considered normal, because they've got nothing to compare it to? Like, for example, how author Mary Karr tells us in one of her memoirs that she never considered that the way her family ate dinner every night—herself, her sister, her mom, and her dad each sitting on the edges of the parents' bed, plates in their laps, backs to each other—was a little odd? Well, that's one answer to my husband's question. When my parents' marriage was falling apart, I observed them passing typed letters back and forth—an envelope tucked into a briefcase during the morning hustle here or left on a pillow there. They must've felt they were being discreet, but I inferred that every reason for the demise of their relationship, every emotion masked by their poker faces, was spelled out on the pages of those letters. There were no screaming matches, no hushed conversations barely audible from behind closed doors. There were only letters, one after another, and the normal daily routine to which everyone was adhering while the ground crumbled beneath. This manner of handling conflict and distress never even gave me pause, until that night so many years ago when my husband asked me, with those loving and genuinely curious eyes, "But why didn't you just talk to me?"

I'm not sure how I responded right then, but I probably said something about being better at expressing myself in writing than out loud, in person. That is a true statement, and most likely it was true of my parents, and that's one reason they handled things the way they did. But what nobody had the psychological wisdom to see, let alone attempt to remedy, is the massive avoidance the letter writing represented. If we don't express ourselves in real time, letting the important people in our lives see the anguish, fear, anger, and pain on our faces, how can we expect to feel fully understood? How can we bear witness to each other's suffering, and help each other through, if the suffering is always channeled—and thereby, in some key way, transformed or distorted—into words on a page?

Writing is one of my greatest passions, and I'll be the last person to deny the power of words on a page. But the Buddhas in my life have shown me that there are elements of avoidance and control in the act of writing about feelings. And so I've come to understand that my parents' modeling of this behavior is really only part of the answer to why I wrote a letter about my feelings, some hours or days after they first rose up in me, to my husband. The rest of the answer is that I didn't have the courage to voice my feelings in a more direct way. I was afraid of my own strong emotions, and determined to get a handle on them before I made them known to anybody else.

This remains a work in progress for me. It's much easier to encourage other people to be direct about what they're feeling than to do it ourselves. As a therapist I help people identify what it is they're feeling and why. Because feelings almost always have an interpersonal context (that is, the feelings tend to originate in our relationships with the key players in our lives), it is not unusual for the dialogue in therapy to include something like, "What's gotten in the way of letting him know how angry you are?" Or "Do you think she knows about your fears?" Or "What's the risk, if you were to tell him that you're really still quite hurt about this?" Meanwhile, I have to ask myself the same questions when I discover I have feelings I've been keeping under wraps.

Tess, too, is learning hard lessons from the Buddhas in her house. I learned early on in our work together that she is haunted by memories of her unhappy mother. She remembers her as occupying a distant corner of the house, rocking vacantly in an old rocking chair. As a child, Tess felt responsible, if not for putting her mother in that state, then at least for getting her out of it. She also felt responsible for keeping her younger siblings occupied, fed, and out of their mother's hair. She swore she would never put her own children in this kind of position. She would not be a chronically unhappy mother about whom her children had to worry. She would not allow her oldest child to be in a parental role with the younger two. She has succeeded with the latter; Tess is very, very careful to ensure her ten-year-old daughter is never expected to tend to her younger siblings. But in all her efforts to be the kind of mom who has fun with her kids every day while also providing for their basic needs, somewhere she has lost her own well-being. She sets up activities and outings for the kids and accompanies them as a hollowed-out shell of herself, worn and weary and quietly despairing. Her intensive mothering—the way she has thrown her whole self into her role as a mother—cannot counter the abiding sadness and resentment she feels about doing it all alone. About living with the man who is their father but who is not a coparent. About being in a relationship with someone who is not there for her.

As she approaches forty, the age her parents were when they divorced, Tess has begun to grapple with some uncomfortable insights about her relationship with David. She sees resemblances between her relationship and that of her parents. She wonders if her efforts to be fully devoted to and available for her children—her commitment to being as unlike her mother as possible—have come at a cost not only to her own well-being but to her partnership. For some women, it is easier to love a child than it is to nurture and maintain a loving relationship with a mate, and nurturing an intimate connection with a child can serve the strategic, if often unconscious, purpose of marginalizing a spouse.

In his book *The Heart of Being Helpful*, psychiatrist Peter Breggin writes, "It's sometimes easier to see the humanity in animals than in people. That's because we're less threatened by animals. It may also be that they are more willing and able to express love in a direct, unadulterated manner. Because we're less threatened, and because they are more open and vulnerable, we become more open to love and to empathy. Similarly, many people find it much easier to love an infant or a small child than to love an adult."[9] In our recent work together, Tess is doing the hard work of confronting this truth. She is realizing that whenever David is more attentive to her, more interested in her, she pushes him away. Being angry with him for not being involved enough in their family life is much easier than contending with her sense of herself as fundamentally unlovable, which is exactly what gets provoked by her partner's attempts to love her and be close to her. Even her desire for another pregnancy, which he did not share, in retrospect seemed strategically timed. Just when the path to restoring intimate connection in their relationship was made clearer by the growing independence of their two kids, Tess lobbied hard to obstruct it again with a third child.

Fortunately, when our spouses act as mirrors and show us things we would not see without them, not everything that appears is unwanted. We can be just as blind to our strengths as we can be to our weaknesses. Sometimes, in order to believe in ourselves, we need believing mirrors*—people who see us in a more positive light than we can sometimes see ourselves, and who reflect that positive image back to us. In the best-case scenario, our spouses play that role regularly.

Recent research illuminates the power of attuned, intimate connection in marriage to propel people toward the best versions of themselves. A team of researchers tracked more than two thousand couples across a period of ten years to determine what role, if any, perceived partner responsiveness plays in a person's trajectory of well-being.[10] The researchers distinguished between hedonic well-

---

* I borrow this term, "believing mirrors," from writer Julia Cameron and her book about cultivating creativity, *The Artist's Way*.

being (generally defined as the presence of pleasure and the absence of pain) and eudaimonic well-being (the kind of fulfillment that comes from achieving one's potential, finding meaning in life, and ultimately feeling comfortable in one's own skin, wrinkles and all). As we might expect, both types of well-being were *concurrently* linked with partner responsiveness; in other words, at both data collection points (when the study first began, and then ten years later), the more a participant felt understood and cared for by his or her partner, the higher that participant's hedonic and eudaimonic well-being. But in a fascinating twist, partner responsiveness at baseline also predicted *increases* in eudaimonic well-being across time, and this was not true for hedonic well-being. Translation? Having an attuned partner does not guarantee an ever-greater bounty of pleasure or protect us from pain as we move through life, but it does bring us the kind of well-being that springs from deeper wells: personal growth, meaning-making, and realizing our potential.

All this is to say that the same guy we resent for pointing out our flaws and unflattering idiosyncrasies may also be the one who helps us lay claim to our competence, our power, and our beauty. But this is possible only if—and this is a big "if"—we can stay in connection and open to his feedback despite the less desirable things we see in the mirror he holds up to us. That's how Julia, the mother we met in chapter 3, came to view herself as a strong role model for the daughter she later had. Her husband's perceptions of her—as the dynamic, self-possessed, determined, courageous woman she could not always see she was—played a key role in countering her worries about what it would mean for her daughter to identify with her. And many women have told me it is their husbands, who often see them at their best *and* their worst parenting moments, whose positive feedback has the most power to cut through their thick and tenacious mother guilt. When we look at ourselves through our partner's lens, we often get a much more forgiving view.

But reckoning with our own *unwanted* qualities, and our habitual ways of being in the presence of those we love, is far from
comfortable. For so many women transformed by motherhood, it
is painful. It is much easier to deny and distort. We can be very
skilled at looking away from the truths our children and partners
try to show us. We can generate any number of excuses and justifications, like I did when my husband first began to suggest to
me that I was no longer acting like myself. I wanted to believe
that if only our son would sleep through the night—and therefore so could I—then I would get centered and become "my old
self" again. I told myself that if I'd been blessed with one of the
easy babies all our friends seemed to have, motherhood wouldn't
be taking such a toll on me. Both of these explanations for why I
was so emotionally off-balance are valid, and I still believe them.
Prolonged sleep deprivation and well-being are directly at odds
with each other, and colicky babies tax even the most patient parents. But I was far more inclined to attribute my distress to these
external factors than to anything internal. Until I had done quite
a lot of work to increase my self-awareness, it didn't even occur
to me that I had some habits, tendencies, and qualities that made
the transition to motherhood quite challenging. It would likely
have been less challenging if I'd had babies who slept through the
night sooner than two years old, or who were less fussy, but what
I know now is that I was in for a rough transition no matter what.
I was especially discombobulated by motherhood because of the
high value I placed on so many of the things that disappear most
quickly when you have a baby: order, neatness, quiet, solitude,
and productivity. Many years and hard-earned epiphanies later,
I've learned to recognize when these core qualities are serving
me, my marriage, and my children well, and when they are not. As
many other wise people before me have pointed out, our greatest
strengths can also be weaknesses.

That our virtues in one context may be vices in another is but one of the many profound lessons our children teach us best. They teach us that with fierce love comes deep fear, and that we cannot have joy without also inviting sorrow. They teach us that life does not go the way we planned. They teach us that we, and they, are imperfect. They teach us that no one emerges from childhood unscathed— that we did not get all our needs met as children, and neither will they. They teach us that the only constant is change. They teach us that we are neither as fabulous nor as horrible as we thought. Motherhood not only transforms us; it also forces us to *relinquish our illusions about who we were all along.*

10

Lost and Found

May it only sting a moment when you dive into that blue
Because by the time you hit the surface, it has rearranged you
—ANTJE DUVEKOT, "SWEET SPOT"[1]

When Quinn was a newborn, we bought a king-size mattress and my husband built us a four-poster bed to accommodate it. He did this not because it was a good time to embark on such a project (it wasn't), but because for Ari, the time to do anything is now. I write things down on my endless to-do list; he walks out to the garage and picks up a tool and gets going. We had a vision of a family bed, the four of us piled in and happily tangled up. A place where hungry babies would be nursed, feverish foreheads would be cooled, little souls shaken by nightmares would be soothed, snores and giggles and stories would fill the air. The building of the big bed seemed to represent a kind of acceptance of the big, sensual, marvelous mess of family life that ours had become.

One morning, I watched that same little person, the one whose new presence in our lives told us we had outgrown the queen-size bed, take big deep sleepy breaths with his four-and-a-half-year-old body. He had come in at four thirty a.m. to tell me he'd had a bad dream, and whenever he does this, he wants not to squeeze in between his dad and me like I imagine most kids would. He says, instead, "Let me trade places with you." By this he means, "You scoot over to the middle because I plan to lie down right where you are." It's as if he needs to sink his little body into the imprint of mine, and rest his head on the exact part of the pillow where mine left its mark, and once he has done so, he is asleep in an instant. And I think, *This is the beauty and the curse of motherhood*. Displaced by a person I love so fiercely that I don't mind.

The thing is, it was a long, twisty road to being able to say "I don't mind." And that mentality doesn't always apply. Sometimes I *do* mind, thank you very much. As Susan Maushart says in *The Mask of Motherhood*, "A woman accustomed to taking autonomy for granted may find the experience of newborn motherhood strangely claustrophobic as she struggles to fit two people into a space formerly reserved for one." Even though Quinn was my secondborn and that claustrophobic experience had been far more pronounced four years earlier when I first became a mother, when he was a baby, there was an almost literal struggle to fit the both of us into a space once occupied by only me. He was deliciously chubby, and he loved his "milka-pilka," as he later came to call it, more than anything. The more pounds he gained, the more I lost. It wasn't just that I was burning calories through breastfeeding; he was also diagnosed with a serious dairy allergy which required me to cut dairy from my diet so my breast milk wouldn't harm him. Between nursing an always-hungry baby and the pretty extreme change to my diet, I went from fairly slender to *really skinny*. I was underweight, and exhausted. He was sucking the life out of me. As he took up more space, I took up less. There is an obvious metaphor here.

All these years later, I'm back to occupying more space in the physical world. I confess I sometimes miss the svelte body I had when I was declining every grilled cheese sandwich and bowl of ice cream I was offered and burning a thousand calories a day just by nursing, but where the metaphor is concerned I'm happy there's no longer such a struggle to fit two into a space formerly reserved for one. Twelve years after the birth of my first child, I have a handle on my life I could not have achieved when my children were younger. While it is certainly ironic, it is no coincidence that I am finishing a book about the strain of *new* motherhood more than a decade after it was new to me. Things are a little—dare I say a lot?—easier now. The strain is not so pronounced anymore, and the emotions are less raw. The chaos of family life is far more bearable. But make no mistake: the life I have a handle on is not the same life I once occupied. It is profoundly changed, as I am profoundly changed. And so are the mothers I've been seeing for six, eight, even ten years of therapy.

Cherished Intruders

I have often wondered if I would be so tired if my sons were introverts like me. Or even if just one of them was. I have two exuberant, extremely chatty, social-butterfly children who are happiest while actively engaged with others. As I've mentioned before, I enjoy my solitude a lot more than the average person, and I especially enjoy quiet, and in these regards I am greatly outnumbered in my house. My husband is the extrovert yang to my introvert yin, and he can resemble the Energizer Bunny as much as our children. Basically, I am surrounded by male humans whose strong presences overwhelm my fragile nervous system, and I didn't ask for this particular arrangement. Another girl,* or even just a male introvert, in the house would have been nice.

It has occurred to me that the decision to have children is not so unlike the decision to invite perfect strangers to come live with you. Forever. The hope is that everyone likes each other, but the reality is that they could be as different from you, and one another, as possible, and they could have many annoying qualities, and everyone might get along poorly. And even if none of this rings true for your family right now, it could have been true in the past, or it may be true at some point in the future, because like us, our children are ever-changing. Sometimes they are barely recognizable as the same children we had last month or last year.

Psychotherapist and renowned relationships expert Esther Perel once referred to children as "cherished intruders." They come steamrolling into our lives and creep into all corners of it, invited or not. They are in our beds instead of their own. Or we *think* they are in their own beds when suddenly they are standing at the edge of ours, asking for a glass of water when we are about to begin—or, God help us all, are in the middle of—lovemaking. They are in the bathroom showing us their drawings while we're peeing. They are climbing all over us while we are on the phone. They are in the back

---

* Truly, I realize that for me in particular, part of what makes parenting my children difficult is their Y chromosomes. The way they want to tell me blow-by-blow accounts of actions. *"Mom! Mom! Check this out! I slammed this into that and then this went flying up and did twelve flips in the air and then it landed on that and sent this spinning across the room!"* The way they are in constant motion and cannot resist climbing and jumping on the furniture. The way their butts make no contact with their chairs at dinnertime. I notice my impatience and irritation peaking at bedtime. When I want cooperation and a smooth transition into cozy, tender, quiet time, I get resistance, frenzied energy, and a sudden loud and enthusiastic chattering about all the things from their day I was so eager to hear about earlier, when they couldn't pause from their living room acrobatics to talk to me. I'm tired just writing about this. Would I be so tired if I had daughters?

seat of our cars, in the back of our minds while we're in a meeting at work, in the center of our dreams while we are sleeping.

All this is as it should be. If all is well in the realm of attachment, kids* don't hold back climbing right up into the laps of their parents to get the sense of safety and comfort they need. They do this without hesitation because they trust they will be held and feel seen and welcomed and witnessed. And that means that with any luck, we will be intruded upon over and over by these little people we cherish so.

Paradoxes abound in the world of motherhood. The same little people who hamper our freedom and spontaneity are also the ones who compel us to savor the present moment. Although parenthood makes us slaves to schedules and planning, it also necessitates extraordinary flexibility and affords new opportunities for unexpected, unbidden joy. Even as they exhaust us beyond compare, children can revitalize adult life. We see through the eyes of our children and the world becomes more tantalizing again. We adopt—if only for brief moments at a time—our children's curious orientation toward what they encounter, and we are more alive again. Babies are sensual and fully present, and this is contagious. It's not hard for me to conjure up memories of all the times I was pulled from distraction and into the present moment by my children's remarks on the experiences we were having, like the time Noah said, while we were enjoying a beautiful day, "The earth is giving us so much love right now."

When Noah was not quite three years old, we started referring to him as Mr. Politeness Man. Our devotion to the task of teaching him manners—all those seven hundred thousand times we insisted

---

* And dogs. Our dog, Poppy, has an uncanny ability to wedge herself right between my husband and me even when we are sitting as close to each other as we possibly can. She makes a place for herself where there isn't one, nuzzles us with her wet nose, and shamelessly asks for the love she seeks. Sometimes I'm annoyed, but mostly I'm glad to have a securely attached dog.

he say "please" and "thank you" and wondered if he was ever, *ever* going to stop needing the reminder—had finally paid off. All requests were prefaced with a "please" and all receipts of snacks, meals, drinks, favors, and assistance were acknowledged with a heartfelt "thanks." It was pretty fantastic. One night he and I were hanging out together, just the two of us, and he was on a thanking roll. In his tiny sweet toddler voice, he said, "Thank you for this mac and cheese! Thank you for these cucumbers! Thank you for my milk! Thank you for reading me that book!" And then, the kicker. I poured myself a glass of wine and he said, "Thank you for having that for you!" I was doubled over with laughter. What was I supposed to say to that? "You're so welcome, Noah. It's the least I could do."

Fast-forward six or seven years, and this same boy is sitting at the kitchen table, about to dive into the big breakfast we had recently instituted as a Sunday tradition. "Thanks, Dad, for being willing to make everybody whatever kind of eggs they wanted." Suddenly, I got teary. This was an expression that went far beyond mere politeness: it was gratitude. Noah was expressing gratitude not just for the food on his plate and for having his egg fried rather than scrambled, but for his father's willingness to accommodate each person's preferences, for his father's effort, his generous spirit. None of this was lost on Noah, and he took a moment to say so.

On that evening years ago when Noah thanked me for pouring myself a glass of wine, I recorded it in his baby book as one of the more hilarious things he had ever said. But what I realize now, and the reason his remark about the eggs struck such a chord for me, is that this child's default mode is to be grateful and *that's because of what we have modeled for him*. The toddler version of Noah was looking around for reasons to feel thankful, and why not the fact that his mommy had served herself a lovely glass of wine? That has become for him a habitual way of engaging with the world. This was one of the happy Buddha moments—the ones that seem not to happen as often as the uncomfortable ones. Noah was showing me something pretty great in that mirror he held up to me. He was reflecting back for me that *my* default is to be grateful, and that this is contagious. We've succeeded in giving gratitude a central place in our family life.

Ari and I have a habit of saying thank you. We say it probably more times each day than we even realize. *Thank you for emptying the dishwasher. Thank you for the delicious dinner. Thanks for making the kids' lunches. Thank you for the massage, the back scratches, the cup of tea. Thanks for remembering that I would need the checkbook today. Thanks for listening. Thank you for being so patient. Thank you for staying up to clean the giant mess in the kitchen when you were so tired. Thanks for being supportive. Thanks for getting up early with the kids so I could sleep in a little. Thanks for booking those plane tickets.* We are giving thanks for actions, gestures, sentiments, attention, consideration, sacrifices, energy expenditures. Big and small. Over and over, every day. If you were a fly on the wall in our house, you might find it a little strange, maybe even a little obnoxious, how frequently the word "thanks" is being exchanged. But it isn't forced or insincere. It has become a way of life, a customary way of interaction. It isn't contrived or saccharine. It's just the truth. We are thankful. And I see this as a key reason for the happiness that reigns over the daily chaos and hardships and frustrations that characterize our overflowing, imperfect family life.

And, Not But

When my boys were younger, there were times I felt pretty certain that I would have been better off with only one child. I know some readers are thinking, *WHAT?! How can she say that!? Doesn't she know her younger son could read this someday and be devastated?* Well, I am not worried about that. I have faith that my second child will recognize the enormous difference between believing I might have been better suited to be the mother of an only child and regretting his existence. It was never *him* I sometimes wished weren't around; it was the dynamic of my two children together and the sheer degree of stimulation in my immediate environment that sometimes made me think, *This isn't the greatest fit for me*. If anyone is disparaging me for having felt that way, and for putting it down here on the page, that is a reflection of the very reason I wanted to write this book. *The complex truths of motherhood will continue to make everyone uncomfortable and ashamed until they're articulated readily and repeatedly.*

My love for Quinn, my second son, is deep and fierce. I do not favor Noah over him. There is nothing I wouldn't do to protect him, and there is no threat more ominous than the threat of losing either one of them. It's silly that I'm even saying all this, but therein lies the problem. We are afraid that if we give voice to the darker, less acceptable facets of our experience as mothers, this will somehow render the prettier, acceptable facets untrue, or at least obscure them from others' view. Why must we preface our expressions of frustration, fatigue, loss, and anger with expressions of love? "I love my baby, but she exhausts me." "I love my baby, but sometimes I just can't handle how needy he is."

We do this with our relationships, too. "I love my husband, but he is so oblivious sometimes." As women we are expected to be unwaveringly nurturing and loving; to waver in those regards is to risk being seen as a lesser kind of a woman. For fear that we will be shunned for voicing a difficult truth about the way we sometimes experience the ones who matter most to us, we package that truth in sentiments of love and fondness. Though this is far better than never voicing the dark or difficult truth at all, I often wonder what it would be like if it was *taken as a given* that the feelings of love and fondness always exist. How much suffering would that alleviate when the not-so-loving and not-so-fond feelings rise up?

A lot, and here's why: Without realizing it, with these *I love my spouse/child, but . . .* statements, we put ourselves in a bind. We are essentially saying, *These two things don't go together, so which of them wins? Which of them will I deny, minimize, banish from consciousness? What can I do to resolve this contradiction?*

Rachael, whose horrifying images of harming her new baby brought her into therapy, has long since moved past the concerns that characterized the early postpartum period for her. A recurring theme in her therapy now is how to accept her wildly fluctuating feelings toward her husband. This has been a real struggle for her, because when she feels negative feelings toward Scott, she feels them hard. The feelings are far from subtle. She hates him sometimes, and there are some moments when she finds him quite unattractive. She wonders what the hell he was thinking in putting that shirt on with those pants, and if he's ever going to shave, and why she even married the asshole.

The thing is, Rachael and Scott are quite in love. They have a very strong marriage. And so it's always such a hard moment when Rachael sits down on my couch and says, sometimes in tears, "It happened again last night. I looked at him and felt repulsed. And when we went out to dinner and he was so silent, I wondered if some other husband would be a better conversationalist."

Rachael must remind herself, again and again, of the full catastrophe. Being close to her husband means, among countless other things, seeing his flaws. Feeling joy and love and passion within her marriage means that she has the "vitality" button turned on, which means she will also feel sadness and pain and aggravation and disgust. She feels the full spectrum. She cannot have it any other way if she wants to live her life in color. It is not her love for her husband that fluctuates, nor is that love in question. What fluctuates are the feelings that come with the territory of love. I turn again to psychiatrist and eloquent author Peter Breggin, who, in *The Heart of Being Helpful*, writes about the nature of unconditional love.[2]

> *We love them not only warts and all, but nasty, self-centered intentions and all. We love them despite, and even because of, the inherent flaws and contradictions that plague all human beings. We love them when they are feeling generous and when they are feeling selfish. We love them when they are brave and when they are cowardly; when they are brilliant and when they are stupid; when they are physically beautiful and when they are ravaged by illness and age.*

On one level, these words capture an *ideal* to which we all aspire; we *wish* we could feel the same degree of fondness for a loved one when that loved one is ill-behaved or looking shabby as we do when that loved one is at his or her best and looking amazing, but we don't always pull that off. On another level, the words are a statement of fact. We do not stop loving our partners when they become wrinkled and gray or when they act like jerks. But we do often feel threatened, deep down, by these momentary negative appraisals. We think they mean something they don't. We think the negative cancels out the positive—that only one can be true, and one day we will realize which one it is.

For Rachael, learning to ride the waves of her changing perceptions of her husband happened with a shift in the story she told herself about her husband. I call it the "And, Not But" shift. When people modify the language they use to describe their experiences, they also modify their perception. When we use the word "and" instead of the word "but," we make room for all emotions. There is no competition between love and hate, no tension between exhaustion and invigoration, no mutual exclusivity between the grief of lost personal freedom and the joy of a new tiny human we love more than we ever thought possible.

It is a simple yet quite powerful shift. When Rachael says, "I feel like we have a good marriage, but Scott is so quiet when we get time together," the words put her in a worried, unresolved place. *Do we have a good marriage or not? Does his silence mean something bad? Am I wrong about our strong connection?* When instead she says, "I feel like we have a good marriage, and Scott is so quiet when we get time together," the feeling in the air is altogether different. One does not negate the other. Scott is allowed to be the quiet person that he is without this having any bearing on the quality of their marriage. And when she untethers Scott's behavior from the quality of their marriage, Rachael sees the issue more clearly. She sees that she simply longs for more of a window into his internal world. Rather than ruminate about the strength of their marriage, Rachael begins to conjure up some creative ideas for how to feel connected with a man of few words. Even the furrow of her brow softens when she uses "and" language. I can see the perplexed feeling, the pent-up tension stemming from the "but" language, dissipating.

Looking upon our internal experiences with benign curiosity is often enough to modify them. Buddhist monk Thich Nhat Hanh has suggested we hold our thoughts and feelings like a mother would hold her crying baby. It's the difference between asking with compassion, "What's going on here?" and asking with judgment, "What the *hell* is going on here?" As we saw with Rachael, something significant happens when we gather up seemingly opposing thoughts and feelings into our arms and just let them be. Maybe even rock them a little and lovingly tend to them. "I love my daughter, and she also makes me madder than I've ever been." "My partner is so supportive, and he also lets me down." There are no dilemmas to resolve or apologies or justifications to be made. There are no angsty questions lurking, like, *How is this possible? What am I going to do about this? Which of these realities am I going to choose as righter or truer?* There is also no shame. There is only the full catastrophe—the cherishing *and* the resenting, the fulfillment *and* the disappointment, the pleasure *and* the pain—where shame finds no home.

So I treasure my two boys *and* I am sometimes completely overwhelmed by the commotion and noise they generate. Every single day, more than once, I consider myself the most fortunate mother in the world because my boys are mine, because they are alive, healthy, kind, beautiful, and smart. Every single day, at least for a minute or two, I quietly celebrate each of my children as the extraordinary, complicated, remarkable, unique human beings they are, and I cannot imagine my life without them. And every single day, I lose my patience with them, and I want all three of the noisy, busy, buzzing-with-energy males in my house to go away for just a few minutes, please. I would never want to trade in my children for different ones, and I remain sad all these years later about not having a daughter. Sometimes the voices of my children fall on my ears like beautiful music, and sometimes it's more like nails on a chalkboard. I want for nothing when I have my children in my arms, and my mind sometimes wanders to an alternate life in which there are no small people making demands on me.

Self-Discovery and Empowerment in Motherhood

As Adrienne Rich first articulated over forty years ago in the 1976 classic *Of Woman Born*, the experience of motherhood is both oppressive and empowering. It is when we embrace all of the paradoxes of motherhood that we can come to understand not just what we have lost, but also what we have gained. Throughout the pages of this book, I have focused primarily on what's difficult about the transition to motherhood—all the loss and constriction it entails—because that is what either gets buried and denied or causes us tremendous shame. We have no trouble speaking to the pleasures of motherhood, because those pleasures are as socially acceptable as it gets. However, the "dark side" of motherhood is also a tremendous opportunity for positive change—for reflection, insight, adjustment, and growth. The dark moments, when not banished for being unacceptable, can call into question our customary way of seeing things and propel us toward personal growth. Embedded within the full catastrophe of motherhood is the potential for self-expansion, even healing and redemption.

Often it is through our perspective as parents that we develop greater compassion for ourselves. I remember vividly a time that my therapist, upon hearing some of the harshly self-critical internal talk in which I'd been engaged, asked, "Molly, would you *ever* speak that way to your children?" She had tears in her eyes, showing me how much my cruel self-talk pained her. She knew, of course, that the answer was no. It was a powerful moment. When my children are hurting, I might sometimes fail to pick up on it because I am only a good-enough, imperfect mother. I might miss their signals or offer a distracted, halfhearted but generally supportive response. But I recognized instantly that I would never say to them the things I was saying to myself that day. As we learn to care for our children, we learn to care better for ourselves. We tap into our wells of empathic concern and compassion for these little people we love so much, and subsequently we find more compassion for ourselves. Our view of ourselves softens just a little and begins to include some of the tenderness we feel for our children. We begin to realize that, as I once heard someone say, we are all adults with little-kid hearts beating inside us.

When my children were just shy of seven and three years old, I walked into a recording studio in the remote woods of central Vermont and emerged five or six hours later with two completed

songs. I sang, with my whole heart, two songs I had chosen because of what they meant to me and represented about my life
and my family. One of them was a lullaby of sorts that Noah had
been requesting I sing to him at bedtime for a couple of years,
and I surprised him with the recording for his seventh birthday.
The other was a song called "Sweet Spot." Some of the lyrics
are at the start of this chapter, which tells you a little something
about the song's significance. Though the meaning of lyrics and
poetry are never the same for everyone, for me it captured where
I suddenly found myself seven years after becoming a mother:

> *Once you stood below a mountain*
> *Now you find yourself surprised*
> This is the sweet spot of your life
> *And this new view compares to nothing*
> *Gone the hardship of your climb*
> This is the sweet spot of your life
> *Well it seems the ice is melting*
> *Seems you've come in from the cold*
> This is the sweet spot of your life
> *And all your streams they are now fuller*
> *Than what their riverbanks can hold*
> This is the sweet spot of your life

That day in the studio, it required more takes than I can recall,
and maybe even a few glasses of liquid courage, to get the vocal
tracks right. I was utterly consumed with anxiety about stepping
up to the microphone, not only because of my extreme* inhibitions

---

* And I really do mean "extreme." The first time my husband played one of my
recordings for some friends at our house, I hid in the garage.

about singing in general, but also because the person with whom I was collaborating to make these recordings had done such a beautiful job with the arrangements on the songs that I was all the more intimidated. Both songs were so gorgeously rendered, with richly layered and emotionally evocative instrumentation all just waiting for my vocal. No pressure or anything! Having taken a giant leap of faith by finding a recording studio in Vermont when all my singing before that had been "in the closet" (or the shower, or the car), it was almost more than I could bear. But this mattered to me. It mattered enormously. And I came to realize how much it mattered only because of the transformations in me set in motion by motherhood.

I grew up in a family of musicians. My parents and my uncle had a band and played at county fairs, bars, and weddings throughout my childhood. My brother played bass and was in several bands starting in adolescence. But not me. Although I took eight years of piano lessons, the lessons were very traditional; there was no improvising and no music theory. It was entirely about reading the sheet music and playing the song, and not at all about self-expression. I was also exceptionally shy, so it's not like I was entertaining ideas of one day being on a stage the way my family members were. The thought of that terrified me, and mostly still does. I always considered myself just a quiet but deeply enthusiastic observer of the music other people around me were making. Music was, in a sense, the air I breathed, but I never identified as a musician. I chose a different path. I was much more comfortable in the academic and intellectual realms.

Looking back, I see that I was drawn to music in a way that goes beyond being an appreciator. I know now that the desire to sing and make music has always been in me. Some of my happiest memories from adolescence are of singing my heart out to Carole King and Aretha Franklin with my friends, all of us piled into my little orange 1976 Honda Civic hatchback that we'd named Tangerine after the

Led Zeppelin song. As I got older, I continued to surround myself with people who made music, in my circle of friends and in my family, and I watched and listened with a kind of rapt attention I now recognize as *longing*. I was longing to be a music maker, not just a music appreciator, but this was a secret I kept even from myself.

It was my children who put me in touch with this longing. In my first few days of motherhood, as I rocked and nursed newborn Noah, I sang. I sang to him without inhibition, without even thinking about it. I sang because it soothed him and because it was natural. It was part of how I expressed my love to him. It became a cherished ritual at his bedtime, and later, the same was true with Quinn. Neither of them would stand for a bedtime without a song. Listening from the sidelines, my husband—who had truly never heard me sing in any audible or serious way—was more than a little intrigued. He began to voice his disgruntlement about my singing shyness ("Why are the boys the only ones who get to hear you sing?"). He even tried to "out" me when we had friends over for dinner by having them listen over the baby monitor when I ducked upstairs to put the children to bed.

Gradually, a part of me that had long ago gone underground was beginning to surface. I thought about singing all the time. Though it's perhaps an odd thing to say, when I open my mouth and sing a song I've written, I feel more like who I really am than ever before. Using my voice in this way has felt like coming home to myself. At first, my trips to the recording studio were construed as being in the service of gifts I wanted to give—there was the sweet song I recorded for Ari on the occasion of our anniversary, and the song Noah loved me to sing to him at bedtime that I gave to him on his birthday—because that somehow gave me permission to spend the time and money doing such a thing. Soon enough, I didn't need that kind of permission anymore. I was immersed in a process of self-discovery or, perhaps more accurately, *recovery*. I was (and still am, years later) recovering a dimension of myself I had denied. Buried. Lost. Until, in motherhood, it was found.

Let me be clear that the story of growth and self-discovery I'm telling is the product of time and hindsight. It is a very, very different story from the one I would've told in those early days of motherhood, or even two or three years out. It's safe to say I had *absolutely no idea* back then what my singing to baby Noah meant, or what road it was setting me on. What I felt then was a mix of intoxicating love for him and acute, unexpected loss—loss of personal freedom, order, productivity, time for self-reflection and self-care, intimate connection with anyone other than the baby, and so much else I held dear that seemed to disappear when I first entered motherhood. If you had told me then that I was undergoing a process of expansion, I would not have believed you. All I could feel was the constriction. The shrinking of possibility, opportunity, and even self.

Doing long-term therapy with the many women who were new mothers when they first came to see me, I have witnessed the same kinds of transformations. Rachael, for instance, left an unfulfilling job and started her own business, which is now quite successful. It was through cultivating the feminist values she was committed to passing on to her daughters that she found the energy and determination to extricate herself from an unfair and stagnant work environment and become her own boss. Today, nine years after the first time I saw her, with her first baby in her arms and a relentless emotional fatigue dimming the light within her, I do a double take when I see Rachael in my waiting room. She is glowing. She has an air of strength and confidence. Anna wrote a poem about the night she soothed her own younger self while soothing her baby after a failed attempt at the cry-it-out sleep solution. Encouraged by a trusted friend's enthusiastic response to the poem, she wrote another, and then another. She submitted one to a small poetry contest, and won second place. Now she is pursuing a master's degree in creative writing, something she may well never have realized was a passion if not for that painful and ultimately redemptive moment with her baby girl.

Neither I nor Rachael nor Anna, nor any of the other women you met in these pages, would have said, at any point in the first several years of motherhood, "I am feeling so invigorated and inspired by my role as a mother! I am so much more comfortable in my own skin now, and so much more in touch with my dreams and passions!" (Just writing this makes me giggle a little, because it's so ridiculous.) And yet, in each case, it was the growing pains brought on by motherhood that ultimately led to greater fulfillment. They are growing pains, indeed. Not shrinking pains, despite how it feels at first. Through motherhood, our identities expand. But we must first survive the long, inevitable slog through the dormancy and constriction of our roles and our possibilities.

The Only Way Is Through

Lynn, a thirty-six-year-old woman with an eighteen-month-old daughter, sat on the couch in my therapy office, a lump in her throat, the gate that would allow the tears to flow never quite opening. Her sadness over the year and a half since her baby was born had been about many different things, but on this day it was about experiencing herself as a "marm" without any sex appeal. She told me a story that, for her, was all the evidence she needed that her sex appeal was gone. At an outdoor festival the week before, she had walked up to the front of the long beer line and asked two men if they would mind getting her a beer, too. Their response, something about how it would be wrong if they did that for her when everyone else had to wait in line, confirmed for my client that she simply had no allure anymore. "Two years ago," she said with such certainty, "those guys would've said, 'Sure!'"

Breastfeeding figured prominently in her view of herself as lacking sex appeal. She could not picture a man finding her sexy as long as she was still breastfeeding her year-and-a-half-old daughter, who had taken to requesting her meals with the word "Boob!" Another factor was Lynn's body image and her discomfort in her ill-fitting clothing. It was noteworthy that the reason her clothes no longer fit was not because she had more weight to lose; she said that she had returned to her pre-baby weight. It was that her body had *changed shape*. There is such metaphor in this. Her body had changed shape, and so had her entire life. The rhythm and pace of her days, the way she related to her partner, the way she related to her friends and family, the way she experienced her body, the way she experienced herself as a woman out in the world.

What especially pained me as I listened to her story and watched her fight back tears was that her view of herself was so misaligned with my view of her. When she walked into my office that day, I noticed that she looked especially beautiful. Radiant, actually. It had been some time since I'd seen her, about five weeks or so, and I wondered what was different, what kind of update I was about to hear. Was her baby finally sleeping through the night? Had the depressive symptoms that had had a hold on her for the previous many months loosened their grip? Was her heartache about the demise of her relationship beginning to heal, maybe with the aid of a new love interest? I was more than a little surprised when what came out of her mouth was, "I feel old. I feel unattractive and unsexy and none of my clothes fit. I've just become a marm with no sex appeal."

My dilemma was whether to share with her that I was seeing a radiance and beauty in her more pronounced than before or keep this observation to myself. There were pros and cons to both approaches. I know well the kind of pain that comes from construing yourself as unattractive, especially when this involves a perceived loss of your former, more attractive self. It can feel like the changes to our bodies after giving birth are permanent, as if we are inhabiting a different body now, much like how when we move from one house to another, we know we are never going to inhabit the previous house again. It can feel like what left our bodies at childbirth was not only the baby growing inside but also any sense we may have had of ourselves as vibrant, sexual beings. It can feel like the "baby weight" is far heavier emotionally than the number of extra pounds that register on the scale. For many women, these struggles begin with their changing pregnant bodies, not just after delivering their babies. But for most women, it's easier to ward off the pain of body image woes when there is a baby inside. We say to ourselves something like, *I may feel like a beached whale, but that's because I'm manufacturing a human being.* After delivery, we no longer have this justification for our changed bodies. In the best of scenarios, we are gentle and patient with ourselves and trust that we will one day recognize our bodies again, but even then we are not immune to terrible bouts of self-loathing.

Knowing all this, having lived it, I see Lynn despairing about her changed body and I want to take away her pain. I want to challenge her current perception of herself in one of the most immediately effective ways I can, which would be to disclose to her that the moment I saw her in the waiting room, I thought she looked beautiful. We could have a tender exchange about this. I could ask, "What is it like to hear me say that? To know how I see you?" We could slowly, carefully, thoroughly navigate this delicate territory of the discrepancy between how she sees herself and how others see her, prompted by my willingness to disclose my own perceptions.

I don't do this. I keep my perceptions to myself, not because I am absolutely certain this is the right therapeutic move to make, but because it feels, for now, like the *better* therapeutic move to make. Lynn can tell her mother and her friends that she feels unattractive, and they will say to her, "Oh, stop. You're more beautiful than ever!" Probably this has already happened, perhaps even multiple times, and yet here she sits in my office, in despair, not the least bit soothed by the reassurances others have offered her. As her peer, as a mother who identifies with what she is feeling, as a compassionate person, of course I feel a pull to offer her those same reassurances. But I am her therapist, and difficult as it is to withhold words that might comfort and buoy her in the moment, I know that my role is a different one.

I draw from my own experience in the client seat—the experience of longing, over and over, for affirmations of various kinds from my therapist. *If only she would tell me how lovely and extraordinary I am, then I'd know it for sure. If only she would tell me I am beautiful, then I'd know it for sure.* We bestow great powers upon our therapists. I can't go deeply into the reasons for that without digressing into an entirely different topic, but I can try to convey the essence of the phenomenon like this: At least in long-term psychotherapy, which is mostly what I know, a therapist comes to know her client very, very intimately. As a result, our therapists' perceptions of us matter enormously; it's as if we are asking, "Now that you know nearly everything about me that I normally keep hidden from view, do you still love me?" Why wouldn't we long for an answer to this question? But if your therapist is any good, she won't answer you. At least not directly, and not right away. We must come by these answers to our questions of self-worth honestly, of our own accord. The most important truths are self-discovered. What Lynn had lost could not be given back to her by anyone else. She would need to discover it again for herself.

For Lynn to make this discovery, she will have to give up the hope of returning to some earlier version of herself. She will have to embrace, rather than resist, what has changed. But human beings have a tough time with change. We find great comfort in stability and certainty, and our relationship with change is often a resistant, defiant one. We see change itself—regardless of the direction of change—as a threat to our strongly held notions of what is true and real about ourselves, the world, and others. Think about the standard yearbook-signing phrase: *"Don't ever change!"* In the realm of marriage, character change is often viewed as the culprit when things go awry; we say or hear things like, "She's not who she used to be," "He's not the same man I married," "I've changed over the years, and he's stayed the same." The irony, of course, is that along with death and taxes, change is one of the few certainties in life.

In *Gift from the Sea*, Anne Morrow Lindbergh writes, "And then how swiftly, how inevitably the perfect unity is invaded; the relationship changes, it becomes complicated, encumbered by its contact with the world. I believe this is true in most relationships, with friends, with husband or wife, and with one's children. But it is the marriage relationship in which the changing pattern is shown up most clearly because it is the deepest one and the most arduous to maintain; and because, somehow, *we mistakenly feel that failure to maintain its exact original pattern is tragedy* [emphasis mine]."[3] It is actually our resistance to change—our fear of what a changing relationship might mean—that renders us victims. We interpret the change to mean, for instance, that we are incompatible, or that we are losing forever something we once had. It's as if we are suffering characters in, rather than authors of, the evolving story of our marriages. Lindbergh acknowledges that the original relationship is very beautiful indeed, even that its "perfection wears the freshness of a spring morning." But subsequent phases of a relationship can be beautiful, too; we move to another phase, "which one should not dread, but welcome as one welcomes summer after spring."

Having a baby changes us, profoundly, and the change itself is a threat to our marriages. But whether that threat ultimately translates to untenable dissatisfaction in the marriage is partly a function of our problematic appraisals of what change means and why it occurs. Change is not inherently damaging to relationships. In fact, many scholars argue that remaining open to the ever-unfolding mystery of who our partners are is a key aspect of keeping love alive. We do not need to know every nook and cranny of our mate's psyche or personality, nor do those nooks and crannies need to stay exactly the same across time. We only need to know the answer to that million-dollar question: *Are you there for me?* And it is when we can't get an affirmative answer—when the strain of parenting and careers and domestic obligations and the endless logistics of life impede our ability to show up for each other and tune into each other—that we suffer.

In the early years of parenthood, that suffering is far more common than most of us realize. It is not reserved for the clinically depressed new mother whose postpartum mood disorder is impacting her marriage. It is the emotional backdrop of a great many mothers, the same ones who are beaming with maternal joy or good-humoredly exposing their domestic disorder in the photos they post on Instagram. It is the unspoken struggle of a great many couples, the same ones who look so happy and in love in their profile pictures that they can't possibly have the kinds of explosive fights we have with our spouses, and they can't possibly have cried quietly into their pillows the night before, their backs turned to each other, wondering when their closest ally started to feel so far away.

Rather than resisting change, we need to find ways to unmask the emotional complexity of the transition into motherhood, a transition that has the potential to rattle and rearrange a woman more than anything else she has faced before or will ever face again. We need to dismantle false dichotomies, like the one that distinguishes between the majority of women who do not develop PPD and the unlucky few who do, and the one that separates the divorced couples whose marriages couldn't withstand the stress of parenthood from the ones whose perfect children only enhanced their already-perfect marriage. We need to connect to the current of our own emotions, where we will likely encounter the truth that *we are fundamentally changed*—not just stressed or depleted or superficially annoyed—by motherhood. We might conclude that our marriages, too, are not the same anymore.

Motherhood transforms us. It is not that we become different people or that we lose ourselves. It is that we discover feelings, impulses, thoughts, and wishes within ourselves that we likely never would have encountered had we not become mothers. Some of these—like the realization that we are as proficient at having emotional meltdowns as our toddlers are, or the wish that we could give our newborn to that woman down the street who seems like a really terrific mother—are not at all flattering. Some—like the way our babies' smiles can produce a jolt of bliss like none we've ever felt—are magnificent and transcendent. In mothering, we come up against the outer bounds of despair and rage, ecstasy and enchantment. We feel more fully the range of emotion our human existence entails. For better and for worse, motherhood holds up a mirror to us, and we see more accurately who we are and what we are capable of feeling.

As if this radical change in identity and self-awareness were not destabilizing enough, for a majority of women it is occurring against the backdrop of a changing marriage or intimate relationship. While we are trying to make peace with the different face staring back at us in the mirror, we are also standing on shifting sand because a marital metamorphosis is under way. It is no wonder at all that so many of us feel we are teetering on the edge of insanity at various points early on in motherhood. If we had the capacity to see any of this *while it's happening* the way I'm describing it now—

with understanding, justifications and explanations, gentleness, and compassion for ourselves—we would be far, far better off.

Years ago I was taken by the beauty and truth of Naomi Shihab Nye's poem "Kindness,"[4] in which it is written:

Before you know what kindness really is
you must lose things,
feel the future dissolve in a moment
like salt in a weakened broth

Nye's poem is about how we come to know kindness, and not necessarily fulfillment or self-understanding, and it's not a poem about motherhood. Still, her words are with me always, somewhere in the background, as harbingers of what happens to us when we become mothers. We lose things. We feel our fictitious futures vanish, sometimes in an instant, sometimes in a slow, steady evaporation that we are most reluctant to acknowledge.

But in the end, it is through loss that we stand a chance to gain. In the realm of our most primitive and most significant relationships—in the realm of mother love and romantic love—our expectations of how things *should be* are most abundant. They are deep and insistent and often outside our awareness, and they cast a constant evaluative shadow over how things are. What if we could let go of our illusions about how things would one day be, or could be, or should be? What if, in loosening our hold on these expectations, they also loosen their hold on us?

To become mothers is to become more fully aware of who we are. To become coparents is to come into greater contact with our partners, and to become more fully aware of who they are. In order to find well-being in the terrain of motherhood, we must accept the loss of so many illusions, not least of which are illusions about the bliss children will bring and the extent to which our spouses will share the burden and support us. The greatest loss of all may be our illusions about who we are and what kind of mothers we will be. When these illusions are acknowledged and grieved, we find some measure of peace in the acceptance of how things *actually* are and who we *actually* are.

The Colors of Love and Fire

One evening as we were cuddling after dinner, then four-year-old Quinn said to me, "I want to paint the living room red and orange." "Why red and orange?" I asked. He looked at me precociously, and even a little wearily, as if he felt the reason was obvious and was dismayed that I did not. Then he declared, emphatically, "The colors of love and fire!"

It's been several years since Quinn said those words, and still they echo in my mind—it was a Buddha moment for sure. With his inspired home-décor ideas, my son was telling me about his perception of the place we call home. I would love to think that Quinn sees our family, and our daily lives unfolding within the walls of this house, as characterized by love and "fire"—warmth, passion, energy. I tell myself that maybe he is declaring he would like the colors of our walls to reflect what already is, to signify a family life lived in vibrant color and anchored by abundant, unconditional love.

Of course, it could also be that there is no greater meaning in his words. Maybe he was just staring at the blazing logs in the woodstove and realized how much he likes hues of orange and red. I don't know exactly what he meant, and the thing is, I didn't ask. I won't ask. The wondering is too valuable to me, too full of promise. I don't want to foreclose it by saying, "Hey, what exactly did you mean when you said that?" Because in my wondering, I consider the possibility that no matter how insistent the guilt, no matter how constantly I aspire to do better or wish I had more patience or more hours in the day to do and say what's important, or how maddening the noise and the chaos is, there is something far more important we are doing right. Everybody is very much *alive* in this house. Love is not contingent upon the disavowal or suppressing of aspects of self, for any of us. Love is not a finite resource. There is enough for everyone, and there is room for everything—emotions of any and every kind, mishaps and messes, creative endeavors and dreams, failures and successes, longings and fulfillments.

It's not that I have arrived at some exalted place where I deserve a gold star for mastering the changes brought on by motherhood. If only that were possible, but it most certainly is not—not for me, or anyone else. It is a constant work in progress. Striving for some unattainable fantasy version of ourselves, our children, or our relationships only brings heartache. It blinds us to the value and beauty in what already is, because we are too caught up in shame or resentment or self-improvement crusades to take in whatever the present moment may be offering. Contentment comes when we embrace, rather than deny or distort or resist or conceal or judge, all of what comes up in the endlessly complicated world of mothering. This is my hope for every woman, every marriage, every child, every family. Love unchained from illusions, and lives lived in full color.

Acknowledgments

This book has been many years in the making, so many that my gratitude for those who contributed to its completion stretches far and wide, and I fear I won't be able to capture it in words.

First, I will forever be indebted to my friend Donna Freitas, who absolutely insisted one fateful day that I show her the untamed beast of a manuscript that I had kept hidden from everyone until then. Her enthusiastically affirming response to what she read not only compelled her to connect me with her agent, but also renewed my faith in my own work and lit a fire in me that burned steadily until the book was finished. Without Donna and the doors she opened for me, I simply would not be here, putting the final touches on a soon-to-be-published book.

For her guidance and support, her insight, and her expert navigation of a world brand-new to me, I am deeply grateful for my incredible agent, Miriam Altshuler. Like Donna, she believed in this book immediately, and I was honored and heartened by her willingness to invest energy in finding the book a home. She took a huge leap of faith in agreeing to represent me, and I hope I have made her proud. My extraordinary editor, Julie Will, took that same leap of faith by signing on for this project with a first-time author, and I really don't know how I got so lucky. From our first phone conversation, I knew this was a meeting of two very compatible minds. Her vision, her editorial skill, and her razor-sharp attention to the nuances of the material are gifts for which I will always be grateful. That she happened also to be a new mother while editing this book was a great fortune that, I am certain, helped to keep every sentence in closer alignment with what new moms most need to hear. Our collaborative process in shaping this book into its best possible form was tremendously fulfilling. Having both Miriam and Julie in my corner, championing this book and what my voice can uniquely contribute, has been dreamy.

To the many other women in my village, both literal and figurative, who have cheered me on and supported me in so many crucial ways, I am forever thankful. I am especially grateful to Kathryn Wyatt for her nurturing friendship, and to Lisa Nading for her sustained and heartfelt interest in the fruits of my creative processes. I'm thankful also to Moira Cook, Kylie Wolgamott, Valerie Racine, Sharon Lamb, Sharon Sullivan, and Gracie Engel Peirce, all of whom contributed to this work in important ways: sharing their stories of motherhood and wifehood, encouraging me and believing in me, engaging with me in thoughtful and inspiring conversation, and celebrating with me when it finally seemed that my years of writing would morph into an actual published book.

I am immeasurably grateful to Kate Longmaid, in whose eyes I see the light of my own possibilities and with whom, through countless hours of dialogue and connection, I have cultivated whatever wisdom is found in these pages.

I offer my enduring appreciation to my clients, who have invited me into their private worlds and entrusted me with their stories. For these privileges I am deeply honored. Again and again, I have been humbled and inspired by the strength and the vulnerability of the people with whom I share such an intimate, brave space of connection and self-reflection.

I am grateful to my mother, Carol Millwood, for whom reading some of the material in this book meant having to revise her story of who I am and how I think about certain aspects of my upbringing. This revision was not easy, I know, and yet in her feedback for me, she led with genuine awe and respect for what I accomplished. She is proud of me like only a mother can be.

For my sister-in-law and brother-in-law, Tally Pucher and Brendan Parent, I am so grateful; they have cheered me on and eagerly anticipated this book as they cross the threshold into parenthood. In return for all their interest, support, and love, I hope my words help them rest a little easier in their new roles.

Finally and most importantly, from the deepest place in my heart I thank my husband, Ari Kirshenbaum, and our children, Noah and Quinn. Besides the grist for the mill of this book they provided to me, they provided also their support and a shared, unwavering confidence in my ability to carry out a project of such epic proportions. Despite the enormous amount of time it took me away from them, somehow it seemed all three of them were genuinely more proud of me than resentful. Noah showed a degree of interest in my work that is very unusual for a boy his age, and speaks volumes about his deep well of empathy and his curiosity about human nature. Quinn—who has never even known a mom who wasn't working in one way or another on this book—brought his characteristic energy, tenderness, and enthusiasm to the table whenever I was weary. I can only hope I have modeled for them how to be a whole person, who loves hard *and* works hard, and that one day the messages in this book will guide them in their efforts to be loving partners and soothe them during their own trying times as parents. Ari, whose generosity knows no bounds, gave to me endlessly through all the years it took to bring this book to fruition. Far surpassing the hundreds of hours of solo parenting and the hundreds of nourishing dinners, his ways of supporting me really cannot be quantified. He has always been the greatest believer in what I have to say, never doubting me even when I so persuasively doubt myself. He is the best thing that ever happened to me, and my biggest gratitude of all is for him.

Notes

INTRODUCTION

1. These false dichotomies, when endorsed as they so readily are, foreclose the possibility of dialectical thinking. "Dialectics" refers to the juxtaposition of conflicting ideas, forces, feelings, and so on. Dialectical thinking, then, means holding in mind, acknowledging as so, the existence of seemingly opposite truths. People generally struggle with this to greater or lesser degrees, and within the psychological literature it has been suggested that difficulty thinking in dialectical terms is the source of much suffering. Dialectical thinking can thus be viewed as a tool to alleviate suffering, and some models of psychotherapy (e.g., Dialectical Behavior Therapy, Acceptance and Commitment Therapy) are predicated on this notion.

2. Writing ten years later about her 1976 classic *Of Woman Born*, author and poet Adrienne Rich says it was "both praised and attacked for what was sometimes seen as its odd-fangled approach: personal testimony mingled with research, and theory which derived from both. But this approach never seemed odd to me in the writing. What still seems odd is the absentee author, the writer who lays down speculations, theories, facts, and fantasies without any personal grounding." I very much agree, and it is in this same spirit that I have written this book.

3. Adrienne Rich, *Of Woman Born* (New York: W.W. Norton, 1986), 15.

1 WOMEN TRANSFORMED

1. E. Perel, "When Three Threatens Two: Must Parenthood Bring Down the Curtain on Romance?" *Psychotherapy Networker*, September/October 2006.

2. "Postpartum Depression: Women's Accounts of Loss and Change," in *Situating Sadness: Women and Depression in Social Context*, eds. J. M. Stoppard and L. M. McMullen (New York: NYU Press, 2003), 133.

3. "Writings from a Birth Year," in *Finding Your Inner Mama: Women Reflect on the Challenges and Rewards of Motherhood*, ed. E. Steinberg (Boston & London: Trumpeter Books, 2005), 5.

2 OUT OF THE SHAME HOLE

1. S. Maushart, *The Mask of Motherhood: How Becoming a Mother Changes Our Lives and Why We Never Talk About It* (New York: Penguin Books, 1999), 57.

2. J. L. Bevan, R. Gomez, and L. Sparks, "Disclosures about Important Life Events on Facebook: Relationships with Stress and Quality of Life," *Computers in Human Behavior* 39 (October 2014): 246–53.

3. R. Kraut et al., "Internet Paradox: A Social Technology that Reduces Social Involvement and Psychological Well-Being?" *American Psychologist* 53, no. 9 (September 1998): 1017–31.

4. R. Pea et al., "Media Use, Face-to-Face Communication, Media Multitasking, and Social Well-Being Among 8- to 12-Year-Old Girls," *Developmental Psychology* 48, no. 2 (March 2012): 327–36.

5. M. Indian and R. Grieve, "When Facebook Is Easier than Face-to-Face: Social Support Derived from Facebook in Socially Anxious Individuals," *Personality & Individual Differences* 59 (2014): 102–6.

6. C. Y. Liu and C. P. Yu, "Can Facebook Use Induce Well-Being?" *Cyberpsychology, Behavior, and Social Networking* 16 (2013): 674–78.

7. W. McCloskey, S. Iwanicki, D. Lauterbach, D. M. Giammittorio, and K. Maxwell, "Are Facebook 'Friends' Helpful? Development of a Facebook-Based Measure of Social Support and Examination of Relationships Among Depression, Quality of Life, and Social Support," *Cyberpsychology, Behavior, and Social Networking* 18 (2015): 499–505.

8. American Psychological Association, *Monitor on Psychology*, October 2010, 21; emphasis added.

9. G. Rubin, *The Happiness Project* (New York: HarperCollins, 2009), 91.

10. J. M. Gottman and C. J. Notarius, "Marital Research in the 20th Century and a Research Agenda for the 21st Century," *Family Process* 41 (2002): 159–97.

11. J. M. Twenge, W. K. Campbell, and C. A. Foster, "Parenthood and Marital Satisfaction: A Meta-Analytic Review," *Journal of Marriage and Family* 65, no. 3 (2003): 574–83; M. J. Cox et al., "Marital Perceptions and Interactions Across the Transition to Parenthood," *Journal of Marriage and Family* 61 (1999): 611–25; D. G. Knauth, "Predictors of Parental Sense of Competence for the Couple During the Transition to Parenthood," *Research in Nursing & Health* 23 (2000): 496–509.

12. M. McGoldrick and B. Carter, "The Family Life Cycle," in *Normal Family Processes: Growing Diversity and Complexity*, 3rd ed., ed. F. Walsh (New York: Guilford Press, 2003), 375–98.

13. The reverse is not true; marital therapy does not treat men's individual depression as effectively. This is quite an interesting finding in itself, in that it points to a stronger relational basis for women's depression than men's. See M. R. Goldfarb, G. Trudel,

R. Boyer, and M. Preville, "Marital Relationship and Psychological Distress: Its Correlates and Treatments," *Sexual and Relationship Therapy* 22, no. 1 (2007): 109–26. Overall, however, research demonstrates a strong link between individual mental health and marital functioning. For instance, D. K. Snyder, A. M. Castellani, and M. A. Whisman, "Current Status and Future Directions in Couple Therapy," *Annual Review of Psychology* 57, (2006): 317–44 reported that people experiencing marital discord are overrepresented within the population of individuals seeking mental health services, regardless of whether marital strain is their primary complaint.

14. In women, depression levels are linked with hostility in their spouses (B. H. Brummet et al., "Hostility in Marital Dyads: Associations with Depressive Symptoms," *Journal of Behavioral Medicine* 23 [2000]: 95–105), but again, the reverse is not true. Longitudinal studies show that among women, marital dissatisfaction is correlated with later depression (Goldfarb et al., "Marital Relationship and Psychological Distress"). In addition, large epidemiological studies that control for distress in relationships with friends, relatives, and colleagues find that marital distress is uniquely correlated with mental health concerns, above and beyond the contributions of general social discord (M. A. Whisman, C. T. Sheldon, and P. Goering, "Psychiatric Disorders and Dissatisfaction with Social Relationships: Does Type of Relationship Matter?" *Journal of Abnormal Psychology* 109 [2000]: 803–8). Indeed, in what are known as "attributable risk analyses," it has been determined that 30 percent of all cases of depression, in both women and men, could be prevented if marital distress were prevented or ameliorated (M. A. Whisman and M. L. Bruce, "Marital Dissatisfaction and Incidence of Major Depressive Episode in a Community Sample," *Journal of Abnormal Psychology* 108 [2001]: 674–78).

15. P. Nettelbladt, M. Uddenberg, and I. Englesson, "Marital Disharmony Four and a Half Years Postpartum: Effects on Parent-Child Relationships and Child Development," *Acta Psychiatrica Scandinavica* 71, no. 4 (1985): 392–401.

16. V. E. Whiffen, "Looking Outward Together: Adult Attachment and Child-bearing Depression," in *Attachment Processes in Couple and Family Therapy*, eds. S. M. Johnson and V. E. Whiffen (New York: Guilford Press, 2003), 321–41. See also M. W. O'Hara and A. M. Swain, "Rates and Risk of Postpartum Depression: A Meta-Analysis," *International Review of Psychiatry* 8, no. 1 (1996): 37–54.

17. V. E. Whiffen, "Is Postpartum Depression a Distinct Diagnosis?" *Clinical Psychology Review* 12, no. 5 (1992): 485–508. Also see Cox et al., "Marital Perceptions and Interactions."

18. W. S. Rholes et al., "Attachment Orientations and Depression: A Longitudinal Study of New Parents," *Journal of Personality and Social Psychology* 100 (2011): 567–86; S. Misri, X. Kostaras, D. Fox, and D. Kostaras, "The Impact of Partner Support in the Treatment of Postpartum Depression," *Canadian Journal of Psychiatry* 45 (2000): 554–58.

3 THE FULL CATASTROPHE

1. Steinberg, *Finding Your Inner Mama*, 20.

2. It was in the work of Marsha Linehan, PhD, that I first encountered the therapeutic potential of helping clients distinguish between pain and suffering. See, for instance, Linehan's *Dialectical Behavior Therapy for Borderline Personality* (New York: Guilford Press, 1993).

3. Steinberg, *Finding Your Inner Mama*.

4. A. Miller, *The Drama of the Gifted Child: The Search for the True Self*, rev. ed. (New York: Basic Books, 1994).

5. J. Berman, *Superbaby: 12 Ways to Give Your Baby a Head Start in the First 3 Years* (New York: Sterling Publishers, 2011). The title of the book seems to imply that parenting is a competition, and that it is not enough to do our best to raise a healthy human child; we must strive for a superhero child instead, and the first three years of that child's life are make-or-break.

4 MOM, INTERRUPTED

1. M. A. Killingsworth and D. T. Gilbert, "A Wandering Mind Is an Unhappy Mind," *Science* 330, no. 6006 (2010): 932.

2. You can use the same app used in the research study to find out about your own mind-wandering propensities by going to trackyourhappiness.org.

3. For a very recent and comprehensive review of the use of mindfulness in psychotherapy for the treatment of depression, anxiety, and other psychological disorders, see S. B. Goldberg et al., "Mindfulness-Based Interventions for Psychiatric Disorders: A Systematic Review and Meta-Analysis," *Clinical Psychology Review* 59 (2018): 52–60. For a comprehensive review of the effects of mindfulness-based stress reduction (MBSR) on physical health and psychosomatic problems, see Grossman et al., "Mindfulness-Based Stress Reduction and Health Benefits," *Journal of Psychosomatic Research* 57, no. 1 (2004): 35–43.

4. D. de Marneffe, *Maternal Desire: On Children, Love, and the Inner Life* (New York: Back Bay Books, 2004).

5. H. Woolhouse, D. Gartland, F. Mensah, and S. J. Brown, "Maternal Depression from Early Pregnancy to 4 Years Postpartum in a Prospective Pregnancy Cohort Study: Implications for Primary Health Care," *International Journal of Obstetrics & Gynaecology* 122, no. 3 (2014): 312–21.

5 IT TAKES A VILLAGE TO RAISE A MOTHER

1. A useful comparative analysis of the costs and benefits, for both mothers and babies, of vaginal versus cesarean births is K. D. Gregory, S. Jackson, L. Korst, and M. Fridman, "Caesarean Versus Vaginal Delivery: Whose Risks? Whose Benefits?" *American Journal of Perinatology* 29 (2012): 7–18.

2. M. Millwood, *Cesarean Birth as a Risk Factor for Postpartum Relationship Distress*. Poster presented at the annual convention of the American Psychological Association, Division 35 (Society for the Psychology of Women), San Diego, CA, 2010. Women were assessed on various measures of well-being at approximately 4 to 6 months postpartum, and scores on the measure of relationship satisfaction were significantly lower in women who had C-sections.

3. Mary Karr, *The Liars' Club* (New York: Penguin Books, 1995) 9.

4. According to the CDC, 32 percent of total births in the US are C-section (2015 data).

5. "Why Are America's Postpartum Practices So Rough on New Mothers?" *Daily Beast*, August 2013. https://www.thedailybeast.com/why-are-americas-postpartum-practices-so-rough-on-new-mothers.

6. Carmen Knudson-Martin and Anne Rankin Mahoney, *Couples, Gender, and Power: Creating Change in Intimate Relationships* (New York: Springer Publishing, 2009), 24.

7. L. Nepomnyaschy and J. Waldfogel, "Paternity Leave and Fathers' Involvement with Their Young Children," *Community, Work & Family* 10, no. 4 (2007): 427–53.

8. One major longitudinal study found that the drop in earnings over the life of their careers was 15.5 percent for men who took time off for family reasons, compared to 11.2 percent when the time off was for personal illness, injury, or other reasons not tethered to their identities as fathers (S. Coltrane, E. C. Miller, T. DeHaan, and L. Stewart, "Fathers and the Flexibility Stigma," *Journal of Social Issues* 69, no. [2013]: 279–302). Other studies (e.g., J. A. Vandello, V. E. Hettinger, J. K. Bosson, and J. Siddiqi, "When Equal Isn't Really Equal: The Masculine Dilemma of Seeking Work Flexibility," *Journal of Social Issues* 69, no. 2 [2013]: 303–21) find that lower performance evaluations, smaller raises, and risk of demotions and layoffs are all associated with taking paternity leave.

9. As noted in C. Cain Miller, "Paternity Leave: The Rewards and the Remaining Stigma," *New York Times*, November 2014.

10. Nepomnyaschy and Waldfogel, "Paternity Leave and Fathers' Involvement."

11. E. Abraham, T. Hendler, I. Shapira-Lichter, Y. Kanat-Maymon, O. Zagoory-Sharon, and R. Feldman, "Father's Brain Is Sensitive to Childcare Experiences," *PNAS* 111, no. 27 (2014): 9792–97.

12. L. Mundy, "Daddy Track: The Case for Paternity Leave," *The Atlantic*, January/February 2014.

13. S. Pinker, *The Village Effect* (Toronto: Vintage Canada, 2014), 16.

14. R. Putnam, *Bowling Alone: The Collapse and Revival of American Community* (New York: Simon & Schuster, 2000), 331.

15. Pinker, *The Village Effect*, 37–8.

16. J. K. Monin and M. S. Clark, "Why Do Men *Benefit* More from Marriage Than Do Women? Thinking More Broadly About Interpersonal Processes That Occur Within *and* Outside of Marriage," *Sex Roles* 65 (2011): 320–26. See also M. S. Clark and J. K. Monin, "Giving and Receiving Communal Responsiveness as Love," in *The New Psychology of Love*, eds. R. J. Sternberg and K. Weis (New Haven, CT: Yale University Press, 2006), 200–24.

17. Knudson-Martin and Mahoney, *Couples, Gender, and Power.*

18. Women have twice the lifetime rates of major depressive disorder, and most anxiety disorders, as men. Subclinical depressive symptoms (i.e., symptoms of depression that do not meet full diagnostic criteria) are also considerably higher in women. See M. Altemus, N. Sarvaiya, and C. N. Epperson, "Sex Differences in Anxiety and Depression: Clinical Perspectives," *Frontiers in Neuroendocrinology* 35, no. 3 (2014): 320–30.

19. D. M. Buss, "The Evolution of Happiness," *American Psychologist* 55 (2000): 15–23.

20. B. Fox, "The Formative Years: How Parenthood Creates Gender," *Canadian Journal of Sociology* 38, no. 4 (2001): 373–90 (quote from p. 388).

6 THE GREAT DIVIDE

1. Cox et al., "Marital Perceptions and Interactions Across the Transition to Parenthood,"611-25. Also see C. E. Bird, "Gender Differences in the Social and Economic Burdens of Parenting and Psychological Distress," *Journal of Marriage and Family* 59 (1997): 809–32; and K. Korabik, "The Intersection of Gender and Work-Family Guilt," in *Gender and the Work-Family Experience*, ed. M. J. Mills (Switzerland: Springer International, 2015), 141–57.

2. C. P. Cowan and P. Cowan, *When Partners Become Parents: The Big Life Change for Couples* (New York: Basic Books, 1999).

3. G. Cappuccini and R. Cochrane, "Life with the First Baby: Women's Satisfaction with the Division of Roles," *Journal of Reproductive and Infant Psychology* 18, no. 3 (2000): 189–203.

4. R. Alexander et al., "Attachment Style and Coping Resources as Predictors of Coping Strategies in the Transition to Parenthood," *Personal Relationships* 8 (2001): 137–52. Also see S. M. Pancer et al., "Thinking Ahead: Complexity of Expectations and the Transition to Parenthood," *Journal of Personality* 68 (2000): 253–80.

5. R. Levy-Shiff, "Individual and Contextual Correlates of Marital Change across the Transition to Parenthood," *Developmental Psychology* 30 (1994): 591–601.

6. S. R. Thorp et al., "Postpartum Partner Support, Demand-Withdraw Communication, and Maternal Stress," *Psychology of Women Quarterly* 28 (2004): 362–69. See also Whiffen, "Looking Outward Together."

7. Knauth, "Predictors of Parental Sense of Competence," 496–509.

8. 2010 American Time Use Survey, Bureau of Labor Statistics.

9. Borelli et al., "Gender Differences in Work-Family Guilt in Parents of Young Children," *Sex Roles* 76, no. 5–6 (2017): 356–68.

10. M. Perry-Jenkins and A. Claxton, "The Transition to Parenthood and the Reasons 'Momma Ain't Happy,'" *Journal of Marriage and Family* 73, no. 1 (2011): 23–28.

11. Claxton and Perry-Jenkins, "No Fun Anymore: Leisure and Marital Quality across the Transition to Parenthood," *Journal of Marriage and Family* 70, no. 1 (2008): 28–43.

12. Milkie et al., "Gendered Division of Childrearing: Ideals, Realities, and the Relationship to Parental Well-Being," *Sex Roles* 47, no. 1–2 (2002): 21–38.

13. Cowan and Cowan, *When Partners Become Parents*, 83.

14. Fox, "The Formative Years," 373–90.

15. S. L. Katz-Wise, H. A. Priess, and J. S. Hyde, "Gender-Role Attitudes and Behavior across the Transition to Parenthood," *Developmental Psychology* 46, no. 1 (2010): 18–28.

16. From Lisa Belkin, "Calling Mr. Mom? Why Women Won't Have It All Until Men Do, Too," *New York Times*, October 24, 2010.

17. Hook, "Care in Context: Men's Unpaid Work in 20 Countries, 1965–2003," *American Sociological Review* 71, no. 4 (2006): 639–60. Also see the 2010 American Time Use Survey, Bureau of Labor Statistics.

18. 2010 American Time Use Survey, Bureau of Labor Statistics.

19. M. A. Milkie, K. M. Nomaguchi, and K. E. Denny, "Does the Amount of Time Mothers Spend with Children or Adolescents Matter?" *Journal of Marriage and Family* 77, no. 2 (2015): 355–72.

20. Fox, "The Formative Years," quote from p. 382.

21. Knudson-Martin and Mahoney, *Couples, Gender, and Power*.

22. M. J. Mattingly and L. C. Sayer, "Under Pressure: Gender Differences in the Relationship between Free Time and Feeling Rushed," *Journal of Marriage and Family* 68, no. 1 (2006): 205–21.

23. S. M. Bianchi and M. J. Mattingly, "Time, Work, and Family in the United States," *Advances in Life Course Research* 8 (2003): 95–118.

24. M. McMahon, *Engendering Motherhood: Identity and Self-Transformation in Women's Lives* (New York: The Guilford Press, 1995), 238. McMahon references La Rossa and La Rossa (1981) for the term "glossing" and Hochschild (1989) for the term "family myths."

25. McMahon, *Engendering Motherhood*, 269.

26. Ibid.

27. 2010 American Time Use Survey, Bureau of Labor Statistics.

28. McMahon, *Engendering Motherhood*, 244.

7 COUPLES ADRIFT

1. Gottman and Notarius, "Marital Research in the 20th Century," 159–97.

2. Ibid.

3. Cox et al., "Marital Perceptions and Interactions."

4. O. Erel and B. Burman, "Interrelatedness of Marital Relations and Parent-Child Relations: A Meta-Analytic Review," *Psychological Bulletin* 118, no. 1 (1995): 108–32. See also P. Cowan and C. P. Cowan, "New Families: Modern Couples as New Pioneers," in *All Our Families: New Policies for a New Century*, eds. M. A. Mason, A. Skolnick, and S. Sugarman (New York: Oxford University Press, 1998), 169–92.

5. P. Cowan et al., "Prebirth to Preschool Family Factors in Children's Adaptation to Kindergarten," in *Exploring Family Relationships with Other Social Contexts*, eds. R. D. Parke and S. G. Kellam (Hillsdale, NJ: Erlbaum, 1994), 75–114.

6. D. Meyer, B. Robinson, A. Cohn, L. Gildenblatt, and S. Barkley, "The Possible Trajectory of Relationship Satisfaction across the Longevity of a Romantic Partnership," *Family Journal* 24, no. 4 (2016): 344–50. Also see Twenge et al., "Parenthood and Marital Satisfaction."

7. M. Marks, A. Wieck, S. Checkley, and C. Kumar, "How Does Marriage Protect Women with Histories of Affective Disorder from Post-Partum Relapse?" *British Journal of Medical Psychology* 69, no. 4 (1996): 329–42.

8. J. Viorst, *Necessary Losses: The Loves, Illusions, Dependencies, and Impossible Expectations That All of Us Have to Give Up in Order to Grow* (New York: The Free Press, 1986), 186.

9. In the interest of preserving the original spirit of John Bowlby's pioneering work on attachment, some of the wording of these key principles of attachment theory (e.g., "attachment is an innate motivating force") has been borrowed from Dr. Susan Johnson's translation of Bowlby's theoretical pillars in her book *The Practice of Emotionally Focused Therapy for Couples: Creating Connection* (New York: Brunner-Routledge, 2003).

10. These are the oft-quoted famous words of John Bowlby, the originator of attachment theory.

11. This language is also borrowed from Johnson; it is language she uses in various interviews and in *The Practice of Emotionally Focused Therapy for Couples*.

12. A. Schore, *Affect Regulation and the Organization of Self* (Hillsdale, NJ: Erlbaum, 1994). As cited by Johnson in *The Practice of Emotionally Focused Therapy for Couples*, 26.

13. Johnson, *The Practice of Emotionally Focused Therapy for Couples*, 25–26.

14. Researchers have found that when couples are happy in the relationship, sitting

next to each other with their thighs touching causes them to secrete oxytocin—the hormone of trust and bonding—and reduces blood pressure in women. The same is not true for unhappily married couples (K. M. Grewen, S. S. Girdler, J. Amico, and K. C. Light, "Effects of Partner Support on Resting Oxytocin, Cortisol, Norepinephrine, and Blood Pressure Before and After Warm Partner Contact," *Psychosomatic Medicine* 67 [2005]: 531–38). Similarly, as Dr. John Gottman discusses in his book *The Science of Trust* (New York: W. W. Norton, 2011), the level of trust couples have determines their physiological responses to looking into each other's eyes. In Gottman's laboratory, couples sit facing each other and are first asked to close their eyes and relax for five minutes. They are then instructed to open their eyes and look at their partners. In couples with high levels of trust, blood velocity (a physiological index similar to blood pressure) remains the same or even decreases upon eye contact, but for those with lower levels of trust, blood velocity increases. It's as if these unhappy couples feel they are looking into the eyes of an enemy, or at least someone who is a predictable source of stress.

15. Johnson, *The Practice of Emotionally Focused Therapy for Couples*, 26–27.

8 IN THE WEEDS

1. Gottman, *The Science of Trust*, 193.

2. De Marneffe, *Maternal Desire*, 9.

3. Mirror neurons are considered to be one of the major discoveries of modern neuroscience, originally identified during a research study with monkeys whose brain activity was being monitored as they watched the humans who were studying them. It became apparent that the monkeys' brain cells were firing the way they would if they were doing what the humans were doing (see G. Rizzolatti and L. Craighero, "The Mirror-Neuron System," *Annual Review of Neuroscience* 27 [2004]: 169–92). But even without brain electrodes or MRIs, there is plenty of fascinating evidence of mirror neurons visible to the naked eye. For instance, hours-old infants will imitate the facial expressions of adults (A. N. Meltzoff and M. K. Moore, "Newborn Infants Imitate Adult Facial Gestures," *Child Development* 54, no. 3 [1983]: 702–9), and any close examination of two people engaged in intimate dialogue—like a therapist and client—reveals incredible synchrony in their body language and vocal cadence.

4. Whiffen, "Looking Outward Together," 321–41.

5. In a fascinating twist to one research study, it was found that what distinguished mothers who engaged in intensive mothering despite their partners' disapproval was their position of relative financial power within the relationship. These women earned more money than their partners. See Fox, "The Formative Years."

9 LIVE-IN BUDDHAS

1. H. Lerner, "Vulnerability and Other Lessons," in *Finding Your Inner Mama*, 24.

2. S. Grosz, *The Examined Life: How We Lose and Find Ourselves* (New York: W. W. Norton, 2013), 107.

3. J. Warner, *Perfect Madness: Motherhood in the Age of Anxiety* (New York: Penguin Group, 2005), 93.

4. A comprehensive review of the research literature on gender differences and gender similarities in not only guilt but also shame, embarrassment, and pride can be found in N. M. Else-Quest, A. Higgins, C. Allison, and L. C. Morton, "Gender Differences in Self-Conscious Emotional Experience: A Meta-Analysis," *Psychological Bulletin* 138, no. 5 (2012): 947–81. See also British psychologist Simon Baron-Cohen's book *The Essential Difference: Men, Women, and the Extreme Male Brain* (New York: Penguin Books, 2012).

5. I. Extebarria, M. J. Ortiz, S. Conejero, and A. Pascual, "Intensity of Habitual Guilt in Men and Women: Differences in Interpersonal Sensitivity and the Tendency towards Anxious-Aggressive Guilt," *Spanish Journal of Psychology* 12, no. 2 (2009): 540–54.

6. See for example S.S. Dickerson, M.E. Kemeny, N. Aziz, K.H. Kim and J.L. Fahey, (2004), "Immunological Effects of Induced Shame and Guilt," *Psychosomatic Medicine* 66(1) 124–31, or see A. Rozanski, J.A. Blumenthal, and J. Kaplan, "Impact of Psychological Factors on the Pathogenesis of Cardiovascular Disease: Implications for Therapy," *Circulation* 99(16) (1999): 2192–217.

7. B. Almond, *The Monster Within: The Hidden Side of Motherhood* (Berkeley/Los Angeles: University of California Press, 2010), 7.

8. Warner, *Perfect Madness*, 102.

9. P. R. Breggin, *The Heart of Being Helpful* (New York: Springer Publishing Company, 1997), 59.

10. E. Selcuk et al., "Does Partner Responsiveness Predict Hedonic and Eudaimonic Well-Being? A 10-Year Longitudinal Study," *Journal of Marriage and Family* 78 (2016): 311–25.

10 LOST AND FOUND

1. Permission to use the lyrics that appear here and later in the chapter was graciously granted by Antje Duvekot. The song appears on the album *Toward the Thunder*, © 2016, Antje Duvekot.

2. Breggin, *The Heart of Being Helpful*, 57–58.

3. A. M. Lindbergh, *Gift from the Sea* (New York: Pantheon Books, 1955), 57–58; emphasis added.

4. Permission to use this excerpt from the poem "Kindness" was graciously granted by the author, Naomi Shihab Nye. The poem appears in *Words Under the Words*, Far Corner Books, 1995.

Index

About the Author

Molly Millwood, PhD, is a licensed clinical psychologist in private practice specializing in couples therapy, motherhood, and women's issues. She is also an associate professor of psychology at Saint Michael's College in Vermont, where she teaches courses on intimate relationships and marital therapy. She lives in the woods of the Green Mountains with her husband and their two children.